Kayaking
Made
Easy

HOW TO PADDLE SERIES

Kayaking Made Easy

A MANUAL FOR BEGINNERS WITH TIPS FOR THE EXPERIENCED

FOURTH EDITION

DENNIS STUHAUG

GUILFORD, CONNECTICUT
HELENA, MONTANA
AN IMPRINT OF GLOBE PEQUOT PRESS

FALCONGUIDES®

Illustrations by Dennis Stuhaug
Photos by Dennis Stuhaug unless otherwise noted

Design by Sheryl P. Kober
Layout by Melissa Evarts
Project editor: Ellen Urban

Library of Congress Cataloging-in-Publication Data

Stuhaug, Dennis O.
  Kayaking made easy : a manual for beginners with tips for the experienced / Dennis Stuhaug. — Fourth edition.
     pages cm
  Includes index.
  ISBN 978-0-7627-8008-2
  1. Kayaking—Handbooks, manuals, etc. I. Title.
  GV783.S88 2013
  797.122'4—dc23

2012050347

Printed in the United States of America

10 9 8 7 6 5 4 3 2 1

To Suzanne,
who is already packed for the next adventure.

Contents

Preface

The last of the orange was bleeding out of the eastern sky, coloring the notches between the forest-dark mountains, when we launched from the head of the small bay to catch the tail of the ebb tide. There wasn't enough sun yet to burn away the low sea fog that rises along the North Pacific on a summer morning, and we glided down a compass course on our way to the edge of the sea.

We would clear the headland at the mouth of this fjord at slack tide, then turn and climb with the flood tide a dozen miles up the next deep fjord to where we'd meet with friends midway into a two-week paddling vacation. It was the wrong time of the year to watch the great gray whales migrate, but there were pods of orca in the neighborhood, and we could paddle close enough along the barnacle-crusted rocks to see the soft, brown eyes of seals hauled out and basking. An eagle crossed over us as we launched, and it came back to circle us twice before powering northward.

The tidal flow eased to nothing as we neared the low rocks of the headland. A parachute-shaped jellyfish, large enough to fill a 5-gallon bucket, pulsated just under the surface as we glided along the rocks, and we delightedly pointed out the great orange disk of a twenty-rayed sun star at the limits of our vision into the depths. A boulder, a dozen meters high, jutted into the sea as the last corner between us and the fjord we came to explore, and as we rounded its sharp prow, an otter vaulted from it and splashed into the quiet water between our boats. Twenty seconds later it popped back to the surface, rising almost like a marmot in the water to see what it had startled.

This is the world of kayak touring: mist, or unexpected sun. A whale rolling up to watch you, a moose standing in the shallows with green strands of grass dripping from its mouth. A day when the loudest sound comes from waves sloshing upon a gravel beach. Seagulls croaking and rasping as they hunt along the fringes of the tide. A good kind of "tired," when even the weariness rejuvenates you.

Your touring kayak is a bridge into this world. The physical skills are within easy reach of most of us, with a little discipline and a little effort, and the foundation of kayaking knowledge may be grasped readily—and may be expanded day by day for the rest of your life.

Comfortably seated in your silent, swift kayak, you become a participant in a natural world unfortunately abandoned by all too many of us. You set your own pace, your own goals: You may enjoy an hour-long cruise along the beach, or you may embark on a monthlong voyage through these North Pacific islands— or along the Maine coast, through the Florida Keys, or from island to island along the north coast of Lake Superior. You may use your boat for exercise, or as a platform for fishing or bird-watching. It may become your vantage point for photography or painting. All those "mays" are at your paddle tips. The truth is that all your voyages will lead back inside yourself, and along the way you'll meet yourself again.

You won't become an expert sea kayaker by reading the following pages. You will start to become a proficient kayaker by going paddling, and you will find your way eased by what I'm passing on to you, knowledge I learned from my friends and from experience.

If we meet and paddle together, say down Kyuquot Sound, the otter may once again leap over our kayaks.

Are you ready?

Acknowledgments

No one ever paddles alone. We are accompanied by generations of silent, invisible companions; we share the water and the knowledge we have gleaned from everyone whose wake we cross. I have been particularly blessed with the privilege of paddling with three extraordinary kayak designers and builders: Lee Moyer, who by example set a standard for stewardship of our waters; Peter Kaupat, who insisted that perfection is attainable; and Werner Furrer Sr., who constantly reminded me that the ultimate reason for paddling is enjoyment. I deeply appreciate the hard work, dedication, and professionalism of the editors at FalconGuides. They make editing a high art and in doing so, unscrambled my syntax. And I take full credit for any remaining mistakes or confusions.

CHAPTER 1

You Can Learn to Kayak

Sprawl back on the beach with me, enjoying the warmth of the afternoon sun. Wiggle about a bit on the fine gravel to form a little depression to sit in, and dig a pair of heel holes more for the fun of it than for any support. A sea kayak with a red deck is carving a long vee through the riffles on the dark water, silently and swiftly. It doesn't look at all hard, judging from the ear-to-ear grin on the lone paddler's face. The smooth pattern of her strokes looks like something you could do.

You shake your head. Anything that looks that easy must be really hard to do, or it must take a long time—a really long time—to learn. She was probably born with a paddle in her

hands, and her folks were paying big money for sports lessons when she was just a toddler.

Sorry to break into your dreams on such a nice day with a cold dose of reality, but at best you are way less than half right. The smile plastered all over that paddler's face is absolutely real, and the grace she exhibits as she almost effortlessly rounds the point off to your left is totally genuine. Paddling a kayak is totally fun. But being so difficult that mere mortals could never learn to do it? Wrong in a big way. This is an activity for today's world: low impact on you, and a light touch on the world through which you pass. Low cost, low technology, and a low learning curve for the person who wants

You can learn to paddle in a day, and you will learn something new every day you paddle.

to explore all the delightful vagaries along the break where the water meets the shore.

I'm willing to bet you that candy bar in your pocket that you can learn to get into a boat just like that one and paddle it in ten minutes or so. Let's keep a handle on reality here. In ten minutes you're not going to show off the grace and elegance of the lady who just glided past. You probably won't even paddle in an approximately straight line. You will splash and you will puff. But you *will* be paddling; you will be in command of your own ship.

Okay, I hedged that wager a bit. I know that you are in good health and physically fit enough for moderate exercise. If we had a question about that I would have suggested having a chat with your doctor, as most of us should before beginning any new exercise. Don't hear this as a warning that paddling is only for the

physically elite. Almost any challenge we may face can be accommodated within the cockpit of a kayak. There's a place for all of us, whether it be camping, cruising, or competing.

I also know that you can swim—although you don't have to know how to swim before boarding a kayak. I know paddlers who can't swim a stroke. However, I also know that folks who can't swim often (and often unconsciously) fear the water. They stiffen up at every pitch or roll of a kayak, and it is more difficult to either lean a kayak or trust their balance to the power of their paddle. Swimmers tend to be more confident and relaxed, allowing them to enjoy the learning experience more easily. Non-swimmers tend to be more hesitant. This is not a bad thing; we'd just have to play a bit more on building confidence and comfort.

With a kayak you are part of the environment you explore.

If you and I spent an entire morning on the beach, you would be able to climb into your boat, push off from shore, and head in a reasonably straight line to a destination of your choice. In a day or so, you'd have all the skills you need to be a welcome addition to just about any group of paddlers. I don't mean a master mariner, with kelp in your hair and a compass clutched in your teeth. That would be lying, and to grasp the essential simplicity of a sea kayak we have to build a bond of trust. Want to try?

First of all, let's change the name of this vessel. We'll call it a cruising kayak. That's only a small difference, but it opens up a whole world of lakes, big rivers, and small ponds as well as salt water. Our cruising kayak, sometimes called a touring kayak or a sea kayak, is designed for an environment where the primary forces are wind and often tide. Wind is the power that generates waves. A whitewater kayak is designed to slide downhill and cope with currents in the moving water. That said, I've been blown all over a river by winds and have played in boisterous currents in the sea.

It's my experience that the cruising kayaker has an entirely different mind-set from that of the whitewater boater. The whitewater boater sits in a tool that is part of the sport. The cruising kayaker, on the other hand, shares a partnership with a subtle and responsive craft in the exploration of an activity. Sure, some people race these long and skinny boats. Others voyage for great distances with all their possessions stored belowdecks. Some plop their boats in the water for an afternoon's outing and a picnic. Still others churn the water over a limited course in search of exercise.

Whatever works. But I notice that a fairly high percentage of cruising kayakers name their boats, while most whitewater boaters plan on replacing theirs every few years.

There's also a difference in execution, even though many of the strokes and skills can be readily transported from one kind of kayak to the other. About three-quarters of a whitewater boater's moves are reactionary, while three-quarters of a cruising kayaker's actions are based on contemplation and preparation.

Neither is more challenging, nor requires a higher level of skill or ability. Neither is a stepping-stone to the other. They are simply two separate ways of having fun on the water with a paddle in your hand.

A Mini-History

Back in the nineteenth century, cruising kayaks were a rarity. Sure, there were guides with canoes who would take curious travelers into the woods, but the wilderness was mainly the haunt of outfitters, "swells," and a handful of folks who made their living in the small byways of the water world. Then, in the 1880s, George Sears glided into the American consciousness with his stories of exploring the Adirondacks alone with a lightweight canoe and minimal camping gear. Sears became one of the most popular American outdoor writers, convincing his readers that anyone could follow comfortably in his wake without the expense and formality of a professional guide.

Across the pond, in England, John Mac-Gregor modified an Inuit kayak design and developed a decked sailing canoe, which he named *Rob Roy*. MacGregor launched the clinker-planked boat in 1865, and, driven by both the wind and his trusty double-bladed paddle, he explored and wrote about the waterways of Europe. His writings, penned as often as not from within a tent stretched over the cockpit, introduced a generation of outdoor enthusiasts in England and North America to kayak cruising. (He called the *Rob Roy* a canoe, a usage that would be understood in Great Britain today, but in North America the trim craft would be called a cruising kayak.)

Maybe it was the times. Economies were vibrating from boom to bust. Americans believed in homesteading; they pinned their hopes on a dozen Western gold rushes, and they strongly valued independence and self-sufficiency. Not a bad combination. "Canoes" became the affordable yacht, whether open in the traditional manner or decked and driven by a double-bladed paddle.

Small boating was a way of life in social clubs and sporting organizations. Name a river or a body of water and odds are there was a paddler chugging along it. By the 1930s paddlers had crossed the Atlantic and had navigated most of the rivers of Europe and North America. Paddling enthusiasts had divided into two subgroups: those dedicated to whitewater thrills and those who sought the pleasures of distance.

And that's the history. The present world of the cruising kayak has its origins in the resins of the first fiberglass-hulled kayaks, constructed in the 1950s. Sure, there had been plenty of wood kayaks and wood-frame and fabric-hull boats up until that time, but fiberglass created a whole new market of affordable boats and a generation of designers and builders aiming for stronger, lighter, and more-efficient craft. They succeeded beyond their wildest dreams. New fabrics were added to the mix, allowing designers to seek the outer limits of engineering. More than a few kayak designers and builders spilled out of the cyclical economy of the aerospace industry.

Delightfully enough, the new pastime was not particularly gender-specific. Women could match their male friends stroke for stroke in the sleek cruising kayaks, whether in circumnavigations of Hawaii or in beach-hopping explorations of remote Alaskan coasts.

With a kayak you set your own destination, your course, your speed, and you are responsible for your own decisions. That can be frightening, and equally liberating.

Kayak cruising is not an exaltation of brute strength, but a bending of skills to fit within the environment.

With the introduction of polyethylene plastic hulls in the closing years of the 1980s, mass production of kayaks became commonplace. The real-dollar price of fine cruising boats continued to fall while the quality of construction and design soared. Today, you can get a good cruising kayak for about the same price as a moderate- to good-quality bicycle. You'll spend a minimum of $1,000 with the basic accessories added in, though the total price may climb to several times that with more technologically sophisticated materials and more specialized designs.

So, what's the allure of this sport? The beauty you'll see . . . the quizzical look on a seal's face, the dip of a gull's wing over a wave, the large eye of a whale. The feeling of being responsible for yourself, the joy in making a boat glide where you want. The exploration of a new skill and the satisfaction of tired muscles at the end of a crossing. What's the appeal? Instead of talking about it, let's go paddling and you'll discover for yourself.

CHAPTER 2

What Is a Kayak?

Lawrence Roberg; licensed by Shutterstock.com

"What," I ask, "is a kayak?"

Your eyebrows shoot up as if I had just reached a new pinnacle of ignorance. Well, everyone knows that a kayak is a long, tippy boat in which you sit and which you propel with a double-bladed paddle. And then comes a long moment of silence. Except when it isn't.

Some kayaks are shorter than I am tall, and I'm no basketball player. Some are stable enough to stand up and walk around in, and others aren't. Some you sit in, some you sit on, and some are as open as a traditional canoe.

I have a short, fat canoe, a bare 13 feet long and a plump 38 inches across, and when I paddle down the bay from my home, as often as not I lean against my backrest and listen to the pattern of droplets flinging free from my double-bladed paddle. A kayak-building friend designs long, narrow, and way-efficient touring kayaks. He strokes along with the power from a bent-shaft marathon canoe paddle. Some canoes are decked over with only a tiny, open cockpit, which is sealed with a fabric spray deck.

Heck—there's even one kayak on the water that is propelled by pushing on pedals with your feet.

You can fly downwind sails to boost yourself along, or you can rig performance-oriented sails that are very competent mini-yachts.

Perhaps you and I can agree on some arbitrary distinctions. While kayaking, we sit down. In a canoe, we kneel. You can stand up, but let's ignore that and the folks who do it.

We'll side with physics. A longer hull, up to a point, requires less paddling effort to move it through the water. A long, narrow kayak may have the same carrying capacity of a short, beamy kayak, but the longer kayak will move forward with less effort. A long kayak will track—that is, will go straight—better than a shorter kayak.

Because we're interested in cruising, or touring, we want a kayak that will carry an adequate amount of gear, will be easy to paddle, and will go in a straight line without all sorts of corrections. We want a long, reasonably narrow kayak.

Kayaks that you sit upon can be great fun to paddle, from the racing surf skis to splashabout pond boats. However, the paddler is exposed to the sun, wind, waves, and temperature. Sitting inside your kayak offers a lot of environmental protection. So, for touring, most of us will choose to sit inside our boats.

Most touring paddlers choose solo kayaks. Some like the teamwork of a double kayak.

There is no single size of cruising kayak. There are solo kayaks for single paddlers, doubles or tandem for two, and some with a center cockpit ideally suited for kids. Length, beam—even the distance from the bottom of the hull to the inside of the deck—all reflect the different ideas of boat designers and the purposes to which those boats are headed.

You'll see a smattering of three-hole kayaks—some with a child in the center, and some chosen for the ease of loading or unloading gear.

Why does a kayak look as it does? Perhaps a kayak is function as well as form—a way of thinking about the act of traveling as much as it is the vehicle in which one travels.

Starting at the bottom, a kayak displaces water. In order to float, the hull must displace a greater volume of water than the combined weight of the boat, the associated gear and equipment, and the paddler. If the hull displaces a volume of water less than this combined weight, it sinks.

Water is not overly particular about the shape of solids floating upon it. As long as we

adhere to the basic flotation rule, and we are sitting motionless, we could be in a sphere, a cube, or a giant pencil. Once we start moving, though, all sorts of other things start happening. We become prisoners of friction and playthings of water movement.

For the fun of it, fill your sink with tepid water. Bring your fingers together so that you make a solid blade of your fingers and palm, put your hand in the water, and push it from one side of the sink to the other, palm first. You'll make a whopping great wave, the water swirling and boiling in behind your hand as it fills the hole you attempt to create. Now, turn your hand so that your little finger is the leading edge, and sweep back across the sink. You've

Kayak Bows and Cutwaters

All bows are not created equal. This figure shows three general styles of bows on touring kayaks, and all of them performing equally well but with slightly different handling characteristics. The dashed red lines show the shape of the hull.

Traditional Bow

With a traditional bow the sides of the hull flare out moderately, offering a reasonably dry ride (spray is thrown outward) and with plenty of buoyancy forward the kayak will rise over most waves. The cutwater—the forward edge of the bow—is steeply angled and so allows a relatively longer waterline.

Greenland Bow

With its long overhang (the distance from the furthest forward point of the bow back to where the bow cutwater cleaves the water) and flaring sides, the Greenland bow provides a dry ride. The long overhang, though, also means the actual waterline of the kayak is significantly shorter than the overall length, which in turn indicates a slightly slower kayak and one that is somewhat less likely to glide in a straight line.

Plumb Bow

The plumb or vertical bow creates the longest waterline compared to the overall kayak length. All other factors equal (they rarely are, but we can assume), the longer the waterline the more efficiently the kayak slips through the water and as a result requires the least effort to keep it moving. Most paddlers find longer waterline kayaks to hold a straight line better, and this means you spend less energy in correcting strokes. This style of bow has minimum flare, and cuts through waves rather than riding up and over them. You might get a little more spray in your face and water on your deck.

Basic Kayak Shapes

These are the three basic shapes for solo or single kayaks, as seen by the outline of their waterlines, which is sometimes called their footprint. The fourth is the footprint of a typical double or tandem kayak.

Symmetrical

With a symmetrical hull, the greatest beam is at the midpoint of the hull. The front and rear halves of the hull will be pretty much mirror images of each other.

Swedeform

With the Swedeform hull (sometimes spelled "Swede form"), the greatest beam is aft of the cockpit and the midpoint of hull. This design is often seen in downriver (wildwater) racing kayaks.

Fishform

With the fishform hull (sometimes spelled "fish form"), the greatest beam is forward of the cockpit and the midpoint of the hull.

Double Kayak

The double kayak has a basically symmetrical hull, with the cockpits moved from the middle of the kayak out toward the ends. If there is only a single paddler in the double, the kayak is unbalanced and more difficult to control. Some, configured with a third cockpit in the middle, can be paddled by a solo paddler, but the beam becomes a challenge.

now created less turbulence—a ripple rather than a wave—and you used much less effort in moving your hand through the water.

You've just seen why a narrow kayak moves more easily through the water than a great wide one. It has to push less water aside as it cleaves ahead, and the water flowing in behind to fill the hole doesn't have to move as far, or as fast. You didn't change the size of your hand; you just changed the angle of attack.

If that were the only variable in the equation, the rest of this would be simple: Narrow kayaks are better. But it isn't, and they're not. To see this for yourself, stand a 2x10 plank on edge and attempt to balance yourself atop it. It's difficult, if not impossible. Now flop it over so a 10-inch side rests on the ground, and you can stand on this board until you get bored.

And now you've demonstrated another principle of kayaking: For boats of equal

Kayak Cross Sections

Don't be misled by too much information. A good designer and a good boatbuilder can marry just about any bow profile to any hull cross section and profile and come up with a functional kayak. There are many factors in kayak design, and the kayak designer balances a host of needs with a broad array of features. In the end a kayak not only has to perform well under a wide range of conditions, but it also must look attractive.

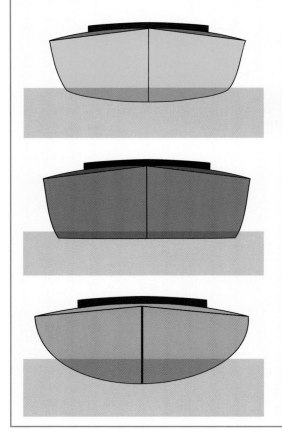

Flared Sides

A kayak with flared sides will normally be a drier kayak in waves and wind. Because of a narrower beam at the waterline, it could feel a bit tippier, but as it is leaned, the flare will make it a more buoyant boat in the water, resulting in a stable ride.

Flat Bottom

A kayak with a flat bottom might initially feel very stable and resist leaning . . . up to a point. It may well pound or slap the water when crossing waves.

Round Bottom

A truly round-bottomed kayak will feel very tippy— and for good reason. It is. It also has the least wetted surface and would probably be the quickest design when upright because of less friction with the water. Most "round-bottomed" kayaks really have somewhat flattened arches, and are reasonably stable.

displacement—you may hear the term *volume* in many kayak shops—broader boats are more stable than narrower boats. To be technical, this principle refers to beam, or the measurement from side to side across the widest part of the kayak.

What you're really looking for is that old golden mean—the ideal compromise. Of course, there are many factors that go into kayak design, but you start with sufficient displacement to keep you afloat, the narrowest hull that will allow you to move ahead efficiently, and sufficient beam to keep you reasonably stable.

What kind of numbers can you attach to this happy, middle-of-the-road kayak? Put the measuring tape on a couple dozen popular touring kayaks, and you'll average out a boat with a beam of 24 inches and a length of just about 17 feet. A narrower boat may have less

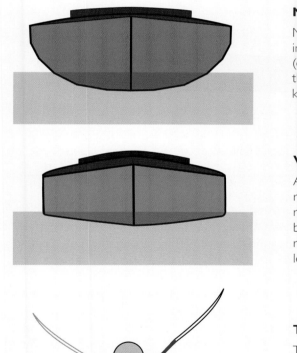

Multi-Chine

Most multi-chine kayaks are an adaptation of building materials to design. They use a number of planks (often thin plywood) formed to shape the kayak with the pleasing and efficient lines of a "round-bottomed" kayak.

Vertical Sides

A kayak with vertical sides, which may be easily married to a vee-bottom (as here), an arched or slightly rounded bottom, or a flat bottom, creates a wide beam at the waterline and, as such, is very stable. It resists leaning, and the amount of support it offers the leaning paddler is not consistent.

Tumblehome

Tumblehome refers to a turning in of the upper part of the sides of the hull as it mates with the deck and flows to the coaming. It allows a more vertical and efficient paddle stroke than does a kayak with a high and wide deck, and it does save your knuckles from thumping on your gunwales.

Keel Profiles

If you look at cruising kayaks in profile, you'll see that some have a straight keel from bow to stern while others have a keel line that is slightly curved. The amount of curve is called rocker, named no doubt from that old familiar rocking chair. Long, straight keels tend to "track," or go in a straight line, more easily than "rockered" keels. This is also a factor in allowing a kayak to turn: Rocker helps. Whitewater kayaks, which are all about quick and precise turns, are rockered like an old-time baby cradle.

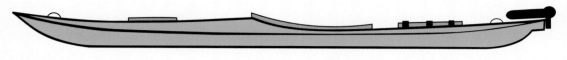

No Rocker
The keel line on this kayak is straight from the bottom of the bow to the stern.

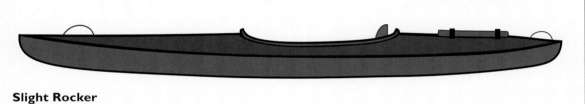

Slight Rocker
Most of the kayaks you'll paddle have a gentle curve, or slight rocker, from bow to stern. Some will have a slight rocker extending from the bow and the stern, with a straight keel line in the middle.

frontal resistance, but you will have to invest plenty of practice time in order to feel comfortable paddling. One rule of thumb is that you'll spend two full days—five to eight hours at a crack—practicing paddling for every inch whittled away from the beam. Miss a few days of practice on these toothpicks, and you'll be wobbling your cautious way one tentative stroke at a time.

Ah, but does that mean the 18-inch-beam boats are bad? Nope. When in their proper environment, they are a delight and a blast to paddle. If that's the type of cardiovascular-workout, high-efficiency, and technically proficient environment you want to inhabit, then the sprint boats are the way to go for you.

Designers keep evolving boat shapes and dimensions. Two-thirds of the way through the last century we saw a lot of touring boats around 5 meters long (that's a couple of inches over 16 feet) and 24 to 25 inches across the beamiest part. This changed, like fashion models, to kayaks that were 5.5 meters long (around 18 feet) and 23 inches wide.

Once that happened, a new generation of "recreational" kayaks appeared, about 4.5 meters long (15 feet) and 25 to 26 inches wide.

The "recreational" kayaks were easier to turn, store at home, and move to the water, and the huge cockpits certainly didn't feel confining.

Most double kayaks will be in the 19- to 21-foot range, with a few stretching to 23 feet.

That's a significant length. Physics and hydrodynamics show that longer kayaks are faster or easier to paddle than shorter ones, with the maximum efficient speed being 1.4 times the square root of the waterline. Up around 23 feet or so, the friction of the hull moving through the water becomes a greater factor than the mere waterline length.

The Cruising Kayak Family

There ain't no such thing as a cruising kayak—unless you mean a kayak of any description that you cruise in, and then it's a perfectly valid definition. There is a big family of cruising-friendly kayaks, and, like most families, they all look a little different. What follows is not a scientific description of genus and species, but a completely arbitrary set of introductions that will provide at least a nodding acquaintance with the various branches of the family.

Traditional Hardshells

When most of us think of cruising kayaks, traditional hardshells are likely what we picture: long and sleek hulls topped by a smooth deck, pierced by a snug cockpit, sharp ends—the picture of efficiency in a marine environment. Today most of them will be molded polyethylene plastic. It is a doggone-good material that produces a fine boat at a moderate cost. Next, in terms of numbers floating about, are made from composites. Some folks lump all of these together as fiberglass, but they're not. They are built of a resin-impregnated fabric, and that fabric can be fiberglass cloth, Kevlar, carbon fibers, and a host of proprietary materials and combinations of fabrics. I've never seen one made of burlap, but I have seen kayaks with a layer of brightly printed cotton cloth. They tend to have sharper bows and sterns and sleeker lines, and they often cost more than plastic boats because there is more hand labor in their fabrication.

We're starting to see elegant kayaks built with a plastic sandwich material, shaped in the pressures of a hot mold. These thermoplastics are marrying the advantages of the crisp lines and shape of space-age 'glass with the cost benefits of mechanized production.

Wood remains one of the materials most favored by people who are building just a boat or two. The rotating and temperature-controlled molds for plastic boats are an industrial process, and out of the realm of possibility for most backyard builders. Composite boats are laid up (fabricated) inside a finely finished mold using fairly toxic and stinky materials. Wood, on the other hand, is an easily worked material for craftsmen. You'll see a few cruising boats on the water planked up with stout materials and graceful lines, but these are increasingly rare. Somewhat more common are kayaks assembled from long and thin strips of wood edge-glued together and bent over removable forms. Most of these will be coated with resins and topped with a layer of fiberglass cloth. Strippers are fun to build, and the result can be a surprisingly light kayak that is amazingly strong and durable. Very carefully shaped planks of very thin plywood can be "sewn" together over removable forms, their seams glued, and the entire boat coated with resin and topped with a layer of 'glass. If you're tempted, I'd suggest looking at a kit boat, letting a computer design the shape of each plank and control the precise cutting of each of these.

And on the fringes? I've seen kayaks made of paper, concrete, and aluminum. Concrete boats were put together by civil engineering students at major universities, who then raced them against other schools. No doubt someone right now is attempting to build a silk craft out of a sow's ear.

Most hardshell kayaks come all of a piece, and that means you have a 17-foot (or more) hull to move or store when you're not paddling. A couple of manufacturers now build hardshell kayaks which they have cut into three sections, each section made waterproof with bulkheads, that can be assembled into fine touring boats. They are heavier than their one-piece cousins, and you pay a premium for the additional engineering and fabrication, but they are easier to move and store.

Frame-and-Fabric

These are the lineal descendants of the original kayak, updated with a few modern components. Think of a series of frames lined up from bow to stern establishing the shape of the boat, and long stringers bent over these frames from the very front to the absolute rear. Then a waterproof fabric is stretched tautly over the frame, just like our skin over our skeleton. Some frameworks are skillfully shaped pieces of wood, while others are fabricated from aluminum. Plastics are beginning to work their way into the mix, progressing beyond mere fasteners to structural frame members.

We don't use hide much these days for a covering. Coverings can range from cotton canvas sealed with marine paint to heat-shrunk and drum-tight synthetics. Many kayaks use a polyester fabric for the base support, sealed with a rubber-like synthetic or a vinyl coating. Kayak decks are traditionally made of canvas, breathable when dry and swelling to waterproofness when wet. Canvas worked just fine for the first modern kayaks crossing the Atlantic Ocean.

Frame-and-fabric kayaks come in two flavors, and, just as with ice cream, some paddlers prefer one and some the other. Some boats have a rigid frame and a permanently attached skin. The other flavor has a frame which may be disassembled with a few clips and nuts, removed from inside the skin, and within minutes, transformed into a bag of struts and braces alongside a rolled-up skin.

Frame-and-fabric designs are not as light as their fiberglass counterparts (true as of this writing, although the next boat out of the shop could prove me drastically wrong). Performance tends to lag a bit behind the hardshells, with a more-flexible hull that drinks up some of your paddling energy and, no matter how tightly you stretch it, still forms little concavities that slow you down. Their invaluable practicality comes rocketing to the forefront when you unsnap those clips and unscrew the nuts, and instead of having a great long dart to lug around, you have at most a backpack and a suitcase. If you must transport a boat, the frame-and-fabric designs become your only real choice. Yes, some of the hardshells can be unbolted into three sections, but they still don't match the tight packaging of the true folding kayaks.

Don't consider these inferior. Folding kayaks have crossed the Atlantic, poked their prows around Cape Horn and the Cape of Good Hope, circumnavigated most of Australia, and bumped into Arctic and Antarctic ice. These boats are tough. Make that *tough*. Hannes Lindemann's Klepper model, in which he crossed the Atlantic, was bought mail order, and the Klepper folks didn't even know what it was going to be used for until after the voyage.

Incidentally, the very nature of the fabric-hulled boats gives them a neat little advantage. Many fabric boats have air sponsons along the outside edges of the hull, providing flotation but also keeping the fabric tight. Most hardshell boats contain their flotation in the tight ends of the bow and stern. As a result, many hardshells tend to rotate freely once swamped, with the bow and stern flotation keeping them buoyant. Folding boats, with their flotation in sponsons on the sides of the hull, are much more stable when swamped— and far easier to re-board.

You will pay a premium for folding boats, and, as often as not, a very healthy premium over hardshells. But if you want to park your boat in a closet, or fly it as luggage, it's a premium well worth the cost.

And now a very personal bias: I love to paddle our big Klepper double kayak. The frame gently and slightly flexes with each paddle stroke and each wave, and it feels as if it yields and cooperates with the water rather than bashing along, fighting the bounce of each wave. It could be my imagination, but if it is, it's a fantasy I choose to live with. That said, we have composite, plastic, and stitch-and-glue wood kayaks, and all get their turn depending on our mood that day.

Sit-on-Tops and Wash-Decks

There are a lot of names for this broad spectrum of boats, encompassing just about every facet of kayaking. Hot rods stretch out to 20 feet and more, necked down to a bare 17 inches wide and used to race across vast distances of open ocean. I think a 30-mile-wide channel between islands rates as a vast distance, and these surf skis race such lengths between the Hawaiian Islands. At the other end of the scale, stubby wave skis shaped more like platters frolic in the crash and froth of breaking surf. Between the two extremes, midsize boats are great for lolling about from put-in to picnic, and at the same time are an ideal platform for serious cardiovascular exercise. Right now, several boats have carrying capacity for camping equipment and food. At first blush, sit-on-tops appear to be creatures of the warm seas. However, with modern protective clothing designed for paddlers, including wetsuits and dry suits, these are truly year-round craft.

Opponents castigated early sit-on-tops, claiming they were not true kayaks because they could not be Eskimo-rolled in the event of an upset. Paddlers, nestled in a slight depression on the deck, simply fall off. Proponents countered by arguing that there was no reason to Eskimo-roll a sit-on-top since it was so easy to scramble back aboard following a capsize. And the advantages are many, they claimed: no claustrophobia, no being hemmed in by a narrow hull and confining cockpit. Confounding both points of view are the new sit-on-tops, with braces that allow you to use your legs to hold yourself on the boat during some radical maneuvers, which include self-rescue rolls.

A powerful argument for the sit-on-tops is their short history. There is no long tradition of the "proper" way to paddle them, the "correct" clothing to wear in them, or even the "acceptable" paddling hat. These are boats floating in the "now"; they simply invite you to splash out and have fun.

Inflatables

Inflatables, in the cruising kayak world, are an acquired taste. In no way am I dissing them. Inflatables have circumnavigated many of the Hawaiian Islands, for example, and cruised for a thousand miles along the rugged and sparsely inhabited Alaska coast. They have skirted pristine beaches in Southeast Asia, poked their bows among icebergs in the Far North and at the other pole, and explored the rivers and canals of Europe.

So why the "acquired taste" caveat? I'm used to narrow kayaks, and an 18-foot inflatable double can be 36 inches across its middle. This demands a long paddle shaft and significant accommodations to the stroke repertoire. Perhaps that's because I'm not used to having a nearly 12-inches-in-diameter tube between my hip and the other edge of the gunwale. It seems to me—and this is purely an unsubstantiated opinion—that inflatables are a little harder to push along. It also seems that they are a bit more affected by wind than their hardshell cousins.

Balancing that, and depending on your specific needs more than overbalancing the above, is the unarguable fact that these boats are portable. A deflated 18-foot AIRE Sea Tiger double kayak, with a beam of 3 feet, can be rolled up and carried in a manageable, conventional wheeled duffel, and its take-apart paddles, personal flotation devices (PFDs), and related gear fits in another. You can hop around Europe by train with one of these and never get a raised eyebrow. They'll fit in a taxi, and will slide into the luggage compartment of a small plane. Easily? Well, the hull tips the scale in the mid-60-pounds range. Most of us can handle that.

What about when you get to a put-in? It takes about ten minutes to use the Sea Tiger's pump to inflate it.

There are a bunch of good inflatables available today. I referred to the Sea Tiger because it is a big boat. You may well find a smaller boat more suitable for your particular needs.

A few other benefits of the puff-'em-up boats: A double can comfortably carry up to 700 pounds. They are amazingly stable, to the point where it is very difficult to even get them to tilt. If you actually manage to flip one, they are pretty easy to pop back up, and, once upright, you can clamber back aboard. It is a good idea to practice this before you need to do it, but it's not daunting.

With today's engineering and materials, they are durable. I know of well-used boats more than a decade old with nary a patch.

Solo or Tandem?

You may carry an archetypal kayak in your mind, comparing the object before you with the reality that you can only see with your eyes closed. For most of us the kayak is a swift, silent, and solo boat—whether slipping along a coastline or cavorting in the froth of a rapid. The sleek Greenland-designed kayaks, with their flaring bows, certainly adhere to this standard, but the baidarkas surging out of the Aleutian Islands in the Far West were cut to a different design. Perhaps in response to a localized need, or possibly born of Russian explorations along the western North American coast, the several-cockpit baidarkas proved themselves superb sea boats as they shuttled from the fringes of Arctic Alaska to northern California. For a half century, folding double kayaks have plied the waters of every continent.

Which leads to the crux of the matter: Which is better?

Sorry. There's no definitive answer. Each has a hatful of advantages, and the art of choosing lies in matching your needs to the conditions in which you'll be paddling.

Most of the time when I paddle with my companions, we look like an undisciplined horde pouring down the surface of the bay. But appearances can be deceiving, as we've paddled together long enough to incorporate the group safety practices that support each of us, even if it may not look like it. One friend is a physical fitness fanatic, and in his long and narrow boat he darts ahead and lags far behind, much like a coursing dog during the first miles of a backpacking trip into the mountains. Another is a fisherman, and his boat is merely a platform that carries him to fishing grounds. A third paddles a high-volume, beamy kayak stuffed with cameras and the paraphernalia of his art. Still another gunkholes along—*gunkholing* being the habit of poking into every nook and cranny along the way.

It's pretty obvious that we don't paddle the same kinds of boats, and that we don't cruise along like a line of trunk-to-tail elephants. With our unique personalities and our different needs, it's also obvious that we're all in solo boats. Any attempt to put a sprinter in with a fisherman inevitably leads to bruised egos and disagreement. So the solo cruising kayak gives us the solitude and control of our immediate destiny that is all so rare in today's hurly-burly world.

Double kayaks, on the other hand, are greater than the sum of their parts.

There are many good reasons for choosing a double kayak. Two paddlers of equal strength and skill will go faster and farther or will arrive at their destination less tired if they are paddling one double kayak rather than a pair of solos. A double is more stable than a single of equal design. A double allows paddlers of differing strengths and skills to paddle as one, with the least emotional friction.

A double enables a strong-paddling parent to carry a child in the bow cockpit, and the station wagon–size boats (that feature a center cargo hatch) can allow a family to paddle together with the floating equivalent of a playpen amidships. In a group, the double can carry a tired or injured paddler.

And now for the real reason to paddle a double: It's fun. You can share, you can chat, you can be a second pair of eyes with a ready *Look at that!* in response to the roll of an orca or the breath-like shadow of a loon across a lake.

My wife and I dreamt of owning a double kayak and saved for years for a Klepper Aerius. This big, folding kayak had been for half a century the boat of choice for explorers and wanderers, and we saw it as the perfect vessel for cruising close to home, as well as for packing compactly on air flights to odd corners of the continent. Coins were stashed in a secret jar; the occasional bill was tucked away and ignored for a while; the check from an odd job was earmarked. I finally ordered our dream boat, and it arrived on the eve of Valentine's Day while my wife was halfway across the country playing in a tennis tournament. I lugged it up to our second-floor family room, put it together, and spent the next couple of hours carefully gift-wrapping the boat—all 17 feet of it—with a big red bow around the middle. My wife flew in at 10:00 p.m., walked into the family room at 11:00, and shrieked at 11:01. We carefully hoisted the (by-now) unwrapped boat out an upstairs window, across the garage, and atop our van. Twenty minutes later, in the drizzle, we were floating on a lake with the lights from the shore glittering in the night.

"Oh," my wife exclaimed. "We forgot to christen her. We forgot the champagne."

There are moments when you don't have to say anything. I handed her a goblet and popped the cork.

You can't do that in a solo boat.

Doubles, especially the bigger ones with the center hole, certainly can carry more gear than a single kayak. You can load aboard the multi-burner stove, the big water jugs—even the kitchen sink. This carrying capacity is a definite plus, but don't be misled into thinking a double can carry twice as much as a single. Two solo boats can easily and efficiently carry more weight than one double kayak. Your double may be 50 percent bigger (I just made up that number, but it's in that range) than one solo boat, but it is not as big as two solo boats. Think about it. Put two solo boats side by side, with the bow of one just about at the cockpit of the other. Then, with a chain saw, cut the bow off one boat and the stern off the other. Scoot the mutilated hulls together sideways and glue them into a whole. The pieces you have left over show the volume you lose.

One way of looking at it is that you can stow the gear that fits into three backpacks into an "average" solo touring kayak. You don't need all that gear, and you sure as heck don't want to push it about, move it from the beach to your campsite, or—heaven forbid—portage it. You can stow the equivalent of four backpacks and maybe a fanny pack or two in your double.

So you're teetering on the edge of laying out a bunch of bucks for a touring double, and you still need a few reasons to take the final plunge. After all, it always helps to have someone pushing at you from behind and insisting that your idea was pretty good in the first place.

Here are four reasons to buy a tandem kayak:

1. You have a family. Once your child is of a size to be trusted in a cockpit alone, a double becomes a necessity. Drop a strong and skillful paddler into the stern hole, and a child into the bow cockpit, and you can kayak-camp and kayak-cruise at your

leisure. One adult can handle most of the touring doubles, giving up a little speed and distance for the real pleasure of watching a child come face-to-face with a beautiful world. If your family includes a child and a pair of adults, add a single to your fleet. The child and one adult can paddle the big boat while the other adult paddles solo. Soon enough the adults will be back in the double while the child paddles off on his or her own. Lifting a double down from atop a car and lugging it to the water's edge is a challenge for one person, but it can be done.

2. Doubles are romantic. Trust me.

3. You'll always be paddling with a partner, if not a whole group. Despite the best of intentions, accidents happen. You might sprain a wrist, develop a blister on one hand, come down with tendonitis, or be weakened by the flu. If you're paddling in a double, your companion can obviously help you out. And with a double in a boating party, an ill, injured, or tired paddler can switch over to the big boat and continue on to camp, or to safety. Your option

in a party of solo boats is to rig a towline, which, while doable, is seldom satisfactory to the towee or to the one doing the towing.

4. Life's about sharing. Sunrises, the ripple rings spreading out from a drop of rain, an otter diving over the midsection of your boat as you glide around a rock on a rugged coast. Ghosting along a line of houseboats while a dulcimer and a recorder play Christmas carols with the stars diamond bright and a lantern on a pole bobbing at your stern.

A caveat: Some people should never be bridge partners nor ride a tandem bicycle together. Paddling should be fun, and if your and your companion's paddling styles clash, you may well be happier in a pair of solo boats.

Whatever you decide, your basic kayak is going to be the kayak you like. You may prefer to paddle in a single kayak or team up in a double; you may embark on a monthlong voyage or an afternoon picnic; you may leisurely glide along or strain to hold top speed. The pleasure of paddling lies in finding your own style.

CHAPTER 3

What Is It Made Of?

We know, right down to our bones, that our toys are the most sophisticated and technologically advanced ever seen on the face of this planet. Of course, everyone before us thought the same. There's a story, perhaps apocryphal, that in the waning days of the nineteenth century there was a movement in Congress to abolish the US Patent Office on the grounds that everything that was worth inventing already had been.

Reset your wristwatch back ten millennia or so, and let's visit an Inupiat exploring the Arctic shore, just emerging from the continental ice sheet of the most recent ice age. He needed to cross glacial melt as well as salt water, and he needed to both stalk game and bring that game home. Wooden rafts or dugout canoes were out of the question, as there were no big trees. Even if logs had been available, his environment precluded their use. Boggy conditions subject to frequent icing over and thin leads of open water surrounded by moving pack ice demanded a light, sturdy, and seaworthy boat. His cultural economy was based on hunting, meaning he had to see where he was going rather than where he had been.

In a flash of technological brilliance he figured out that he could build a skeleton of wood and bone strikingly similar to his own rib cage, and over that stretch a treated hide to make a floatable object—the first kayak. Remember that the great ice sheets were barely retreating and that these people were exploring what then was a resource-poor environment. Those first boats were a magnificent utilization of the available resources meeting the demands of an unforgiving environment.

It is likely that the first kayak was a hunter's boat. But these were nomadic people, moving in search of food. The same design was

expanded, the deck removed, and it became a cargo and passenger vessel—the *umiak*.

Was that first kayak-building Inupiat male or female? We have no idea. It probably took every member of the family or village to find the pieces of wood and bone for the frame, hunters to bring back the sea mammals that would yield hides for the covering and sinews to lash the frame together, and craftsmen to shape the pieces and prepare the skins. Sort of like the space shuttles of their time.

Most amazing to me is the truth that despite our wider choice of available materials, today's kayak bears the recognizable stamp of

An Arctic hunter from two millennia ago would immediately feel at home in one of today's frame-and-fabric kayaks—the direct descendants of the boats he built as the ice melted.

that first builder. How many other machines or devices are in use today after ten to fifteen millennia?

Each of the hand-shaped wooden components in this replica has been lashed together. There are no nails, screws, or glue used in the entire frame.

Fact is, that first Inupiat hunter would probably feel pretty much at home in today's frame-and-fabric Feathercraft or Klepper kayaks, and could drop right into a Necky plastic cruising kayak with only a few grunts of amazement at the rigidity of the skin.

Virtues of the Common Materials

The overwhelming majority of today's kayaks are built from one of four families of materials: polyethylene (plastic), composites (flexible fabric supported in resin), frame-and-fabric, and wood. What's best? To answer that, you have to paddle into the builder's mind. The choice of hull material teeters atop a pyramid of strength, weight, and cost, measured against the builder's vision of how the boat must perform in the changing conditions of the real world. It's important to remember, and to repeat, that you're buying a kayak and not a material. You should start with a dealer you trust and with whom you can communicate, a design that fits your desires and needs, and a reputable manufacturer. You want a boat that fits you, that will carry you safely and efficiently on the voyages you dream of, and that you can learn to love. The function you seek determines the incidental material of the hull.

Frame-and-Fabric

The first kayak ever was a frame-and-fabric boat, and a lot of paddlers firmly believe that nothing since then has surpassed the original. Over the last century they've poked around on every continent, explored whitewater rivers and remote lakes, and crossed oceans. Scientists, explorers, the military, and casual recreationists have used them.

Imagine a peeled banana. Cut it crosswise into seven or eight pieces. (It's okay if you nibble one, because this is only an example.) Each of those cuts is the shape of a frame. Now run a half-dozen or a dozen little strips of wood from one pointy end of the banana to the other. Those are stringers. Between the frames and the stringers you've created the shape of the banana. Slip this shape back into the peel, which we'll now call the fabric skin, and you'll perfectly understand a frame-and-fabric skin kayak. Other than the fact they don't have bananas growing in the Arctic, this matches the original kayak.

Many of these designs have wooden frames and wooden stringers, with metal fittings clipping everything together. Many, but not all. Some have structural components fabricated from aluminum, others molded from plastics. One paddler prefers aluminum, saying it requires less maintenance, while the paddler in a boat with a wood frame counters (while varnishing) with the claim that aluminum must be equally cleaned and protected from saltwater

corrosion. The wood-frame advocate says that wood is easier to repair in the wilderness, while the aluminum-frame paddler simply points to the tube repair kit that comes with most aluminum boats. The plastics aficionado may boast of economy, ease of care, and precision molding.

I suspect that, blindfolded, most of us couldn't tell the difference between one and the other.

Most of the skins come with a synthetic fabric base, with a heavier coating on the hull to cope with greater wear. Some boats are wrapped in a woven fabric—originally cotton canvas, but now in many cases a stout

A hand-sewn kayak gives and moves with the waves, feeling almost as if it is alive. The strength of the hull is that it can bend and give to the forces in the sea, rather than rigidly resisting them.

synthetic—all sealed with several coats of marine paint. Often the painted base fabric is tacked securely to the frame.

The big difference in this family of kayaks is that some have frames that can be easily disassembled and slipped from within the skin. The skin can be rolled up and the frames and stringers separated and stowed, so the whole kayak fits in the corner of a closet. Others have a rigid frame and do not come apart.

The convenience of a take-apart boat is matched by the additional price when you buy it. Your choice hinges on how you want to transport or store your boat. As with hull color, the choice really boils down to the taste of the paddler.

A more significant choice may involve cockpit layout. Some frame-and-fabric tandem boats have individual cockpits for each paddler, while others have a large cockpit holding both paddlers with a two-hole spray skirt or spray deck covering the cockpit.

A second major option involves methods of keeping the fabric skin taut on the frame. Some boats have a snug-fitting skin snapped to the frame, with the final skin tension coming as the paddler inflates air bladders within the skin structure. The military version of the Klepper, for instance, has four such bladders that provide a near-rigid skin along with amazing stability and flotation. Other manufacturers go with a skin that must be pulled tight and hooked to the frame—a slower, more difficult, but less expensive alternative. Assembly time can range from five minutes to half an hour, depending on model and manufacturer.

Wood

Wood-hulled cruising kayaks have been around for a century or more. Historically, hulls were laid up with lightweight lapstrake or smooth planking over steam-bent ribs, much like traditional canoes. Today there are two common techniques in building wooden kayaks. *Strip-built*

boats are constructed out of narrow strips of thin wood fitted over a mold (or frames), with each strip of wood edge-glued to its neighbors. Hulls and decks are formed separately and removed from their molds before being coupled together. Most are covered with a layer or two of fiberglass and resin. *Stitch-and-glue boats* are shaped out of accurately cut "planks" of thin plywood that are wrapped around molds and then "stitched" together along each edge with wire "thread." They are also covered with one or more layers of 'glass and resin.

The first kayaks were sewn together—not only the skin, but also the frames and the stringers that formed the skeleton of the boat. Today many builders use wire rather than sinew, and stitch their kayaks together from carefully shaped strips of plywood rather than animal hide. It's still a lot of hand-sewing.

Strip-built and stitch-and-glue boats really mark a huge step in kayak technology, the development of the monocoque hull. Dictionary words aside, the monocoque *hull* is one in which the skin is the structural component rather than there being a rigid skeleton supporting a flexible and yet watertight skin.

Some home builders construct kayaks that are the link between frame-and-fabric-skin boats and wood kayaks, in which the hull is supported without frames—the strip-built and sewn-together hulls we've already discussed. They have the frames and stringers of a frame-and-fabric skin craft, but instead of a flexible fabric hull, they are planked with sheets of plywood fastened to the frames. Sometimes these frames are sawn from marine plywood, and sometimes glued and bolted together from shaped pieces of solid wood

Wood boats tend to be very strong, very light, and expensive. Part of the cost is in the nature of the raw material. Straight-grain, knot-free wood usually comes from old trees and is pricey. At the same time, craftspeople who work with wood are willing to put in the extra touches that transform an eminently practical hull into a work of art. You're likely to find inlays, painted decorations, and a host of other special flourishes. Since it takes somewhere between 100 and 150 hours to hand-build a wood kayak, it's easy to see how costs can quickly mount. Yes, some builders can launch a boat out of their shop in less time (some will take even longer), but the creation of a wood kayak is as much an act of love as the manufacture of any quality product, and the buyer will pay for that time one way or another.

It's all in the eye of the beholder, but wood kayaks look warm and just so darned pretty.

Composites—Fiberglass and Its Cousins

Composite construction revolutionized kayak building. Frame-and-fabric kayaks and wood kayaks to a large extent were the products of individual craftsmen. Composites coupled with molds industrialized production. Hey, don't belittle the skill involved. I've built composite boats and it is challenging. Laying the fabric wrinkle-free, properly wetting out the fabric with just the right amount of resin (too little and you get a dry spot void, too much and you add weight), avoiding runs and curtains as you apply the resin, mixing consistent color . . . and you're working with pretty potent chemicals—that stink! All the time you're under the time gun of resins that will harden all too soon. Building a composite boat is a wonderful blend of craftsmanship and art.

In principle, it's simple. Visualize a few layers of fabric soaked in a resin (usually polyester, vinylester, or epoxy) and draped tightly within a female mold. That's not sexist. A female mold is hollow, and you lay your layers of fabric inside the hollow. The first layer, next to the mold, is the outer skin of the kayak, and subsequent layers build inward. This results in a mirror-smooth outer layer. I don't know anyone building composite hulls with a male mold. A male mold would be solid, for all practical purposes, and the layers of fabric would be laid over the mold. The outer layer, the outside of the finished hull, would be rough and would look unfinished. Wood can be bent over a male mold for a wooden kayak. The fabric may be traditional fiberglass, or one of the high-strength materials such as Kevlar, carbon fiber, or any of a number of proprietary cloths. Don't be surprised if the boat you find is a sandwich of a number of materials, combining the virtues of each.

The resin sets and becomes rigid, and a sleek and stiff hull is created. That's in principle. In the real world, builders have concocted an incredible variety of resin formulas poured over an equally staggering number of fabrics in their search for the strongest, toughest, and lightest hull. A hull's strength is indicated in its ability to retain its shape under stress, without

Composite kayak hulls are amazingly light, wonderfully strong, and precisely molded, and with the evolution of composite technology and chemistry, pretty darned cheap. All that and you get to explore the edge of the sea!

cracking or splitting. Its toughness depends on its ability to withstand the sandpaper-like abrasion of landings, as well as the dings and nicks of day-to-day existence. Everyone is concerned about weight, but few people stop to think that the bare hull of a boat only accounts for about one-fourth of its total weight. The other three-quarters comes from the seats, coamings, hatches, hardware, bulkheads, and the gizmos that you hang on or around your craft. Even at that, you yourself will outweigh your boat by two to three times. Nevertheless, you don't need to pack around a lot of excess weight, so if you can pare away a few unneeded pounds from your kayak and equipment, you will be better off.

Most composite sea kayaks have a layer of pigmented resin on the outside of the hull and deck. It's called the *gel coat*. This layer, in addition to carrying the bright colors of the boat, also provides a wearing surface against the abrasion of beach landings, as well as shielding the resins and fabrics from the piercing rays of the sun.

Where does cost come into this? If you add strength or toughness, or if you reduce weight without diminishing the first two, you're going to add money into the pot.

A composite hull should be rigid. It shouldn't creak and flex underneath you, and it shouldn't develop patterns of hairline cracks at stress points, nor have its tape pull away from its seams. When you shift your weight from the shore to the cockpit rim, you shouldn't feel the deck slump in, and when you slide your weight onto the seat, you shouldn't feel the cockpit rim compress toward your hips.

Run your fingers along the seams, or under the edge of the cockpit. A smooth finish is a good sign—not an ironclad guarantee of a fine boat, but certainly a good sign. Stick your head deep into the cockpit and look out through the

You can paddle anywhere on this globe and you're probably following in the wake of another kayaker. And yet each day's paddle is a new experience.

side of the hull. If the gel coat is of uniform thickness, the light coming through the hull will be uniform. If you have splotches of light and chunks of shadow glimmering through the gel coat, you should suspect an uneven gel coat or a hull of unexpectedly varying thicknesses.

Unless you're an Olympic racer, don't be enticed by claims of lightness. First of all, in the real world of boat production, reinforcement means both strength and weight. You can build a light boat of superlative strength, but you will pay for it. Pay for it originally, and pay for higher repair and upkeep from the everyday knocks of paddling. If you desperately need to spend money, pop for a really good paddle and let the boat rest in the hands of the water.

Look for bubbles, scabs, or what looks almost like colorless rust—these are all symptoms of flaws in the manufacturing process.

They may just be cosmetic, or they may be cosmic.

Last, take a look down the hull or the deck. Don't expect a mirror-smooth finish, but are you looking at a major wavy surface? That's worth being a bit concerned about.

A few manufacturers can supply "take-apart" fiberglass kayaks. These are rigid-hulled boats that have been cut into three or four pieces. The sections can be bolted into a single, strong, and waterproof hull—and since the sections can nest somewhat, the take-apart hull is a bit easier to store or transport.

What would that original Inupiat builder think of a composite kayak? Well, he might opine, it looks like a real kayak. If he stuck his head in the cockpit he might be puzzled because he wouldn't be able to see the supporting framework. Then he'd touch the hull and all would become clear. Someone, probably one of the ladies, had found a way to make the hides stiff. Other than that, it's a kayak just like his.

Plastics

Back in the Dark Ages of chemistry, ethylene was one of the oddities of petrochemical production. It was a kind of waxy-feeling substance, apparently without a lot of practical use. But one day someone discovered that you could string huge numbers of ethylene molecules together as polyethylene. A whole new plastics industry was born. Not only was it a new material, but it was also a radical new way of molding complex shapes. Pellets of polyethylene plastic could be melted in a temperature-controlled mold, and a complete kayak hull could be fabricated right inside the molding machine. It's not that easy, but that's the basic idea. Once you learn how to pop a serving bowl out of the mold, you can shape a kayak.

In addition to two kinds of polyethylene, there are two ways of forming polyethylene boats. Both methods produce fine hulls. Each starts by melting polyethylene pellets within a mold. Rotating and tilting the mold to spread the polyethylene and to allow thicker buildups in such wear areas as the keel, stem, and stern form rotomolded hulls. The other method, blow-molding, uses air pressure to force the molten plastic into every nook and cranny of the mold.

If you string ethylene molecules together into long chains, you have linear polyethylene. Hook the molecules so that the chains also extend sideways, and you have cross-linked polyethylene. Cross-linked is a more rigid material, more resistant to damage and requiring less interior bracing. Linear polyethylene is a tad less rigid and strong, but it is far easier to repair by an amateur if it is damaged. The other major difference is that with current technology, linear polyethylene is very easy to recycle, while cross-linked is out on the fringes of the possible. That could change with one twist of a test tube, of course.

Concerned about recycling? Figure that just about any blackish part of a plastic kayak probably first saw the light of day as some other part. Virtually every boat manufacturer uses recycled plastic in seats, coamings, deck plates, and other non-hull components. Remember when you puddled every one of your watercolors together? The resulting mess was sort of a deep muddy gray—certainly not one of the more appealing shades on your palette. The same thing happens with recycled linear plastic. As of yet, there is little color separation of the plastic going back into the hopper to be re-melted, and with the blues and the reds and the greens and the yellows going in, a mucky gray oozes out. While manufacturers could add a very substantial amount of pigment to the new plastic (and beef that up with more plastic to make the mix as strong as it was the first time around), it's more efficient and practical just to add a little black to bring the mix to a marketable color.

Even with this information about the recycled portion of the boat, you might as well admit it: You have a nagging feeling that somehow plastic just isn't socially correct. Yes, plastic is made from petrochemicals, but isn't it better to create a renewable resource from the crude bubbling out of the ground than to burn it up in making electricity or creating auto exhaust? You can cut down forests to make wood boats, dam rivers to produce electricity to refine aluminum, or . . . well, the point is that just about anything we use carries an environmental cost. A piece of polyethylene plastic lying on the ground is inert and won't be leaching toxic substances into the earth. Collect that piece, chop it up, and it can be re-melted into new forms. That includes the sad moment when your boat is thoroughly thrashed. It can be recycled into the raw material for a new boat.

Plastics revolutionized kayak building. There is a lot of hand work and art in the top kayak, a German frame-and-fabric boat. On the bottom is a plastic sit-on-top. The design is art, the fabrication of the mold shaping it is painstaking, but the actual building is an industrial process that yields very affordable and top-quality kayaks.

In most linear plastic boats, you're likely to find interior supports such as bulkheads, walls, ribs, and even stringers. These aren't a sign of a "weak" boat that has been beefed up, but are a mark of sound engineering taking full advantage of the structural characteristics of plastic.

Unfortunately, we don't have a single plastic that is the best choice for every part in a kayak. Some builders are working with panels made of a sandwich of different plastics, which when shaped in a hot mold appear to offer superior design possibilities.

If you were to weigh plastic and fiberglass hulls of equal quality, odds are that the fiberglass hull would be a touch lighter. You might also notice that the corners and edges of the fiberglass hull are a little sharper than those of its plastic counterpart. Most of us, though, wouldn't perceive these minor differences once the hulls are in the water. What we would notice, however, is the weight of our wallets after buying the boat of our choice.

Given boats of equal quality and design, mass-produced plastic hulls tend to be more economical than labor-intensive fiberglass hulls.

Generally speaking, you can bang a plastic hull around pretty good and it will pop back into the shape it memorized in the mold. Whack a composite boat like that and you'll see a spiderweb of stress cracks in the surface. However, the plastic hull can be cut more easily than a composite. Treat either one with the respect they deserve and they'll serve you long and well.

Other than wondering how we turned perfectly good hide into this new, slick substance, our Inupiat would recognize this plastic boat as being much like his.

Inflatables

Inflatable kayaks seem, at first look, a long step away from their forebears up on the Arctic shore. Take some time for another look, and you'll be surprised.

Imagine two elongated bananas. Well, they're not really bananas, but they are shaped quite a bit like them—other than the fact that they're about 5.5 meters long and about 26 centimeters (10.5 inches) in diameter. Put 'em side by side and glue the pointy ends together. Wedge out the two tubes to about a half-meter (20 inches or thereabouts) back, a comfortable seating distance from the pointy end you call the bow, and about the same distance from the stern pointy end.

Span the area between the tubes with a flexible floor and glue the floor to the tubes.

Without the design skills, engineering, and technical abilities needed to build a real one, you've just fabricated an inflatable touring kayak. You're still short a few things: seats, backrests, foot braces, and probably a rudder and foot-operated rudder controls.

Some inflatables will have the floor right down at the bottom of the side tubes. If water splashes in, you'll bail or sponge it out. Others will have a floor elevated to about the water level, with valves or slots in the floor to let water drain away. Some inflatables are decked, with a conventional cockpit. Others are open, but in many cases can have fitted tarps lashed over the open areas.

Multiple air chambers offer more security. If one chamber oozes air, the others will continue to support the kayak and passenger; however, the additional walls and seams do add weight to the craft.

An inexpensive kayak may be built of unreinforced or unsupported polyvinyl chloride (PVC) plastic or rubber. The low initial cost is counterbalanced by a more-fragile hull and normally a less-efficient design.

Most enthusiast-caliber inflatables are made with a base fabric topped with an airtight and abrasion-resistant coating. Nylon has been the most common base material, with polyester catching up in popularity. Some manufacturers are now fitting inflatables with fabrics such as Kevlar—used in bulletproof vests—incorporated into high-wear areas for light weight and durability.

The most common coatings are neoprene, Hypalon, PVC, urethane, and ethylene propylene diene monomer (EPDM). Not all fabrics or coatings are created equal, even those with the same name. As a rule of thumb, the higher the percentage of coating compound in the coating material, the better the quality. For instance, a compound with 65 percent neoprene would probably be of better quality than a compound with 40 percent neoprene.

The fabric's fineness is measured by *denier*, which is the weight in grams of 9,000 meters of yarn. The greater the denier, the heavier the yarn. Don't grab this number too quickly, assuming that heavier yarn indicates strength. The weight of the yarn does not indicate the tightness of the weave, or the bursting or tear strength of the fabric.

A balanced weave is a fabric with its warp and weft—that is, the lengthwise and crosswise threads—made of the same denier yarn. An unbalanced weave has the warp and weft made of different denier yarn.

What would our ancient Inupiat think of your inflatable? He knew how to build air-filled floats, which he used for hunting. He may not understand why you stuffed floats along each side of your kayak, but he will recognize their shape and function. He'd be surprised at the beam of the kayak, until he understood the function of the structural air tubes. The idea of using air to support the hull structure would be alien, because he didn't have easily available and durable materials to fabricate large airtight structures. The hull material may seem a little more familiar because of its resiliency. All told, he'd decide you were limited by your materials, but that you did manage to build a serviceable boat despite those limitations.

Christopher Day; licensed by Shutterstock.com

CHAPTER 4

Outfitting Your Basic Kayak

Think about your kayak for a minute. Not the kayak of your dreams, compounded out of reverie, brochures, advice, or sales talk, but the essential hull of your boat. It's a tube with a pointy end and a place for the paddler. A cruising kayak is simply basic transportation. You can keep it simple, or you can turn it into a floating advertisement for every accessory and gadget your wallet will bear. Somewhere in between is that golden mean where you match your paddling style with the equipment necessary to support it. I'm pretty sure that you're going to find that simpler is better, and that rugged quality trumps fashion.

What's your paddling passion? This wash-deck kayak is rigged with permanently mounted rod holders, bait tank, tackle storage, fish finder (on the pedestal between the paddler's knees), anchor, and drogue as an ultimate fishing machine.

The basic hull of your kayak, just sitting here on the beach, looks awfully bare. What do you really need for a safe and comfortable day on the water?

You're not going to have much of a choice on some things, because they are integral parts of the kayak. These may be "upstream" choices—things you have to consider when you're still searching for the object of your desire. The kayak itself will limit your choices. There are some things the folks in the kayak shop might insist you must include, and they could be right. It might also be that they haven't listened to your plans for how and where you want to paddle, and they are offering a generic package of accessories in a one-size-fits-all approach. Don't ignore them, thinking they're just trying

to make a bigger sale. You might learn that most of these goodies are really important, some are vital, and some are just plain convenient. Most of the folks in paddling shops are passionate and knowledgeable about our sport, and they are willing to share their expertise. It's up to you, though, to listen to that advice and pick out that which is applicable to your kayak; you're the one that will be paddling it.

Seats

You ought to start with the seat, well before you settle on the brand, model, or color of your kayak. If you're uncomfortable at the end of a paddling day, no matter how great the rest of the boat is, you're going to have a bad relationship with kayaking.

What do we mean by a seat? It is a structure that provides your sit-bones a degree of comfort and your back just the right amount of support, all the while letting you transmit the energy of your muscles into movement.

Many kayaks, but not all, offer a molded seat supported from the cockpit coaming. It will have foam supports on each side, between the seat and the hull, to curb any sideways sway, and foam under the seat itself to prevent sag. The seating platform itself is usually 1 to 2 inches above the hull.

So far, so good. Some seats will have a back-band, or lumbar support, that is essentially a several-inch-wide strap. You adjust the length of the back-band, and its support, with small bolts through the side supports of the seat and a series of holes in the back-band itself, sort of like the holes in a belt. These work pretty well.

Some back-bands are adjusted with a line from one end of the back-band leading through a jam cleat on the side of the seat itself. You can easily adjust the angle of support even while out on the water.

Some adjustable seats have a curved back panel hinged in some fashion on the bottom, with an adjusting mechanism that allows you to dial in the angle of the most comfortable back support. These seats come in two flavors. One is the frame suspended from the coaming, with the back support hinged to the seat base. The other has an independent seat, not dangling from the coaming but supported on the bottom of the kayak hull. I first had these for a sit-on-top kayak and have on occasion moved them into more-traditional boats.

I find the least comfortable backs are those solid and nonadjustable ones molded directly into the boat. Some of the frame-and-fabric boats have seat backs directly fastened to the coamings, and while they do rotate—which means being a bit more form-fitting—they can't be adjusted fore and aft.

Some touring boats are made with no back-support system built into the boat. The idea—in terms of the fact that most of us like some sort of back support—is that the paddler would place a dry storage bag filled with gear behind the cockpit and gain support from that. Do you really want to cram a full and heavy touring bag into your boat just for a couple of hours of evening paddling?

Beware, however, of seats that are suspended well above the hull. Low is beautiful, because low means you have a lower center of gravity and thus more stability.

Darned if I know what seat and support system you like. I usually paddle with an inflatable pad (the same kind used with wheelchairs) on the floor of my kayak, with a fabric back-band adjusted with a line and a jam cleat. It works for me.

In terms of fit, you should check the front of the seat for an upraised lip, and you should be aware of your own position within the seat. If the front edge of the seat presses against the back of your thighs when you're in a normal paddling position, you'll soon be in extreme discomfort. After a few minutes of paddling, the pressure of that seat lip can send your feet into tingling sleep, and in a few more, numb them totally. Answer? Pad the bottom of the seat with thin layers of tapered, closed-cell foam (closed-cell won't hold water like a bath sponge) until you're comfortable.

The Cockpit

Your kayak's cockpit is another upstream choice. Unless you're building your own kayak, you're not going to be able to select the size of the cockpit as an option with the color of boat you want. But, like the seat, you'd be well advised to first choose a cockpit size and then look for kayaks offering that configuration.

Here are some of the pros and cons you'll have to juggle.

The cockpit on this **Current Designs Caribou** is somewhat larger, allowing for an easier entry, but, equally important, also allowing for gear to be stowed more easily. The paddler is using a quill or traditional Greenland paddle.

Most "expedition" kayaks are built with small cockpit openings. What's an expedition kayak? A kayak that will take you camping for more than a weekend, or one prepared for more-exposed waters. The cockpit opening itself may be round or oval, a rounded triangle, or much like a keyhole. "Small" is a flexible term, but figure there will be deck on both sides of the cockpit, the back of the seat will be close to the back of the coaming, and your knees will be under the foredeck. On some cockpits that means your knees will be about even with the elongated end of the cockpit, and outboard of the opening.

Knees under the deck is pretty important. Pressing your knees up against under-deck pads with your feet on your rudder controls or on footrests will hold you comfortably in a powerful paddling position. If you don't want all that power, just throttle back, but stay firmly in position for a low-energy and effective paddle stroke.

Small cockpits mean small spray decks; a small spray deck may be set more tightly, and is less likely to be blown off than a larger one. I paddled a friend's boat with a large cockpit and a far-from-taut spray deck on a blustery day and ended up with what felt like a large bowl of water sloshing in the concave deck. I didn't get wet, but that was a cold passage. You are also less likely to lose a smaller, tighter spray deck when Eskimo-rolling your boat. Generally speaking, if you're launching your boat from an exposed beach and with any kind of wave action, a taut spray deck is a big advantage. You certainly don't want to power into any kind of wave and have the crest of that wave peel your spray deck away. Believe me—paddling a kayak half full of cold water is not a happy-day scenario.

On the other side, some paddlers feel hemmed in and almost claustrophobic in a confined cockpit. While the thinking part of your brain knows you are not trapped, the emotional part is convinced that you're sloshing into danger. Emotional comfort is just as important as physical comfort. It's harder to slip into a small cockpit opening than into a larger one. It's also harder to stow all your gear through the confined opening of a small cockpit.

Larger cockpits mean boarding and exiting are easier, and larger items may be stowed in the cockpit itself. Again, it's a matter of perception, but some paddlers are more comfortable in a larger cockpit.

What is a larger cockpit? Think of a "recreational" kayak, which is sort of a silly term, because almost all of us kayak to recreate. A recreational solo kayak will probably be a bit shorter than an "expedition" kayak, maybe 4.5 to 5 meters (just under 15 to maybe 16 feet) long, and an inch or two wider (25 to 26 inches) across the beam. If you were paddling one without a spray deck, your knees and the upper parts of your shins would be exposed to the sun. Side decks would be narrower.

Recreational kayaks tend to be found in more-protected waters, free of waves that can wash over the entire deck. The larger surface area of the large spray deck is harder to support; it's harder to firmly snap around the edge of the coaming; it's perhaps more likely to sag, and in doing so, to create a pool in which spray and rain may collect; and it's more vulnerable to popping loose from the coaming when struck by a significant wave. These are not bad things. You'll soon learn more about the conditions in which you are comfortable, and more about the voyages you plan to make. Find the kayak that best suits your paddling needs.

Spray Decks

Why are we jabbering about seats and cockpits when they are already in our kayak? Because the size of the cockpit determines one of our most important paddling accessories: the spray deck. The spray deck, sometimes called a spray skirt, is a doughnut-shaped piece of stretchy, waterproof fabric. You fit through the center hole, and the fabric grabs you in a near-watertight grip. The outer edge of the fabric snaps over your kayak's coaming, and is held in place by the lip of the coaming. It keeps the rain, spray, and other bits of water

Want to adjust your temperature while paddling? The upper edge of this Seals Tropical Tour spray deck has a hook-and-loop tab that allows you to ventilate or seal up your spray deck.

Suspenders can keep the tunnel of your fabric spray deck high, if conditions warrant, or it may be removed. The choice is yours with this Seals spray deck.

on the outside, where it belongs, and keeps the warmth and dryness inside, where you can appreciate it.

Most touring kayakers will choose a nylon spray deck. This provides a pretty dry ride under most conditions, offers a looser and more-comfortable fit, and allows plenty of ventilation for when you're really cranking on the paddle. Most nylon spray decks offer some sort of waistband (often an adjustable elastic cord), a similar elastic at the top of the tunnel, and possibly suspenders. Relax the elastic cords to ventilate your cockpit, and tighten them down when conditions get sloppy.

Most nylon spray decks snap onto the coaming much more easily than their heavy-duty neoprene cousins, but they don't offer the grip of neoprene. Paddlers venturing into surf or turbulent water often exchange the more-comfortable nylon decks for neoprene. Neoprene tunnels create a more-waterproof seal around your torso, grip the coaming like a bulldog, and are considerably warmer than nylon. In fact, most neoprene decks have a grab loop at the front of the cockpit, used to tug the deck free. Neoprene decks tend to be more taut than nylon.

Neoprene spray decks, like this **Current Designs** deck on one of their boats, are taut, dry, and warm. This cockpit has an expedition-size opening, which is smaller and offers a more-secure environment when the waves and wind kick up.

Some spray decks are made of neoprene—that stretchy, rubber-like stuff used to make wetsuits. Others are made of polyurethane-coated nylon or other waterproof and breathable materials. Whatever the material, all spray decks are made with the same three parts: the *tunnel,* which literally fits around your waist and up your torso a bit; the *deck,* like the name implies, extends out from the bottom of the tunnel in all directions and covers the kayak's cockpit; and the *rand,* the elasticized outer edge of the spray deck that snaps securely around the lip of the coaming.

You might come across a few hybrids, with neoprene decks and rand for waterproofness, warmth, and security, and a nylon tunnel for venting and comfort.

What's the best? For me (and for most of us, I think), nylon is the way to go. For frigid winter paddlers and those crashing into turbulent water, break out the neoprene and enjoy.

What should you look for in a spray deck?

I like a fabric band or handle across the narrow point at the front of the deck. It's a handy way to pop the deck when you want to remove it. When I was making my own neoprene decks I'd always tie a practice golf ball to the elastic cord within the rand and let it bounce free on the forward point of the deck. It was easy to find and easy to grab if needed. Closer to the tunnel, within hand range, I like a small mesh pocket with a secure zipper. That's the home for sunscreen, lip balm, maybe a snack . . . well, whatever small things I might want at hand. Mesh allows any water to drain away.

Under the deck I like an arched batten—sort of like a low-profile tent pole, something to lift the fabric up and let water drain away. I don't appreciate a cold tub of water in my lap.

Lastly, I want the deck to be in a bright color. In a kayak (or out of it), we are low, slow, and hard to see. Anything to make me more visible is a plus.

Unless for some reason you want a wet lap, get in the habit of always wearing your spray deck. Most paddles come with drip rings, and most drip rings allow a steady trickle of water to slide down the paddle shaft, destined to fall onto your lap. You may be quick, but I doubt you can pop your spray deck into position in just a few seconds, between the time you hear a wake-making powerboat and the moment when the wake rolls up on your boat.

For paddling in protected waters and when you want quick access to your belowdecks, half-deck spray decks are available. Think of an awning stretched over a frame, spanning the distance from the front of your cockpit to just before your torso. They'll shed water drops from your paddle, as well as not-serious splashes and spray sneaking over your bow.

Foot Pegs

A wise woodsman has noted that in order to keep your feet warm you must wear a hat. Counterintuitive? Well, it works. And in order to let your hands twirl your paddle about to move forward, you need a firm footrest. Well, it works.

To paddle, you must have your feet solidly placed on a structural support. That's part and parcel of how we kayak today. You can do this a number of different ways, depending on your particular kayak. Some foot-peg assemblies (where you brace your feet) are molded right into the hull itself. That might be a wedge-shaped block that is part of the inner surface of the hull, or it might be a platform protruding from a bulkhead. Another kayak may have a foot peg sliding front or back along a channel that may be locked into place when the proper distance from the seat back to the arch of your foot is determined. As a starting point, when you can push your knee tightly into an under-deck pad while your foot is on the peg and your back is against the back-band, you are just about right. A third alternative utilizes your left and right pedals for your rudder. Without getting into the pros and cons of equipping your kayak with a rudder system (okay, I will—I think a full rudder system, used properly, is invaluable), bear in mind that most control pedal systems may be adjusted for proper fit. If you are fortunate enough to be exactly the same size as the model used in setting up a nonadjustable system, then I suppose you could live with one. But most of us couldn't.

Remember as you adjust your pedals that your mother was right. Sit up straight and don't slouch.

If your feet rest against a solid bulkhead, you can glue foam blocks to the bulkhead as footrests. It will take a while to get the fit right, and you'll spend most of that time upside down in the hull, gluing or shaping foam. Adjustable foot pegs are a *lot* easier, especially if more than one person may paddle the boat.

Bulkheads and Hatches

Go ahead and stick your head down into your cockpit. Take a good look forward and another one aft. What you see are the two styles of kayak interior design. You might prefer an open interior from bow to stern, or you might divide your kayak into a series of rooms with waterproof (so they say) walls called bulkheads.

Today, *bulkhead* is the trendy word in kayak fashion, and you'll find satisfactory reasons to flow with the crowd. Front and rear watertight bulkheads create air chambers at each end of your kayak, which in turn provide you with substantial buoyancy (remember all those awful submarine war movies in which the crew clangs massive doors shut as they wait out a depth-charging?). Those bulkheads also limit the amount of water that can flood through your cockpit following a (fortunately rare) miscalculation.

Doesn't such a design radically limit the amount of stuff you can pack with you? What about camping? Not to worry. If you erect

It's hard to see a bulkhead once a kayak is assembled. Here's a bulkhead—a waterproof wall—as it is being built into a wood kayak. The wall separates the paddler's compartment from a stowage compartment.

If you seal off the stowage compartment with a waterproof wall, doesn't that limit its use as a place to store things? Nope. Just cut a hole in the deck over it.

waterproof walls within your hull, you can still gain entrance to the two holds via hatches. There are two common types of hatches. One is circular and, much like a short, fat bolt, can be screwed into or out of a deck fitting. The other type may be of any shape—usually rectangular or trapezoidal—and is held in place by clips or by lines passing over it. These commonly have a gasket between the hatch and the deck fitting to keep them watertight.

There is no perfect hatch. Take it as an article of faith that all hatch systems will, at the least convenient moment, choose to leak. This is not bad. Remember to pack anything you want to keep dry within a waterproof or "dry" bag. That's the old "belt and suspenders" theory. Even if a hatch does leak, it will take a long time for enough water to trickle in and affect your buoyancy.

It might seem that bulkheads and hatches are the wave of the future, but like the song says, "It ain't necessarily so." You are limited by the physical size of the hatch as to how big a package you can load. Your cockpit opening is larger than just about any hatch you can find, and that makes loading your gear easier. You do want to have a seat back you can move out of the way when stowing stuff under your rear deck.

If you don't have hatches, obviously they can't leak. No hatches, though, means no bulkheads, and that in turn means you can accidentally fill the entire interior of your kayak with heavy, cold water. The answer to that comes in the next section.

On one of our boats we have a rear bulkhead and hatch, but just a void under the forward deck. Some folks would suggest that in this arrangement I should have a small screw hatch up near the bow, which would allow me to reach in and push or pull on the small gear bags I tend to shove forward. Instead, I have a long cord lashed to the first bag that is crammed in the bow. It is not elegant, but

Wouldn't the hole in the deck let in water, ruining the whole idea? Not if you cap the hole with a hatch, line the hatch with a gasket, and secure the hatch in place with stout straps.

when I tug on that cord and pull the first bag out, all the bags I loaded after that one come with it. My mountain dulcimer, which I could never fit through a hatch, goes up under the bow.

Flotation

Have you ever watched an air-filled kid's balloon skip across the water? It doesn't sink. Kayakers use 'em to keep their boats afloat, but instead of balloons, we use stout, plastic, inflatable "flotation" bags. Cone-shaped flotation bags can be placed in the bow and stern ends of your kayak, lashed into place, and

inflated. Most will have a longish air tube for inflating, so that you don't have to squirm into the ends of your kayak. A couple of D-rings or other tie-down points can be mounted way up in the ends, to secure the flotation bags. Some paddlers just push their flotation bags into their kayaks, and while that saves a wee bit of time and work, it's embarrassing to watch your kayak sink while your flotation bags drift merrily away.

In addition to providing buoyancy, flotation bags also limit the amount of water sloshing around the inside of your kayak. No paddler I know really wants to spend time bailing out a swamped kayak, but most have done so at one time or another. Flotation bags speed up the clean-out process.

Flotation bags can be dual-purpose, doubling their value. Many have a large opening, and items you really don't want to get wet may be placed inside. The opening is then shut with an airtight and waterproof seal, inflated, and stowed in your boat. The cost isn't much higher than for a plain flotation bag.

Consider safety. If you have the ends of your boat sealed off—by bulkheads or flotation bags—with one just behind your seat and the other just ahead of your foot pegs, you have limited the amount of water that can enter your kayak in the event of a miscalculation. "What's a little water?" you might say. A big, high-volume cruising kayak with no interior walls or flotation bags can swallow up a ton or more of that liquid. That's a lot of weight to move, and a lot of water to pump out!

Don't be smug if you have a folding kayak with air sponsons built into the hull. That's not enough. Sure, those sponsons will keep your boat afloat if swamped (with decks awash), but you'll still be left with a lot of gallonage sloshing about. Secure flotation bags in bow and stern, and you'll displace some of that water.

I've been told in all seriousness by some sit-on-top or wash-deck paddlers that they do not need flotation bags because their hull is a huge flotation chamber. They shouldn't be so complacent. A friend paddling 5 miles off the Puerto Rican coast realized his sit-on-top was sluggish and popped open the inspection hatch to take a look. Significant water lurked inside, to his surprise and dismay. Fortunately, another paddler in his group had a portable pump, and the crack in the hull that had let in the water was small enough so that only one drop at a time could ooze in.

Another friend, paddling a composite kayak with bulkheads and really good hatches off Canada's Vancouver Island, felt his kayak become logy and unresponsive. The stern was nearly submerged. He and his paddling buddy opened the rear hatch and found the stern nearly filled with water. A small crack in the stern had opened. Fortunately, they were able to pump out the water and make shore before the slow leak became unmanageable.

When you consider a hatch for your own needs, you must realize I've made an assumption. I thought you might like to load your boat up with gear and paddle off on a multiday expedition. If you look at your kayak as an exercise machine, with the potential of serving as a ferry to an occasional picnic, don't even bother with a hatch. If your idea of camping is a short paddle from inn to inn, you don't have to worry about stowing tents, sleeping bags, and stoves. The simpler your needs become, the more elegant your boat becomes.

Rudders and Skegs

Kayaks are designed to perform well in a variety of wind, wave, and current conditions. Each kayak, however, will respond just a bit differently to its environment, to how well and how much it is loaded, and to the paddling techniques of the person in the cockpit. That's neither criticism nor praise; it's just the way it is. There are a couple of tools that you can use to improve performance, and if your kayak didn't

Most double kayaks are easier to control or guide with a rudder. Some single boats have rudders, but you're more likely to see a skeg on the back.

come with one of them, it's likely one could be added.

We'll chat more about them later (in chapter 12), but you should be aware of the value of rudders and skegs. They look a lot the same, hanging off the stern end of your kayak. *Rudders* can be swiveled back and forth, and can be lifted from the water. *Skegs* look like a rudder blade, but are rigidly held in line with your keel. They can be adjusted from fully immersed to fully retracted, and any position in between. You'll discover as we go out on the water that although a rudder can turn your kayak, its principal benefit is in helping you go straight when wind or waves are attempting to push your bow or your stern sideways.

Kayak rudders are normally controlled by pedals. Push your foot down on the left pedal and the cable controls will pull the rudder blade to the left, and your kayak will swivel leftwards. A cord is tied to the top of the rudder blade. Tug on the cord and the rudder blade is lifted from the water. Some blades will wiggle in the air, while others will nestle against your rear deck. Some rudder systems have a loop of cord leading through a block (a pulley) by the paddler. Pull on one side and the rudder blade rises; pull on the other and it is lowered back into the water.

Not all rudder systems are foot-operated. Easy Rider has a one-line control system quite suitable for physically challenged paddlers who cannot use a foot system. Basically, there is a line from one side of the rudder, while the other side is connected to an elastic cord under pressure. Loosen the line and the kayak turns one way; apply a moderate pressure on the line and the kayak goes straight; pull even harder and the kayak turns in the opposite direction. You don't always have to hold the line, but can secure it with a jam cleat.

Your chief concern shouldn't be the rudder-retracting design, but the linkage between the rudder and the foot pedals. First, is it smooth? Second, is it likely to foul on anything? Third, when it breaks, can you jury-rig a repair?

Rudder pedals may be mounted on hinges at the bottom of the hull, like these, or may be mounted in tracks on each side of your hull.

Since a skeg will not swivel to one side or the other, it won't require pedals. You'll still need to rest your feet somewhere, and that's why some bright paddler invented adjustable foot pegs. The skeg, like the rudder, has a cord from the top of the blade to the paddler to raise or lower the fin.

Once in a great while you'll come across a kayak rudder or skeg that is permanently fixed in the down position. Best to shoot it to put it out of its misery. The last one I saw had a cotter pin holding the rudder blade fully immersed. Even if you believe you'll never run into shallow water, never try to land on a beach, and never have to adjust your rudder depth to counter a crosswind, this design is still a pretty stupid idea. Kayaks are nosy, prowling-shallow-water-and-tiny-bay boats, and you don't need that barn door permanently hanging down back there when you do venture into all those nooks and crannies you thought you'd never explore.

All the talk here of rudder and skeg options assumes (I did it again) that you are paddling a single kayak. If you're in a double, there is no debate. I have yet to see a double kayak that doesn't perform better with a rudder.

Paddles

Paddles don't break. They don't get lost or go adrift. And if you believe that . . . In my paddling circle we always carry at least one spare paddle, just for those incidences that aren't supposed to happen. Heck, I usually have a spare take-apart paddle, not a super one, stowed on the rear deck of my kayak because if I do break a paddle, the group's spare won't be in easy reach.

Carrying Toggles

A canoe is easy to carry. Toss it up on your shoulders and you can take it along for a comfortable walk over a pretty good distance. Your kayak won't cooperate like that. For a short distance you can hoist it up with the cockpit resting on your shoulder and crab along—this difficulty is not a function of weight, but of bulk—and odds are you'll be tired well before you get to your destination.

What's the solution? For short distances and a lightly loaded boat, we can use the handles at the bow and stern.

Your kayak most likely has one of three kinds of handles. You might have a loop of webbing (sometimes rope) running through a hole in the upper bow and matched by a similar webbing circle in the stern. The holes go through solid fill, and don't (if done right) leak water into the hull. You might have a similar loop of webbing, but this time running through the middle of a piece of plastic pipe, perhaps an inch or so in diameter and around 4 inches long. Possibly you'll have webbing extending up through your deck at the bow and stern, hooked inside a T-shaped molded handle.

The basic webbing loop is hard on your hand, and painful after a few steps. The webbing-through-a-pipe handgrip is more comfortable, and allows you to carry the kayak a bit farther. Some paddlers like a T-grip, not liking the webbing on each side of their hand.

Whatever style you have, make certain that the webbing or line is easily replaceable. I've seen handles molded into the hull itself, and they were a pain to replace.

I haven't seen any kayaks made in the United States with a handle through the center of the rear deck just behind the cockpit, but I did see a few kayaks with this feature in England. I was told that when everything else went wrong, a swimmer could ride the rear deck of a rescuing kayak to safety, clutching that handle. It sounds as if it might work, but I never saw (or tried) it.

Bow and Stern Lines

You really don't want your kayak leaving without you. A bow line will help prevent that. A bow line is a stout but not large diameter line secured to your bow loop and long enough to tuck under your spray deck. A stern line works the same way, from the other end. Use one or both to tie your kayak securely after landing, or at a dock. I've seen folks beach a kayak and walk away from it . . . only to find it snatched back to the waiting arms of the water by the tide, a wave, or even the wind. That may never happen to you, but like the belt-and-suspenders theory, it is far better to be safe than sorry.

Bow and stern lines can also be used to help secure your kayak to your car when transporting it between paddles.

Most cruising kayakers like to run lines fore and aft from their bow to their stern along both sides. A kayak, especially when wet, is as slippery as a greased pig. If for any reason a person in the water or another boater has to grab on, those lines will allow it. You can also tie little eyes or loops in those lines, for securing odd bits of gear.

I have four pad eyes arranged on a largish square just ahead of my cockpit. Elastic cord is strung through each of the eyes, for the perimeter, and then twice across the middle in the shape of an X. This is my chart table, as well as the spare pair of hands I use to temporarily hold a floatable object. If it doesn't float, I tie it to one of the eyes on the fore and aft lines I mentioned earlier.

Paddle Float

Just behind my cockpit I have two pad eyes and two cleats, the lashing system I use in setting up a stabilizing system in the unlikely (I hope) event that I capsize. A *paddle float,* made with a spare paddle and a float, is a temporary outrigger used to stabilize a swamped kayak, allowing me to re-board. (See chapter 14 for information on rescues and a look at the arrangement.)

Some kayaks are molded with a groove in the deck to help hold the paddle at right angles to the kayak. Handy, but not vital.

Whatever system you use, it has to be hell-for-leather stout. You'll put a lot of strain on the mountings, and, as with parachutes and life jackets, you can't afford a failure. Make sure the fasteners holding the cleats to the deck will not pull out and that the deck itself is stout enough to resist tearing. I've seen cleats mounted with screws and with pop rivets—neither of which would prevent the cleat from ripping free. I have a reinforced deck and hold the cleats in position with bolts mounted through a steel backing plate under the deck.

Because I know these cleats are securely mounted, I'll use one as a towing bitt in the unlikely event of having to tow another kayak. Incidentally, the expression "to the bitter end" doesn't refer to a bad taste at the end of an experience. The "bitter end" of a line or rode (rode is just nautical talk for the rope holding an anchor) is the last part of it that is secured to the bitt. When you're at the bitter end, the whole rest of the line is stretched out and you're at the last of it.

Sea Anchor

A sea anchor looks much like a small fabric parachute, and when opened underwater, it pretty much holds you in one place despite the forces of the wind. You need only a few deck fittings to stow or deploy one. The bitter end of the sea-anchor rode is usually a loop or bridle that fits around your cockpit rim. This rode leads forward and through the bow loop, keeping your bow pointed at the sea anchor when it's deployed, and into the wind and usually the waves. When voyaging, the sea anchor is kept folded under the elastic cords on your deck, all set to use with the rode simply kept through the bow loop.

There's another use for a small sea anchor, requiring one additional deck fitting. I do like to fish, and I do like to take pictures—and a kayak can be blown all over a bay with just a light breeze. I'll fly a small sea anchor off the midpoint of my kayak, right next to the cockpit. I have a fairlead and jam cleat right to hand, to secure it. With the sea anchor out 10 or 15 feet, I can sit rock-solid over the precise place that will deliver dinner as soon as a fish lurking there bites. My kayak turns sideways to any wind, and I can fish or make images from my chosen position. Doug Simpson, the founder of Feathercraft, taught me this trick.

A cautionary note: Your sea anchor will hold you against the force of a wind. If you deploy it in a current, you're going to follow that current as far and fast as it wants to carry you.

Paddle Parks

A paddle park is a place to (temporarily) park your paddle. I've seen paddlers mounting something that looks like a broom clip on their deck, snapping their paddle into the jaws. I use one of the cleats on my foredeck. I put my paddle up against one of the horns of the cleat and then slip a loop of elastic cord over the paddle and under the opposing horn. Quick and simple, and it secures the paddle from drifting away.

Another way of doing the same thing is a paddle leash. Think of a length of elastic cord with a strip of hook-and-loop fabric at one end and a snap at the other. The hook-and-loop strip fastens around your paddle shaft and the snap clicks through a fitting on your kayak. For around twenty bucks you'll keep your paddle and kayak together.

Compass

If you paddle anywhere except on a very small pond you should both have a compass and know how to use it. Permanently mounted compasses are easy to read, safe from the casual thief when your kayak is unattended on a rack, and often provide illumination for paddling in the dark or in lousy visual conditions. Removable compasses hook onto your deck fittings, and can go back into your bag when not on the water. A handheld orienteering compass—one of those guys with a red needle pointing to magnetic north, and a protractor base to shows bearings from you—is way less convenient, but will do in a pinch. I have a compass, toggling between true north and magnetic north, in my Garmin GPS. Unfortunately, mine doesn't tell me which way I am looking, only in which direction I am moving at the moment. We'll chat about these when we discuss navigation in chapter 15.

Bilge Pumps

Water stays on the outside of the hull and you sit inside the hull—separate and distinct existences. Right? Well, not really. Every kayak I know has at one time or another been filled with water. If you and a friend are in a shallow, warm pool, you can invert a water-filled kayak and rock it from end to end in order to dump the last of the water. But outside of that pool, it's a different story. Let's say, because it's an easy bad habit to slip into, that you were paddling without your spray skirt snapped around the coaming. Since your mind was a thousand miles away and you weren't paying any attention, you didn't notice that you'd drifted out of the channel and were gliding right along the edge of the dredged drop-off. You also didn't notice the yacht plowing up the channel. Really—all of these things can (and do) happen. The wake from the yacht hit the shallows, mounted into a curl, and right in the middle of your daydream dumped all over you. You prevented an upset with some quick paddle moves, but now you're hip-deep in channel water.

Your first instinct is to rant and rave at the inconsiderate jerk who drenched you. Your second instinct . . . well, I hope you planned first, because your second instinct is going to need a bit of preparation. You want to get the water out of your kayak. Bailing is awkward at best in the narrow confines of your cockpit, and probably won't do more than irritate your already-frazzled nerves. If you thought ahead, you probably have a bilge pump in your kayak. You could start working the handle, and a steady flush of water would immediately sluice overboard.

Some kayaks have a built-in bilge pump, with its handle mounted on the exterior of your rear deck. These can move a lot of water. You may have purchased a portable pump and stowed it safely under some of the elastic straps on deck—with a lanyard tying it to your boat in case of a mishap. Shove the bottom down into the bilge and start working the handle up and down. Remember to direct the stream of water overboard. You can snap most of your spray deck in place and still be able to insert the pump into the cockpit. It's possible that you ordered a spray deck that comes with a mini-hatch just for your pump.

You should also have a big sponge tucked alongside your seat. You can mop up the last few dribbles of water with it.

Safety Equipment

If I'm paddling close to home, I usually carry a couple of communication devices: a cell phone to alert family if I'm delayed for dinner; and a marine VHS handheld radio for contacting other boats, commercial marine traffic, or the Coast Guard. The VHS radio floats, is waterproof, and includes all the National Oceanic and Atmospheric Administration (NOAA) weather channels. Our group has been known to carry small walkie-talkies for kayak-to-kayak chatter. If you're paddling out into the far blue, you might want an emergency position-indicating radio beacon (EPIRB). You have to license and register each EPIRB, which is pricey, but if you pull the little tab, it will shriek out a distress call on constantly monitored frequencies. If you're out of cell-tower range (and that is a good thing), you can rent a satellite phone. Many paddlers think staying in touch is worth the price. There's always the risk that any electronic gizmo will fail at the worst possible moments, so you want to pack spare batteries.

As the operator of a real boat, you have the obligation to carry signaling devices in case of emergency. The law says that this includes an emergency flashlight (blinks an SOS), a strobe, or flares. The first two are down near the "not-good-enough" mark for those who paddle close to the sea, as we kayakers do. I keep a two-faced (clear and red) signaling mirror and a piercingly loud whistle taped to my personal flotation device (PFD) (see chapter 5). A bright flashlight is also needed for any night paddling, just to tell other craft where you are. Some paddling friends keep extremely bright strobe rescue lights pinned to their PFDs, to help locate them in case of an accident at night. Some paddlers I know use "light sticks," chemicals in a tube that when activated glow with a green or blue light. Start one, and it's good for most of an evening, and allows you to keep track of other boats in your party.

Some paddlers place red reflective tape on their left paddle blades and green reflective tape on their right blades, as well as white reflective tape at the center of the shaft. They also stick red and green reflective tape on the left and right sides of their kayak bow. If your PFD doesn't have reflective tape, you might adhere some white across the shoulders and back.

You can attach a small light tower with a white light on your rear deck to attract notice. A radar reflector might be a good idea, but any study I've seen—the Maine Association of Sea Kayak Guides and Instructors did a good one—raises some good questions about your visibility on a screen. I'd hate to rely on something that isn't reliable.

If we're out for an afternoon we'll carry along a roll of duct tape and a sharp knife. That takes care of most minor problems. For a longer trip, we put together a more-complete package: epoxy, fabric, and a mixing pot (for wood or composite boats—doesn't work with plastics); baling wire; a Gerber multitool; a folding saw; clamps to fit a paddle shaft; scissors; a sharp knife; and a bag full of screws, bolts, nuts, clamps, and miscellaneous fittings.

A paddle float is a sort of do-it-yourself outrigger that can be mounted in an emergency to let you clamber back aboard your kayak. You lash your spare paddle to your rear deck and attach a float to the outboard paddle blade. A bleach bottle provides 8 pounds of buoyancy, enough to support you as you slither into the cockpit, and a commercially made float that slips over your paddle blade can provide as much as 30 pounds or more of buoyancy. Never use your personal flotation device as the float on the end of your paddle.

There's one last piece of safety equipment you should have with you, and it can be priceless—your own good sense. You'll probably never need emergency or rescue equipment if you paddle within your own capabilities. Accidents can happen, but it's up to you to reduce the possibility of one.

CHAPTER 5

You and Your PFD

The single most important piece of equipment on my kayak is my PFD. Period. No debate. It's not only on the kayak, it's on me. The proper name is personal flotation device (okay, most of us call all flavors of them "life jackets"), and I take that first word to heart.

Why so fussy? Aren't all life jackets the same?

Nope. There are four distinctly different classes of PFDs, each available as inherently buoyant or inflatable. Each type has its own characteristics and advantages. Some are designed for specific purposes or uses. Most of 'em come in a range of sizes, and many of those have an array of straps and buckles to shape them to you or me. While all of them

will support us in the water, they offer that support in different ways.

After putting mine on and fussing with the straps until it was adjusted, I dropped into the water to see how I floated. And I tried swimming to see how I got along. After all that, I readjusted everything.

Yes, I rinse it after being out on the salt, and check for rips or discolorations before heading out on the water. Perhaps I am a bit obsessive, but I really don't want to start making repairs or adjustments after ending up in the water.

For now, though, let's find a suitable PFD for you.

The US Coast Guard flatly states that you must have at least one Type I, Type II, Type III, or Type V PFD on your kayak for each person aboard. If you want the numbers, that's US Coast Guard Regulation Title 33, Chapter 1, Part 175, Subpart B. The regulation stipulates further that they all have to be wearable PFDs. In the boating universe there are actually five types of PFDs, Type IV being throwable devices such as square cushions or life rings. Those are not approved for kayaking.

Those are the minimum federal requirements. States may (and do) set stricter standards. Some states demand that PFDs be worn at all times, usually as a move to protect children, but the laws are changing across the country. Get a copy of your state's boating laws and regulations from your state boating law administrator, normally located in the Department of Natural Resources or Parks (but at times in Game or Fisheries), and, in a couple of cases, in the offices of the state police. If you can't find the office, call the nonemergency number for a local metropolitan police force and ask for the marine patrol division.

You're probably going to end up with a Type III Flotation Aid, configured for kayak, canoe, raft, and sailing. Most of us find them the most comfortable and versatile, and well inside the safety envelope we desire.

The Type I Offshore Life Jacket provides the most buoyancy, a whopping 22 pounds, and is designed for open, rough, or remote waters where rescue may be delayed. It will turn most unconscious wearers in the water to a face-up position. It's bulky, enough so to make paddling a chore, and fitting it (and you) in a narrow kayak cockpit might be a chore.

It doesn't matter if you are playing in the waves, along with this skilled paddler, or drifting along on a mirror-smooth pond: **Wear your PFD.** Yeah, the Man says you just have to have one with you, but Mom Nature trumps that with the conditions she may unexpectedly throw at you.

Photo courtesy Ocean Kayak

Even if you didn't know the name, you'd recognize the Type II Near-Shore Buoyant Vest. It wraps around your neck and extends down your front, and is usually tied with a couple pieces of webbing a bit below your chin, and a webbing belt around your waist. It contains at least 15.5 pounds of buoyancy and is designed for calm, inland waters where there's a good chance of quick rescue. This type will turn some unconscious wearers to a face-up position in the water. The downsides include

This Ronin PFD has adjustable shoulder straps, adjustable side compression straps, an adjustable and buckle-able belt, reflective strips on the shoulder straps and on the pocket (and on the back), a four-way tab on the right shoulder (for a knife or whatever), a similar tab on the back for a light, and a small pocket for a whistle (on a lanyard) and a signal mirror. Small is good when it comes to PFD pockets; don't weigh yourself down with things you can carry in your kayak.

their bulk, and, for some of us, a lack of comfort. I don't like the rubbing on my neck, but that's personal.

Type V, Special Use Devices, are intended for specific activities, and may be used only according to the approval conditions on the label. Depending on the type, they can have from 15.5 to 22 pounds of buoyancy. Varieties include kayaking, waterskiing, windsurfing, hybrid vests, and deck suits.

So that leaves us with Type III Flotation Aids. They are intended for conscious users in calm, inland water, or where there's a good chance of quick rescue. They contain at least 15.5 pounds of buoyancy. Type IIIs are designed so wearers can turn themselves face-up in the water, but won't necessarily turn an unconscious wearer. They can be configured for various sports activities, but are not limited to those activities. A Type III for kayaking will be waist-length (for comfort in a high-backed seat), and will feature a deep neck, narrow shoulder straps, and large armholes for paddling, along with a host of straps or cords to adjust the fit exactly to your specifications.

Your PFD is not complete coming off the rack. First of all, let's add a god-awful loud plastic whistle on a lanyard. I have a Fox 40; my paddling buddy has a Storm. Either one will stop rush-hour traffic three blocks away. You can signal with a whistle much farther than your voice will carry. We can also add rings of reflective tape around your shoulder straps, just for visibility. I have reflective tape across the front and upper back of mine, and you might look for the same. Look for a couple of lash tabs. I have one on my upper rear shoulder where I can clip on a strobe light for night paddling, and one in front that as often as not is home to a knife. You should have a very sharp stainless-steel knife, foldable or fixed, that is kept separate just in case of that rare emergency. You can get tangled in fishing line, or a fish net.

You might run across a "float coat," which is a full jacket that offers the buoyancy of other Type III PFDs. These have a place in the boating world, but I wouldn't want to wear one in a cruising kayak. They're warm (to hot) jackets to begin with, and as you build up plenty of body heat while paddling, you may be tempted to strip off that hot coat.

Before you start adding up how many PFDs it will take to keep you afloat, remember that the PFD is keeping you afloat in the water—and most adults require only an extra 7 to 12 pounds of buoyancy to keep their faces dry. The amount will depend on your body fat, your

PFDs for kids are sized by the weight of the user, and this is clearly stated on the label.

There's a label inside every PFD. For an adult, it gives the type and intended use, the size (and the chest size), uses for which it's approved and not approved, the Coast Guard Approval Number, and the manufacturer. Size, small through extra-large, is determined by the chest size of the wearer. All adult PFDs of each type supply a minimum amount of buoyancy regardless of size.

lung capacity, the water state, and whether or not you have 5 pounds of fishing weights in your pockets. That 15.5 pounds of buoyancy is quite adequate, thank you.

All of us adults are not the same size, and that's why Type IIIs come in sizes from small to extra-large. That's not based on your weight, exactly, but on the girth of your chest when you're wearing your paddling clothes. One manufacturer may not use the same range of inches for a given size as does another, so read the label.

When you're all duded out in paddling clothes, you're about 44 inches around the chest. That translates into a large/extra-large for a guy using a PFD like mine.

You notice I said "guy." That's 'cause the better PFD manufacturers realize that genders are shaped a bit differently. Princess seams, a longer torso, and contoured cups make PFDs a lot more comfortable than they used to be, for some of us, and with the growing popularity of the touring kayak, maybe the majority of us. If you see a PFD marked "unisex," that probably means "doesn't fit anyone very well."

Some PFDs open on the side, which might make for a more-comfortable fit. Most open

On most kayak PFDs there are buckles at the top of the shoulder straps. Release them and extend the straps as far as possible. Don your PFD, with the bottom edge at your waist. Tighten the shoulder straps so that they snugly hold the PFD at this level. This PFD is a Kokatat Ronin kayaking Type III flotation aid.

with a stout zipper right down the middle of the front. Either design works equally well. Mine has a mid-chest webbing-and-snap as well as an adjustable waist belt. The mid-chest strap is a backup in case the zipper fails, and the belt is to adjust the fit.

Look at the sides, below the armholes. A pair of pull-through jam buckles on each side cinches the PFD to your body. The shoulder straps are adjustable, too, allowing you to place the waistband at (surprise) your waist.

Great; you found a PFD you think you might like. Loosen up all the straps, including the shoulders, and slip it on over the clothes you might wear on the water. Zip it up. Tighten the waist belt at your waistline, and then pull the side straps snug. Don't squish yourself, but make the sides snug. Last, lightly tighten the shoulder straps.

Wiggle. Twist. Bend over. Wave your arms. Pretend you are paddling. Lift an imaginary weight. Is the PFD staying in place? Is it binding or constricting you? Looks pretty good to me. Sit down on the floor and rotate your arms as you twist back and forth. Still comfortable?

Come on out to the lawn. There's a kayak sitting there. Get in and twist about.

I'm going to straddle your kayak, just behind your cockpit. Lift your arms over your head. I'm going to lift up on your shoulder straps. Your PFD should stay in place. If the front panels ride up and you can touch the zipper with your nose—or almost—or if the PFD almost comes off, it is too loose. Either adjust it tighter or try another size.

You look pretty comfortable. A few folks, though, will find the PFD shoulder straps up around their ears and their nose rubbing on the zipper. *Don't* attack your PFD with a pair of scissors in an attempt to get a better fit. It isn't the PFD's fault. Odds are the foot pegs/rests inside your kayak are adjusted too far forward and you have to stretch to reach them. As a result, you're slumping in your seat, almost like in a chaise lounge, and that's why the PFD is all scrunched up. If you sit up, like your mother

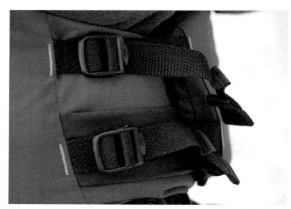

Your PFD most likely has side "compression" straps and buckles much like the ones on this Ronin. Snap and zip your jacket closed (most have both buckles and a stout zipper) and pull the side straps until the PFD feels snug. If a friend standing over you can pull the shoulder straps up easily at this point, you either have a too-big PFD or you haven't tightened the sides. Check the fit each time you paddle. A PFD might fit over a sweater and paddling jacket, but not be snug when you're wearing a T-shirt.

said, you'll paddle better, breathe easier, and your PFD will fit much more comfortably.

Plan a stop at the community pool on the way home. Don your PFD and test it toward the shallow end. Relax and tilt your head back. The PFD should support you with your chin out of the water, and you should be able to breathe easily. If your mouth isn't well above water in the pool, it won't be in a wilder environment. Change your PFD for another!

You've been in chlorinated water, so once you're home, rinse the PFD well and hang it to dry. Store it out of sunlight.

Color

Fashion mavens have discovered PFDs, and you can find them in any color you want. I figure that international orange or lime green can be seen in most conditions. Considering a camouflage pattern? Why would you want any bit of survival gear in colors that are hard to see and thus hard to find? As for me, I choose even my packs and dry bags in the brightest colors I can find—or, more properly, in the brightest colors that I find hardest to lose.

Care

PFDs don't last forever, although with sensible care they will hold up for a number of paddling seasons. To test your PFD once you've had it for some time, plop yourself in the water with it on and see if it can support you with your chin out of the water while you have your arms and hands motionless underwater. If the waterline is up to your eyes, it's time to retire this piece of equipment.

Most Type IIIs fasten with a zipper. I think a big-toothed plastic zipper works better than a small-toothed metal one, but neither will work if it is filthy with sand and dried salt. Keep the zipper clean! Many PFDs also fasten with snaps and buckles. Do the same drill, and keep them clean. Once they start to visibly corrode, or rust, it's time to replace the snap or the

PFD—unless you want to hang your life on a corroding and weakening piece of gear.

It's not hard to kill your PFD. People have been known to use their PFD to cushion their boat and protect their car finish while driving to the launch, to cook a damp PFD dry by draping it on a hot radiator or over a fire, to cut off the bottom of their PFD if it seems a little long, or to use their PFD for a kneeling pad or a boat fender. Dumb, right?

PFDs for Children

Children are not adults. That seems obvious, and yet some supposedly adult folks attempt to dangle their kids in PFDs that are far too big for them. The kid will be uncomfortable and in an emergency could well slide out! I've seen kids literally slip down in their PFDs until only the shoulder straps can be seen above the surface and their arms are hanging up in the bottom of the armholes. So use PFDs that fit your children. Today, you'll find PFDs for infant, child, and youth—with sizes on the labels.

Sizing for a youngster depends on weight (not chest size):

- Infant PFDs: 8 to 30 pounds
- Child PFDs: 30 to 50 pounds
- Youth PFDs: 50 to 90 pounds

For infants and children, look for:

- a padded head support to help keep the head above water;
- a handle to assist you in retrieving the child out of the water; and
- a crotch strap to help keep the PFD from riding up.

Youth-size PFDs look and have the features of adult PFDs. The more straps, the more adjustments you can make for sizing.

Most kids will probably prefer a Child Type III, because they offer more freedom than a Type II. That said, the Type II has advantages—especially for those who can't swim, or are weak swimmers. Kids, like adults, might panic

This dapper little dude is wearing a child's Type II PFD, one that (since we tested it) is likely to support him with his face well out of the water. There is also a grab loop on the back of the collar in case he decides to jump overboard. This model has a strap going from the back of the PFD between his legs and hooking to the front—just one more safety feature to keep him properly in the PFD.

when they topple unexpectedly into the water. They will thrash about wildly and they will attempt to climb from the water. The Type II is more likely to keep their face safely out of the water. Let the little ones get used to their PFD in a pool, to see that it expands their fun, and that they can relax and simply float. Let your children, with discreet supervision, control part of their lives by learning to don and wear their PFD. Teach them by example.

Don't expect your child to grow into an oversize PFD. PFDs don't work if they don't fit. And for goodness' sake, if a PFD doesn't fit, don't attempt to trim or alter it. One snip of the scissors and you've invalidated the USCG approval on the label, but more importantly, you've placed the wearer at risk.

Federal laws don't demand you wear the PFD you have with you; common sense and Mother Nature do.

You aren't worried, though, because you aren't planning to paddle far out to sea where most drownings occur. Well, nine out of ten people who drown are in inland waters, and most of them are within a few feet of safety. According to the Coasties, who are charged with collecting such information, most of the victims own PFDs but die without them.

CHAPTER 6

Power to the Paddle

I do believe you're about to leap into the air, shout, and click your heels, just out of sheer joy and excitement. It's understandable. You've figured out which kayak is perfect for you, tricked it out with a few essentials, and even taken a spankin' new PFD out of the bag. Something, though, seems to be nagging at you. I'm not sharing your urge to get going.

What's the problem? Even with your boat and PFD in hand, we're not going to go anywhere. Why? No paddle.

A paddle is the final link in that power train that begins when your feet press against the pegs and ends with you moving briskly through the water. Let's spend a few minutes here on the beach considering why paddles are the way they are. First of all, kayak paddles have one

thing in common: They have a blade at each end of the shaft. Now, you don't actually need a kayak paddle to paddle a kayak—historically, people have gotten around in long, skinny boats quite well driving a single-bladed paddle. But we're not going to talk about them. Let's focus, for now, on the basics of double-bladed kayak cruising.

From drawings and descriptions it appears that for thousands of years, dwellers of the Far North used a fairly short kayak paddle with unfeathered and narrow blades. *Unfeathered* means that the two blades are in the same plane—if you put an unfeathered paddle on the ground, both blades will rest flat. (*Feathered* paddles have the two blades set at an angle to each other.)

Those canny early paddlers, hampered by a shortage of raw material, knew that long, narrow blades worked quite well if one had to maintain a steady paddling cadence over hours and hours. The narrow blades were (and are) a masterful design given the two parameters of physical strength and available materials.

If the sport had grown only in a linear fashion, the narrow, unfeathered blades would be the only paddle we have today. About a hundred years ago, however, outdoor enthusiasts who adopted the kayak as a sport discovered that while narrow blades were great for high-gear cruising, the narrow faces would cavitate, or lose their grip on the water, during powerful bursts of acceleration—such as when sharply turning or leaping ahead out of a standing start. Wide blades didn't have such trouble. By the late 1960s you could find paddle blades wide enough to hold a large pizza. The wide blades offered a massive grip, but on the downside, they were nearly impossible to paddle for any great distance.

Around this time sprint racers figured out that a big, broad blade waving around in the air during a race was an aerodynamic no-no. Those racers discovered that if you canted the two blades of the paddle at about right angles to each other, then, while one blade was planted in the water, the other would slice cleanly edge-first through the air. And thus was born the feathered blade.

If you're cranking out a hundred paddle strokes a minute, this design makes a difference. But if you're gunkholing and exploring with me, you'll probably stroke at a more leisurely pace and never feel any air resistance, regardless of the paddle design.

Some open-water paddlers, who venture into the wilds of the ocean or the tumult of wind and storm, claim that if you're paddling with the wind on your beam—anywhere on your side—a feathered paddle can be wrenched right out of your hands by a gust. The theory is that while the blade presents a knife edge to any wind coming toward your bow, it presents a big sail to any winds coming from the side. A fierce gust can grab the upraised blade and flip it right over your head. "You have to learn to drop your shaft when the wind hits," is the conventional wisdom.

About 80 percent of all enthusiast paddles are feathered at an angle of 80 degrees. Some folks believe that a 90-degree feather leads to wrist inflammation and tendon damage, and that a less-severe rotation prevents this trauma. Less is not necessarily better. Reducing the blade angles to 45 degrees or less eliminates most of the aerodynamic advantages, but doesn't seem to reduce the possibility of wrist pain or damage.

The "big sail" theory doesn't seem to detract from the feathered paddle's popularity. About three out of every four solid-shaft paddles have feathered blades. A totally unscientific survey indicates that most adjustable paddles have feathered blades. Okay, so what else is important in a paddle?

Length

Let's start with length. Let's shuffle through some guidelines and with luck we'll come up with a fair approximation. Keep in mind the beam of your kayak and your paddling style, and we'll go from there.

Your kayak has a beam side to side beam—maximum side-to-side width—of about 23 inches, close to the average for an efficient cruising hull. The cockpit is at the widest part of your hull. This indicates a paddle with an overall length of 220 centimeters. If you wanted to paddle a skinny kayak, say 21 inches wide, you would choose a paddle perhaps 5 cm shorter. Paddling a recreational kayak, 25 to 26 inches across, translates into a 5 cm or so longer paddle.

That's for solo kayaks. A beamy, 33-inch-wide, cruising double might call for a 240 cm paddle.

Some paddlers like to hold their paddles low, with the midpoint of the paddle between their sternum and navel. To get their paddle blades in the water without banging their hands on the edges or gunwales of their kayak, they'll need a longer paddle. Add 5 cm or more. Although it doesn't necessarily affect paddle length, the lower paddle position translates into a slow stroke rate.

If you like to paddle with a higher paddle position, you'll discover that you don't need as much paddle length to reach the water. Your paddle will also be more vertical in the water. That translates into a paddle around 5 cm shorter.

The beam of a cruising double, along with its height, pretty well precludes a high, quick paddle stroke.

If you're very short you may need a slightly longer paddle to clear the side decks of your kayak. If you are quite tall, you may find that you naturally develop a more-vertical stroke and don't need a longer paddle.

Styles also change. Some years back we saw many more very long paddles, 240 cm or longer for 23-inch-wide solo boats. Then all of a sudden we saw short paddles, 210 cm or less, used on those same boats. Long paddles make it harder to sprint, and for most of us, cause our bows to wiggle back and forth with the looping path of a forward stroke. Really short paddles are a hoot to sprint with, but they make turning your kayak more difficult. That's compounded in some winds. Some paddlers using short paddles developed shoulder issues over long distances.

Tandem paddlers usually find it better to have paddles of the same length. Different paddle lengths mean different stroke rates, making it a challenge to keep your strokes synchronized.

In other words, you're going to have to play around a bit to find the length that works best for you. If you're enrolled in a kayaking class, take full advantage of the full quiver of paddles available and experiment with different lengths. If you're going to furnish your own paddle, start with a 220 cm, two-piece fiberglass shaft and blades paddle, one with at least some adjustability at the center joint. Get a mid-priced paddle, somewhere in the $150 range, not a super-light or super-expensive one. With experience you'll find the length you like, and then you can move this pretty good stick back onto your rear deck as a spare.

A minor note: Most paddles are measured from tip to tip. Paddle blades may come in different lengths. When you experiment with different paddle lengths, try to use the same size blades. This will give you a more-consistent feel.

Blade Size and Shape

You're pretty clear about what you want your kayak to do: You want it to cruise effortlessly at a good rate of speed, crank into turns exactly where you want, powerfully support the braces, and accelerate like a jackrabbit. Your goals are good, but you're talking about the paddle and its capabilities rather than about the boat itself. One paddle won't be excellent at all of these things, but you can shave a bit of the edge off each of your desires and reach a pretty good compromise design.

What kind of paddle blade do we want hanging off the ends of our paddling sticks? For your first season on the water, let's put the traditional Greenland paddle back up on the shelf. Most will have a shaft barely wider than your shoulders and very long, very narrow blades. You could probably carve one from a piece of 2x4 lumber. While many paddlers swear by them for long-distance touring, maybe you should learn with a more-forgiving paddle, suitable for a wide range of paddling environments. Wing paddles with their curled or scoop-shaped blades are a huge plus for fitness or racing paddlers, great for covering long distances or having to get somewhere in a hurry (hurry, that is, in the kayaking world). Support strokes—braces—and sculling or sweeping strokes are harder to do, and in some conditions, some paddlers have a few more control issues (or lack thereof). No disrespect intended regarding either of these concepts; they are very efficient paddles, and you may want to follow in their wakes. For now, though, let's stick with the "European" blade. It's that kind of plump, oval shape, slightly curved on the power side (that's the blade face pointing to the rear of your kayak).

When it comes to paddle blades, size *does* make a difference—but not necessarily the difference you'd expect. There's not a huge size difference between large and small touring kayak blades—perhaps 95 square inches for a small blade, and 110 square inches for a large blade. Let's put one of those small blades in the hands of a strong, monstrously fit, and skilled paddler. That paddler will stick the blade in the water and really yard on it, accelerating the kayak toward the paddle. With the power of all those uncurling muscles, the paddler is literally drawing the paddle back through the water. A skilled paddler will feel that paddle movement, knowing that the energy in moving the paddle is misspent and not moving the kayak.

Exchange the small blade for a big one, and the kayak will leap forward with renewed vigor and far less slippage.

So, does that mean bigger is better? Put that same smaller paddle blade in the hands of a less-powerful paddler, someone like you or me, and we can put all our force on it and that blade won't slip. It will transmit all our muscle power into forward motion. Swap it out for a huge paddle blade and at first we won't be able to pull our kayak up to the paddle blade any quicker than we did with the small paddle blade. We already were at our maximum efficiency. What will happen is that we'll burn a lot more energy lifting and sticking that larger blade, and in a short time, we'll actually be

moving more slowly. That's with two identically shaped blades, one just an expanded version of the other.

Paddle-blade width makes a big difference. A long, narrow blade takes less energy to make one paddle stroke (or a whole bunch), and that's a big plus when cruising for miles. On the other side of the compromise, a narrow blade gives you less grip on the water, which translates into slower acceleration. It takes more strokes to get you going.

A wide blade gives you better acceleration, meaning that it takes fewer strokes to get going. It will turn your kayak faster. It also eats up more energy for each paddle stroke you make, a significant factor over a day's paddling.

As noted, the narrow blade excels at the forward, long-distance stroke. A wide blade is better for bracing strokes, sculling strokes, ruddering, and backing up. A narrow blade is really good at bracing strokes, at sculling strokes, at strokes that skim the surface of the water and that turn your kayak. But narrow blades tend to be a bit more finicky. They desire a precise blade angle to the water. Wider blades are more willing to work if your blade angle isn't spot-on. And a wider blade is less like to say "Angle's not right—let's dive!"

You've already pointed out to me that some paddle blades are flat, and some—generally higher-priced and over at the enthusiast end of the paddle rack—seem to be curved or almost spoon-shaped. Good call on your part. A spooned blade inserts more easily into the water and sticks in place better than a flat blade. (If you'd rather, think of "grabs the water" instead of "sticks," although they mean the same thing.) The spooned blade also isn't as likely to wobble back and forth when you're putting power to the paddle.

At the same time, the spooned blade isn't quite as easy to use in a bracing or sculling stroke, and the same holds true for ruddering strokes.

Put your paddle flat on the ground and draw an imaginary line right down the middle of the paddle shaft and across the blade. Some paddle blades have exactly the same shape above and below this imaginary line, and those blades are called *symmetrical*. Some have markedly different shapes above and below the line, with the upper half being longer than the lower half, and these are called *asymmetrical*. In the water during a forward stroke you'll see them in a different light. Since your paddle goes into the water at an angle, the surface area of the top and bottom halves of an asymmetrical blade will be pretty close to equal, and the paddle will have less of a tendency to twist or roll in your hands. With a symmetrical blade, the bottom half of the blade will have more-submerged surface area than the top, and the blade may want to twist.

So, is the asymmetrical paddle the answer to all your paddling needs? You spotted the challenge immediately! If you're bracing, high or low, doing a draw stroke, or sculling, one side of the blade will have more area than the other, and your effort will be unbalanced. The paddle wants to twist. As with the spooned blade, an asymmetrical blade may want to dive or rise more than you expect.

I don't have any scientific basis for this bias, but I'd stay away from any paddle (usually a flat, symmetrical blade) that has a raised structural support down the power face of the blade (the side facing you when you're pulling on the shaft). These seem to slip more rather than grabbing ahold of the water. A lot of paddles, and darned good ones, have a raised structural support on the non-power face, and that's fine.

What does all this "on the one hand—but on the other hand" chatter mean? In the end, you want to start with a middle-of-the-road paddle. Look for a blade that is 7 inches (or a little more) wide, especially if you are paddling a 22- or 23-inch-wide efficient cruising kayak. If you're paddling a recreational kayak, 25 or 26 inches across, you may want a slightly wider blade to give you a bit more acceleration power to get moving.

Down the road you may fall in love with a 4-inch-wide Greenland blade, or you may have the power for a much wider blade, but for your first paddle, stick in the middle.

A curved or spooned blade is more efficient going forward, our most common stroke, so opt for a slightly or moderately curved blade. You'll get most of the forward-stroke efficiency with a blade that's easier to use in your bracing, sculling, or ruddering strokes. That's a good compromise.

Over the next year you might find that you prefer a stroke with the paddle held low over the deck. In that case, you'd probably prefer an exaggerated asymmetrical blade. You may like a higher stroke, with the paddle held at a more nearly vertical angle, and that translates into less of an asymmetrical shape. Whatever your eventual style, you don't want to give up the asymmetrical advantage of the forward stroke. Your best bet would be a middle-of-the-road, somewhat asymmetrical blade.

I suppose someone could have described that paddle to you and ordered you to use it for a year, but I figure you can make better decisions if you know what compromises and advantages come in the box.

Shaft

The shaft does more than just hold the blades. It allows the paddler to apply power, and to control the angle of the blades. Many paddlers prefer an oval shaft. The oval shape fits comfortably within the hand, and the muscles in your hands and forearms soon learn the relative position of grip and paddle-blade angle. Some builders, and paddlers, prefer a round shaft.

Some paddle shafts are a single tube extending from blade to blade. That's super.

They are strong and light. My wife paddles with such a paddle, in wood, and it suits her perfectly.

Other paddles are designed to come apart, usually in the middle, into two equal lengths. Makes them a lot easier to stow. Most of those paddles will allow you to vary the angle between the blades, some with preset angles and some, infinitely variable. Those joints add a small bit of weight, but being in the middle of the shaft don't impact you overmuch.

If space is really at a premium, some manufacturers turn out paddles that break down into four pieces. You add some complexity, more areas for potential problems, but they sure can be handy.

All shafts are not created equal—at least equal in diameter. If you have small hands, and a "standard" shaft feels uncomfortable large, ask to see a paddle with a smaller shaft. A lot of manufacturers offer several different shaft sizes, especially with the growing number of women paddlers. On the other end of the scale, it is possible to pad out a shaft if the paddle is uncomfortably small in your hands.

I suspect that a fair amount of beginning-paddler wrist and shoulder pain comes with a white-knuckled death grip on the paddle shaft. That's usually accompanied by a tenseness that leaves the paddler looking like a robot with a nearly flat battery. A loose grip and a comfortably sized shaft will dramatically improve your outlook.

Some paddle shafts are solid, and the blades are held in a fixed position. That's super. My wife paddles with such a blade, and I just ordered a new touring paddle for myself with a fixed shaft. Other shafts come apart in the middle, with a variety of locking mechanisms, which allows you to switch between a feathered and an unfeathered paddle. A take-apart allows you to find your favorite configuration. Not only that, but a take-apart is also a lot easier to stow as a spare. I would be hard-pressed

to find a 220 cm space for a full-length paddle on my rear deck.

You can improve your grip with a couple of simple tricks. First, put drip rings on your shaft near the blades. These prevent water from running down the shaft. Second, wrap the paddle shaft with an appropriate tape or pad. You can, if you shop about, find paddle shafts of different diameters. If you have small hands—and this may be important to women paddlers—find a small shaft.

It stands to reason that paddle shafts should be straight. While reasonable, that isn't always true. Instead of being a straight tube between the paddle blades, *bent shaft paddles* have a couple of bends or twists on each side of the hand-grip areas. Why would you want to have such? Some paddlers believe that the bent-shaft paddle allows you to keep your wrist better aligned with your forearm at the start of your forward stroke, which is a mechanical way of saying that you might be reducing the possibility of carpal tunnel distress. Others think the twisty shaft allows you to extend your reach a bit, right at the beginning of the forward stroke.

Other folks claim the bends make your wrist position worse in reverse strokes, rudder strokes, and in low braces. They also point out that you can have proper wrist alignment and extended reach with a conventional paddle.

If you have a history of repetitive wrist-use injuries, you may want to consider a bent-shaft paddle under the tutelage of a skilled coach/teacher. If not, either style will probably work as well for you if you remember to keep your hands loose and learn proper stroke technique.

If you learn with one style, there's no reason why you couldn't switch at some later date. It takes a while to switch from straight to bent, and I'd imagine the reverse is also true.

Wood is pretty. A fine-crafted wood paddle is a thing of beauty, and could cost you as much as $500. At the other end of the scale, a moderately good paddle can be found with an aluminum shaft and plastic blades for under $100. An elegant, featherweight, bent-shaft touring paddle can run you close to $500. Is one paddle worth five times the price of another? If your idea of kayaking is sitting on the bank of a pond watching the kids splash back and forth on a hot day, you can make do with an aluminum shaft and plastic blades, a way-stout paddle that's available for well under a C-note. If you're interested in some limited camping, with short distances and sheltered waters, you can pick up middle-of-the-road paddles with fiberglass shafts and fiberglass blades, probably in the mid-$100s. These do good duty and will take the abuse of pushing off from a beach and driving all day. If you plan on paddling eight hours a day for days on end, you'll appreciate (and darn near require) one of the exotics, priced at $400 and up. Same holds true for the paddler in a wicked-fast sprint kayak, in which a good day means a few minutes of incredible effort culminating in exhaustion (and the many, many hours of training leading up to that sprint).

So is the price worth it? What do you want to do?

It's hot here on the beach, so let's cool off. Grab your paddle and let's walk out until we're thigh-deep in water. That's close to how much of you will be above the waterline in your kayak when you're bobbing about. Close your eyes, loosen up, and relax your hands, and try a sculling high brace. Do a sculling draw stroke. Some paddles will twist and dive for the bottom unless you hold them back. Others like to find the angle in the water that will support you.

Finding the "best" paddle for yourself is a matter of patience and experimentation. Start with a paddle that fits you and your paddling style, and as you grow comfortable with it start to explore slightly different lengths, blade sizes, degree of feathering, and even shaft diameters. As your paddling skills evolve, you'll discover the paddle that suits your needs.

CHAPTER 7

On the Way to the Water

Daniel Desmarais; licensed by Shutterstock.com

There are two distinct sports, which, although they use many of the same terms and techniques, are vastly different: whitewater kayaking and kayak touring. *Whitewater kayaking* is basically reactive, demanding near-instantaneous reactions to a changing environment. *Kayak touring* is reflective, where the environment is assessed and a course of action deduced. In the real world, both are just waypoints on a spectrum, but kayak touring allows you to build through a series of steps on your way to a destination.

So we're going to head down to the beach for part of the morning, laying out some of the

building blocks which in turn will let us have a heck of a lot of fun paddling. You won't be graded on them. You don't have to learn them; you don't have to use them. They have made paddling more fun and more efficient for a lot of paddlers in our joint history, and that's why I want to share them with you before we get a little more involved out on the water. Let's grab our gear and head over to the grassy meadow just above the beach and reflect on some of the skills that get us out on the water.

You've heard from all kinds of people that kayaks—especially touring kayaks—are tippy. And you're a tad concerned. Well, are they? Nope.

If they're not tippy, then why do they wiggle?

A kayak's center of buoyancy is concentrated right in the middle, just about at the waterline. Just about where you're sitting. With you in the boat the weight is still right over the keel, but the center is higher, up close to your sternum. As long as you're sitting still and vertically, the center of the weight is over the center of buoyancy, and the boat is in a state of dynamic repose. You can sit there all day if you want.

Now, kind of lean over to one side—just a bit. That moves the center of weight out a bit from over the center of buoyancy, and that side of the boat is going to be pushed a bit deeper into the water. Think of two people balanced on a teeter-totter. If one moves out a bit on the board, that side of the teeter-totter will sink.

Now comes the magic of boat design and secondary stability. As your boat shifts with the changing position of your weight, it pushes the *chine* (the line between the bottom and the side of your boat) deeper into the water. As that side of the boat goes deeper into the

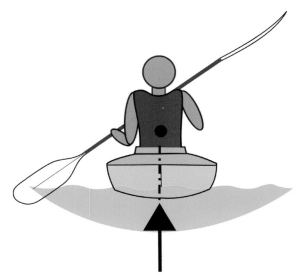

When your center of gravity (the black circle) is directly over your kayak's centerline (the dashed line), you are balanced on the center of buoyancy (the black arrow). In other words, your kayak feels stable.

When you shift your center of gravity to the side, you add weight to that side of your kayak, pushing that side deeper into the water. By going deeper, the kayak displaces more water on that side of the centerline, creating more buoyancy on that side. You are back in balance—yes, your deck is canted to the side, but you and your kayak are stable.

water, it displaces a greater volume of water. The more water it displaces, the more buoyancy it creates, and in doing so the center of buoyancy shifts outward from the keel toward the weighted side. The center of weight and the center of buoyancy will come into balance, and once again your kayak will be dynamically stable. Shift your weight a bit back, and the boat will come to rest level. You can shift your weight to the other side and it works just as well.

So how come it feels so tippy? Because your inner ear, which keeps track of your balance, hasn't learned about kayak balance. Once the balance point of your kayak shifts, your inner ear sends a panicked message to your brain. "Hey, this thing is wobbly—we're going to slip, and then we're going to fall!" Maybe it's the lizard part of your mind, just a centimeter or so off the brain stem, that's so worried, but whatever part of your thinking system it is, believe me, it will be persuasive. Wrong, but persuasive. You'll simply need to show this precursor of rationality the error of its ways.

Do all boats react this way? Nope. If you tried this in a perfectly round cylinder, you'd flop over and get your hair wet. If you were in a boat with a truly flat bottom and sides that were absolutely vertical, you'd find it very difficult to lean it even a little bit. If you tried to force the lean, all of a sudden the boat would flop over.

Learn to Lean

If you want to turn your kayak or if you want to go straight, if you want to move through waves or land in surf, or even thwart the efforts to the wind to turn you about, you're going to have to learn to lean. Most of us start off with the wrong idea about leaning, and spend way too much time having to correct less than desirable habits.

Watch those paddlers coming around the point over there, coming through waves and

No lean

The bell buoy lean

a crosswind, and even the collision of two currents. They are sitting straight up in their boats, and if you hung a string and a plumb bob off their noses, the line would be centered on their navels. Concentrate on their backs as they turn. Their backs stay vertical, but they use their hips and knees to rotate their boats. If you drew a line down their spines, from head to tailbone, it would form a J, and that's why it's called a *J-lean*.

Some of us took guidance from a big old bell buoy out on the water. The superstructure—that's our bodies—is rigidly joined to our boat at a right angle. To lean, we just topple over

to one side or the other and the deck leans with us. We have little balance, almost no control, and at any moment we might dive head-first into the water. The buoy has a honking big counterweight on the bottom, much like those inflatable punching-bag clown toys that come back up no matter how many times you knock them over. Our kayaks don't.

And sometimes we get fixated on the erroneous security of not leaning our boat at all. We keep our boat flat on the water and bend from the waist out, over the side. I've found when doing this that I'd lose all the control of a lean, my balance was on the way to Davy

The J-lean

The body-only lean

Jones's locker, and it was uncomfortable. But I did it anyway.

I've also been known to keep my boat flat on the water with my body stiffly erect. Lean? Well, I'd twist my neck over to the side so that everything looked canted over. It didn't work.

If you learn the J-lean first, and use it, you'll save yourself a lot of paddling grief. It's your call.

Getting to the Water

Your first challenge is getting your kayak from here to the water's edge. Or, in this case, to the meadow. The easiest way for one person to move a kayak, over relatively forgiving ground, is atop a kayak cart. That's what I used when I moved my boat over there a bit ago. Think of two wheels and a frame that supports your kayak and that you trail along behind yourself like a wheelbarrow in reverse. Some get pretty elaborate and fancy—a boat trailer you can tow behind your bike—and some are bare-bones simple. If you're going to pack it along when we paddle away, you'll want one that will disassemble and fit inside your boat. If you think we'll be moving across soft terrain, such as muddy trails or wide and uncompacted beaches, you might want one with really wide tires. No matter what the countryside, the cart will take most of the heavy lifting out of moving your boat.

If you're by yourself and you don't have to go too far, it's pretty easy to pick up an unloaded boat and carry it. Squat down next to your kayak at the cockpit, facing the bow, and reach across the boat to the far edge of the cockpit. With your hand inside the cockpit, fingers underneath the coaming and your thumb sort of hooked over the upper edge of the coaming, roll your boat toward you and boost the coaming up on your shoulder. Your shoulder should be at about the middle of the cockpit, but that varies with the weight and balance of your boat. Then use your leg muscles to stand.

You just noticed two things: First, you have 6 feet or more of kayak sticking ahead of and behind you, and it has its own mind about teetering; and, second, the kayak itself blocks your vision to one side. Your hand still gripping the coaming just ahead of your shoulder balances the boat and curbs the bow's desire to rise and fall. If either the bow or the stern stubbornly refuses to rise off the ground, either your shoulder is not at the balance point of the boat—slide the boat forward or back a very little bit at a time to fine-tune your position—or possibly you left some gear in one end of the boat.

And your diminished vision? Live with it. Be aware that a tree might suddenly jump out in front of you from that obscured area—I say that with the voice of inattentive experience—or you might discover an equally encumbered kayaker on a collision course.

Why squat down? Because when you stand with the unfamiliar weight of the kayak on your shoulder, you'll rise with the sturdy muscles in your legs. If you bent over to pick up your kayak, you'd be putting a lot of unbalanced weight at an awkward angle on your back.

Because there are two of us here, things get easier. Stow your PFD, spray deck, paddle, and jacket in your cockpit, and we'll carry your boat together.

Most kayaks have a "grab loop" of rope at the bow and stern, and most of these loops include a rigid handle. They might be as simple as a short length of plastic pipe through which the loop is threaded, or as specific as a molded T-grip. They're good for moving a kayak a very short distance, but are uncomfortable after just a few meters.

Why don't you squat down next to your kayak, a foot or so back from the bow; I'll move on the other side, about a foot in from the stern. Let's reach over the top of the deck and around the hull, until you can grasp the lower edge of the bow with one hand and I'll grasp the lower edge of the stern. Give a signal when you're ready, and we'll stand using our leg muscles

With one of us on each side of your kayak, we counter the boat's inclination to roll. Just makes it a little easier to balance.

If your kayak is loaded with gear, four people are better than two. One option is to have the two of us in the same positions we just used to lift your boat, and with the other two on each side of the cockpit lifting at the coaming. Since it is unlikely we're all just the right height to lift equally, this can be awkward.

Some folks fabricate a pair of straps (or rope or webbing), with a comfortable handle at each end of the strap. The straps should be long enough to go under the hull a couple of feet in from the bow and stern, with the handles just above the gunwales (or deck) so you won't bang your fingers. Four people, one at each handle, make light work of the carry.

Tandem kayaks are heavier than singles. You and I can carry one at the bow and stern, just like we did with your single, but four bodies make lighter work of it. Carrying straps work just the same. You can also have two people at each cockpit, each grasping the coaming with one hand.

Since we're being efficient rather than hardworking, let's lash your kayak and gear atop a cart and roll on over to the meadow just above the beach.

If this is all about going paddling, you ask, why are we heading for the meadow?

Simple enough. We're going to learn the easiest way to slip into your kayak and slip your kayak into the water, and we can make the first practice runs easier on level grass than on sloping sand and rocks. Right over there looks level.

First of all, there is no right or wrong way of boarding a kayak. I knew a lady that preferred to step into her floating kayak and then slither bonelessly down into the cockpit. She was the only person I ever met with that kind of balance and flexibility, and that could always find a suitable launch. We're going to use a different method that is fairly easy, somewhat graceful, suitable for most beaches or launches, and one that's probably less likely to abruptly transform you from a paddler into a swimmer.

Start by stepping into the tunnel of your spray deck (or skirt) and squirm it up until the deck is at your waist and the top of the tunnel is around your chest, close to your armpits. Once you're in your kayak you can slip the spray deck down and into a more comfortable position. As long as you have it scrunched up high on your chest when you're boarding, you're less likely to jam it between your body and the cockpit coaming or rim.

Some paddlers like to hold their spray deck over their head and wiggle up through the tunnel hole. I've never had much luck with the skirt-over-head technique; whenever I've tried it, I've seemed to end up stuck partway through the hole.

Now put on your PFD. Yeah, you're on grass and not water, and this is just practice. Put it on anyway. It's a good habit to get into, it's the right example for the kids, and it shows proper respect for the water. Besides, boarding your kayak is a lot different with a PFD than without.

Sometimes you'll see people put on their PFD and then pull their spray deck atop that. Aside from being uncomfortable, it doesn't work. Any spray splashed up on your PFD will trickle down until it puddles against the upper edge of the spray-deck tunnel, and it will then ooze down between the deck and your PFD and onto you. If your PFD is on the outside, as it should be, any stray drops will run down its surface and drip off the lower hem onto the exterior of the spray deck, and then overboard. Think of it as shingling, just like on a roof.

Now, with your paddle in hand, go stand right next to your kayak, beside the cockpit and facing forward. Squat down so that you are more or less sitting on your heels. If you find squatting uncomfortable, you can sit on the ground, but this will take more arm muscle. Kneeling doesn't work at all well. You should be just nudging the gunwale, or at least within an inch or so of it. Swing your paddle around behind your back so that the shaft is just behind your cockpit coaming and the blade is barely beyond the far side of your boat. The paddle should be sticking out at right angles to the keel of your kayak. That will give your balance the most support, and will keep you in the right spot to slip into your boat.

Lower the paddle blade on your side until it touches the ground. If you have a spooned blade or an asymmetrical paddle, make sure the *back* face of the blade is on the ground. If you put the power face down, your weight will be on the thin and more-fragile tip. The sound of that tip splintering is very expensive. If you have a stout blade, with the front and back sides of the blade the same, it doesn't matter which side (or face) is down.

If you have a feathered paddle, the blade on the far side of your boat will be somewhat vertical. If you're using an unfeathered paddle, the far blade will be parallel to the ground. In either case, the blade should be beyond the deck.

With your hand next to the kayak, reach over and rest your palm on the paddle shaft while wrapping your fingers firmly around the cockpit coaming. You're holding the paddle in place with this hand. Place your other hand on the paddle shaft, at about the small of your back. Push up, so that your weight is supported by your feet and your hands. You might hear your kayak creak a bit, because it's not accustomed to supporting your weight while aground, but it will do so without complaining too much.

Lift your leg that is next to your boat and put it in the cockpit. Supporting yourself with your arms, shift your weight laterally until you are poised over your cockpit. Not *in* your cockpit, but above it and close to the aft part of the coaming. Balancing yourself with the support of the paddle blade on the ground, bring your other leg aboard and into the cockpit.

If you're paddling a recreational-style kayak with a big cockpit, you'll lower yourself into your seat and then extend your feet forward under the deck. If you're paddling an expedition-style kayak with a small cockpit, you'll have to slip your feet forward as you

Begin by squatting next to your kayak's cockpit, grasping your paddle behind you. The blade on the ground must be power-face up, to protect the tip of the blade. Support part of your weight on the paddle shaft.

Shift your weight from the paddle shaft to your hand at the rear of your cockpit coaming, and slide sideways so that you are over the rear of the cockpit opening.

Bring your foot into your cockpit, balancing yourself a bit on the paddle shaft. You don't want to place your weight on the far side of the kayak, lest you topple over. That's not dangerous, just embarrassing.

Lower yourself, or slither down into, your kayak. You're aboard!

Think of your paddle shaft as a handrail, and balance yourself with it as you exit your kayak.

lower yourself into the seat. Your body already knows how to do this, and will do so if you don't think about it too much.

Getting out? Just the reverse.

Stick your paddle out to the side. With one hand grasp the paddle and coaming, and with the other, grasp the paddle shaft a foot or so beyond the gunwale. Lift yourself up above the coaming, with your weight on the paddle blade against the ground to maintain your balance. Slip one leg out of the cockpit and plant your foot on the ground. Using your paddle for balance, shift yourself from over the cockpit to over the ground, and stand erect. Step out of your boat and you are ashore.

You'll see at least one person paddle to the beach, become discombobulated, and capsize on the beach only to crawl from the overturned boat. While it does get you from the boat, this approach does have its obvious drawbacks.

You'll notice I didn't say "left hand" or "right hand" when talking you through your first boarding. That's deliberate. Practice a few times boarding (and exiting) from each side of your kayak. That way you'll be (very quickly) comfortable when Mom Nature dictates the preferred boarding side.

Sitting in your kayak you realize something: Your spray deck is wrapped around your chest, and there's nothing preventing rain, spray, and waves from pouring into your cockpit. Fortunately, you can be all neat and tidy in a moment.

Spread your spray deck out from your body, somewhat aligning it with the shape of the cockpit. The elastic edges will pull it right back, but all you're trying to do is eliminate tangles. Lift the back edge of your spray deck up so that it can clear the rear portion of your coaming, and lean back in your seat. Hook the center of the spray deck under the rear edge of the coaming, and then extend your hands out along the edges of the spray deck a few inches, to where the back of the coaming just begins to sweep forward into the sides. Feed the lower, elastic edge of the deck under the outside lip of the coaming.

Now lean forward. This pulls the spray deck snug against the coaming lip and holds it in place. Run both your hands forward until you're holding just before the pointy end of the deck, and snap this point over the front of your cockpit coaming. Look for a handhold at the front of the spray deck. This might be a fabric webbing loop, an elastic cord threaded through a practice golf ball, or a molded rubber T-grip. Don't be neat and tuck this under the spray deck; this is the grip you'll use to remove the deck—optimistically, when you land at the end of a day on the water, but equally important if you find yourself upside down and think you're trapped. The deck won't—no matter what you fear—hold you in the capsized boat. One good push and you'll be free. You'll see this afternoon.

Once the elastic edge of the spray deck is tucked under the coaming all around, scoot the tunnel down until it's comfortable, but still high enough to keep the deck bowed or arched slightly upward. A flat or concave deck creates a bowl for water to sit in.

Use the grab loop to stretch your spray deck over the front of the cockpit while keeping the back edge of the spray deck tucked under the edge of the coaming. Practice it a few times before showing off your skill in public.

Come on out of your boat and let's take a look at the beach. In particular, let's look at the waves.

On some beaches, depending on the wind and geology, the waves come straight into the shore in orderly rows. This little beach is more typical: Waves come in at an angle to the shoreline. We're going to find it more comfortable if we launch more or less bow into the waves. Our bows will split oncoming waves, we won't be rolled from side to side by wave energy, and we'll be pointed into the waves for a more-efficient passage through the surf (small as it might be) and the shore break.

Launching the other way, angled out from the shore but parallel to the waves, will give us a number of problems. The launch will be wetter, because the waves will be slapping the full length of the side of our kayaks and splashing up. The waves will be rocking us, perhaps a good deal more than we'll find comfortable. The waves will also be pushing us back to shore, and it will take a fair amount of energy to turn our bows out and head into the comfort of deeper water.

Launching is always a compromise. Many new paddlers attempt to take the shortest path to deeper water by aligning their kayak at right angles to the shoreline as they board. That doesn't work well. The beach plunges at an angle to the surface of the sea. Your narrow bow, with little buoyancy or stability, will be bobbing on the water while your narrow stern will be teetering on the beach. The broader midsection of your kayak will be unsupported above the beach, and you'll be attempting to board this unstable platform. When you do get aboard you'll have to drag that 7 feet or so of kayak behind you down the beach as it attempts to plow a deep rut. Hard work, and hard wear on your boat.

The alternative is not to place your kayak parallel to the shoreline right at the edge of the water. Sure, your boat will be flat and balanced, which will make it easier to board, but to push off into floatable water, you'll have to shove the entire length of your boat sideways—dragging on the beach and slogging through the water. You won't be able to use your shoreside blade to turn into deep water because that side is shoveling sand. Strong strokes on the seaward side will swing your bow back up on the beach.

Don't be frustrated. The magic number is to align your boat somewhere in the neighborhood of 30 to 45 degrees off the shoreline. You'll board from the shore side of your kayak, staying sheltered from any wave action.

Once you're fastened in, just put your hands on each side of the boat a bit in front of your hips and push down and simultaneously backward. Your unweighted kayak will slide forward and you can make a strong forward stroke on your shore side to glide out onto the water.

If you're paddling in salt water, you can just load up your kayak, clamber in, and wait for the rising tide to float you away. Don't laugh. On a really wide beach and with heavily loaded expedition boats, this is a perfectly sensible option. I've loaded a boat on a rocky ledge with only nasty rocks below and was very grateful for the moon's assistance in floating me off.

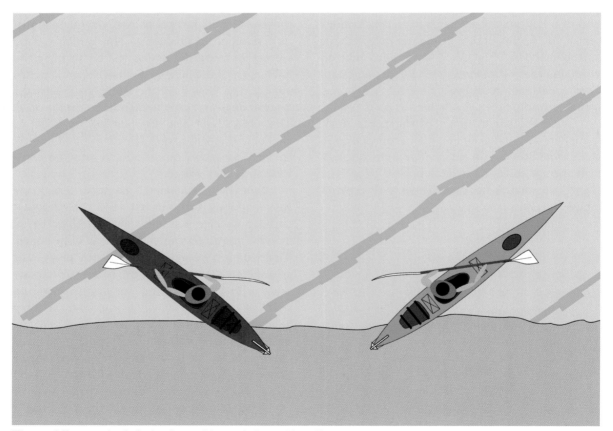

The paddler on the left, in the red boat, is launching directly into the waves. With a few strong strokes that kayak will be through the shore waves easily and with complete control. The paddler on the right, in the green kayak, is launching parallel to the waves. The paddler will get wet from spray kicked up by waves hitting the side of the kayak, and the kayak's bow will be shoved toward the shore with each wave. The paddler will fight to get the kayak off the beach and into water deep enough for a full stroke.

We're not going to launch through waves like this—at least, not on the first day. A launch like this will be well within your skill set, however, very quickly. To blast through the waves just put your head down and paddle forward at full power until you clear the surf.

All of a sudden you realize why we've practiced boarding from both sides. Sometimes the waves come from the left, and you board the left side of your boat. And sometimes the waves will come from the right.

The same angles work for double kayaks. When launching, the bow paddler boards first, with the stern paddler supporting the boat. If water conditions and the angle of the beach require it, the stern paddler may slide the kayak forward until the bow paddler is well afloat. The bow person will then brace as the stern paddler boards, and with a couple of strokes the duo is on the water.

One last thing before we grab a bite to eat and a mug of tea. See that red coaster wagon over there in the grass? Why don't you go sit in it, bracing yourself against the front. Comfortable? Reach as far forward as you can and firmly grab a couple of tufts of grass stalks. Pull! As your arms pull the grass you'll feel yourself edge forward in the wagon, and since you're braced inside, you'll roll ahead. Congratulations. That's the essence of paddling. After lunch you'll place your paddle into the water, and with a combination of muscles pull your kayak up to your paddle.

Don't Like That Wiggly Feeling?

First of all, leaning your kayak is the basis for controlling your direction, coping with wind and waves, and crossing the line between two currents. If you lean your kayak, you're in control. If you don't, you are controlled. The "wobbly" feeling in the cockpit of a kayak is your boat telling you that it's ready and willing to do your bidding. Some folks, though, are a bit uncomfortable with the motion at first.

Some quick tips:

1. Keep your nose vertically over your navel. Use your hips (and knees) to cant your kayak. This will give you the most precise control over your stability.

2. Keep your shoulders inside the gunwales (or widest part) of your kayak. If you lean way over and get your shoulders outboard of your kayak, you'll be out of balance and will find it more difficult to control your boat.

Smile. You're out here to have fun. If you are wound tightly—if you're rigid, with your knuckles and the corners of your mouth white, you will lurch and stab at the water. You'll quickly exhaust yourself. Think of the water as music, and dance to its rhythms. It sounds sort of New Age, but a smiling paddler will go farther, faster, and with far less effort than an uptight companion. Trust me.

Daniel Desmarais; licensed by Shutterstock.com

CHAPTER 8

Strokin'

Your First Launch

We've had a bite to eat and a chance to reflect on what we went over this morning. Now let's head on over to the beach for your first time out on the water. You have an expedition-style kayak, and I've been paddling a shorter, recreational kayak with a larger cockpit and a slightly broader beam. For your first launch, why don't you take my boat?

This little bay stacks all the cards in your favor. The water is shallow and warm, and the sand beach gently slopes into the clear water.

There's not a powerboat in sight, and that means no wakes to slosh up the side of your boat. We're in luck. Most of us get a little case of stage fright when we attempt a new thing before an audience, and there isn't another person on the beach close enough to watch you. I've already adjusted the position of the foot braces and seat back so you'll be comfortable.

Slide the kayak bow-first into the bay so that the front of the cockpit is right at about the shoreline. Then swing the whole boat until the angle between the keel line and the

69

shoreline is around 45 degrees. No need to fuss with this; the angle is not critical.

Climb aboard just as we practiced up on the grass. Your paddle goes just behind the cockpit, with the back side of one blade on the sand and the other blade a bit on the far side of your boat. Squat or crouch down next to your cockpit, just forward of your paddle. You naturally gravitated to the shore side of your kayak, or else you'd be squatting in the water. That's why we practiced boarding from both sides. Since most of the time you'll keep the bow of your kayak pointed into the oncoming waves while boarding, you'll soon be proficient at boarding from either side.

Normally this would be the time to snap your spray deck around the cockpit coaming. For this launch—and you'll soon see why—we'll skip that. If you were doing the whole

I'm going to give you a boost off the beach as we explore just how comfortable you can be on the water.

launch by yourself, this is the point where you'd lean forward and put most of your weight forward, on the floating end of your kayak. Just scoot your weight (and hips) forward and your boat may slide easily onto the water. If the beach is a little sticky, or you have more weight tucked away in the stern, you might need an extra boost. Put your hands on the ground just ahead of your hips, lean forward, and push down at the ground and back toward the stern. A couple of these and you'll be afloat.

This morning you're not going to need those techniques. I'll grab your bow and tug you off the beach and out to waist-deep or so water.

First, and partially to reassure that little voice in the back of your brain, you're going to lean your boat just to prove how stable it really is. Most likely your first lean will be just like a bell buoy, rigidly tilting off to one side. You won't like the way it feels, even though you know I'm resting my hand on the cockpit coaming.

The second time you'll flop your body to the side, bending at your waist and looking down at the water. That's no better, and still uncomfortable.

The third time will be a charm: Keep your nose vertically over your navel and angle your hips to cant your boat over. I can tell by your grin that you can feel how stable your boat is, and how easy it is to rock your hull back and forth with the J-lean. Without any coaxing you twist your hips to the other side and then splash back and forth as you send waves booming out from the sides of your kayak.

You're doing just like I did, for some reason lifting your hands until your forearms are close to parallel with the water surface.

What's the purpose of all this fun (as if fun needed a purpose)? You steer your kayak by shifting your weight and canting the hull from side to side. You'll paddle for a little while before grasping the subtle elegance of this technique. All of a sudden you'll utilize your energy in gliding your boat ahead rather than wasting it, slewing your bow back and forth, trying to hold to a course.

With your hips loose and flexible, you allow your kayak to find the kindest path through the lumps and riffles. You don't have to fight each roll of your kayak as you glide over waves and currents.

Put your hand over the side and test the water. It's warm, and so is the air. You'll understand just how warm it is because in a moment, after you take a good breath, I'm going to capsize you and your kayak. I'll be right here, to give you a hand up.

Sorry, I didn't catch what you said. Or tried to say, because part of the time you were underwater and part of the time sputtering.

That little voice in your mind warned you that you could get stuck in the narrow confines of a kayak. Take a look at the kayak. It's floating right side up, with just a couple of inches of water in it. When it was up on its side, you simply fell out and the boat flopped back, right side up.

I know what you're going to say—that this wasn't fair . . . that this is a recreational kayak with a big cockpit. Let's do it again, with your kayak. A kayak with a smallish cockpit and one that has a spray deck snapped into place around the coaming.

The spray deck will most likely come free the moment you've turned over. If it doesn't, just grab the loop at the front edge and pop it free with a tug. Put one hand on each side of the cockpit and shove—just straighten your arms and don't worry if you are shoving up or down. You're really just shoving out. As you straighten your arms, your rump will lift out of the seat and your legs will slide right out of the boat, just like taking off a stiff pair of overalls. You might actually (albeit unintentionally) push the boat ahead a bit while straightening, and

During a forward paddle stroke, your upper hand will be about shoulder-high.

Photo courtesy Brian Henry / Ocean River

that will just speed your exit. And an exit it is. Or, more precisely, a wet exit. See how easy it was?

This isn't about self-rescues and Eskimo rolls and all that stuff. It simply shows that you won't get stuck when you've exceeded the limits of your stability. That's a very good thing. If you're terrified to *huli*—that's Hawaiian for capsize—you'll paddle in a tight little ball and you'll never explore the limits of this extraordinary little craft.

Your kayak has a wall—a *bulkhead* in boating talk—sealing off the back half of your hull just behind your seat. While it has a waterproof hatch that allows you to stow stuff inside, this big chamber also provides a lot of flotation to keep your kayak afloat if swamped. Since your kayak is still upside down, all we have to do is lift the bow and most of the water inside will drain out through the cockpit.

I didn't build bulkheads in my kayak. Instead, I have big airbags crammed into the bow and stern. With mine we'd alternate lifting the bow and stern until most of the water had drained away. A thirsty sponge will mop up the last water. Just two approaches to solving the challenge of displacing water with air inside a kayak; both work equally well.

Let's splash back to the beach. You can dry off while I mop the last of the water out of the boats. Then we can head out onto the water for some serious fun.

Holding Your Paddle

We're in our kayaks and we're bobbing on the water. If we want to go anywhere, though, you're going to need your paddle.

Hold your paddle with both hands so that the middle of the paddle shaft is centered between your thumbs. At first it's easy to grab it off center, but that results in putting more effort on one side than the other, tiring you out and making it more difficult to glide in a straight line.

You don't need a death grip on the paddle shaft; just wrap your fingers loosely over the top of the horizontal shaft and cradle the weight of the paddle on the balls of your thumbs and the web between your thumb and index finger. If you grip tightly, you'll wear yourself out.

If you want to practice a bone-crushing grip, just squeeze a chunk of broom handle or a piece of 1½-inch pipe as hard as you want for as long as you can. After about a quarter of an hour you'll get the urge out your system and you'll be willing to paddle with relaxed hands.

Where should you hold the paddle? Raise it up over your head with the shaft horizontal. Keep your upper arms horizontal and slide your hands in or out until your forearms are vertical and the middle of the paddle shaft is

Power Position: To apply the most power to your paddle blade, you need the most leverage. You'll find that power spot by raising your paddle horizontally over your head and sliding your hands out until your upper arms are horizontal and your forearms are vertical. The midpoint of the paddle should line up with your nose.

in line with your nose. This is the maximum power position for paddling. No, no, no—not the position in which you have to work the hardest, or make the maximum effort. This is the hand position that gives you the maximum mechanical advantage and the maximum leverage when manipulating your paddle. It's a good spot from which to start.

Don't worry overmuch about precise placement. You're not competing on the international level, and it really doesn't matter if you are a bit off. If you really have to check, just flip your paddle above your head with your elbows at right angles, and there you are. If you want, keep your hands in position and lower your paddle in front of you. Have a friend loop a thin strip of duct tape around the paddle shaft just beyond your little fingers on each side. By the time the tape wears off, your muscles will remember where to reach.

Your First Strokes

We've covered a lot of new ideas and techniques, and you're doing great! Reward yourself by splashing off on your first voyage. You're wobbling about and your course is as straight as a snake's trail, but you're paddling. It's an exciting moment. You're a captain, in total command of your craft. The boat does what you tell it to do. Not necessarily what you *want* it to do, but certainly what you tell it to do.

After your first excitement burns away a bit, let's see if we can increase your fun quotient by making your paddling a little easier. You were pulling with your upper arms as you splashed about, and even after ten minutes or so—if you're honest—you'll admit that your upper arms are a bit tired.

Let's figure out why. First of all, I'm going to thread a thin rod from armhole to armhole across the back of your PFD, Now, take a couple of paddle strokes. It is easier to see from my viewpoint, beside you, but that rod sticks straight out from the side of your boat. It barely wiggles as you put your paddle blade

in the water and attempt to horse your boat forward.

How come? Because you are powering your boat with your relatively small bicep and forearm muscles. You don't have to wrinkle your face at that. The muscles in your biceps and forearms are not the strongest in your body, and that's true for all of us. If we switch your paddling power to the big muscles of your torso, back, and buttocks, you'll glide almost effortlessly along. You'll be able—with some practice, for sure—to be able to paddle for hours on end at a comfortable cruising speed without collapsing in exhaustion when you land at the end of the day.

You're going to sit up straight in your kayak, just as your mother taught you, and you're going to rotate or twist your body gently until your

Bring your shoulder forward by rotating your torso. This will extend your reach, as well as allow you to use the big muscles of your body as you unwind.

paddle-side shoulder is pointing just about to where your paddle blade will enter the water. Your shoulders will create a line about 45 degrees from your boat's keel line. That's not critical. Just rotate so that you're comfortable. You had to strain a bit against your leg muscles, your buttocks, your torso, and your back.

Guide your paddle into the water with your arms and hands, and rotate your torso with those big muscles until your other shoulder is pointing to just about where you'll place the paddle blade on that side. Confused? Let's break that down into small steps.

The first step will be back to the beach and out of your kayak. Hold your paddle vertically in front of you. Turn it so that the power face of the blade on the ground is facing you. (Some

Stand your paddle vertically in front of you, with the power face of the paddle blade on the ground facing your feet. Look up at the blade overhead. If it faces to the right, it's a right-hand control; to the left, a left-hand control. If it faces you, it's not feathered.

instructors call the power face the "front," but we all mean the face of the paddle that "pushes" against the water.) Look up at the blade in the air. You'll have to look up, because most touring paddles are 220 to 230 centimeters long, and few of us are 7 feet tall. If the power face of the upper blade is aimed at your right, you have a right-hand-control paddle. If the power face faces your left, you have a left-hand-control paddle. If the power face faces you, you have an unfeathered paddle.

And what if the power face faces away from you? You've either let the paddle twist as you gape at the upper blade, or you have a paddle with a serious identity problem. If you have a break-apart paddle, you might have simply slipped the two halves together incorrectly. If by some strange chance the two halves match up backward, release the lock (often a button) and twist the paddle blade around to where it should be.

If you are using a feathered paddle, your control hand (right for a right-hand-control paddler and left for a left-hand one) will lightly grip the paddle shaft and will allow you to rotate the paddle with your wrist to put each blade precisely into the water vertically. You won't change this grip as you paddle. Your other hand forms a ring within which the paddle shaft rotates as you immerse first one blade and then the other. Your non-control hand guides or aims your paddle, and puts the heel of your hand against the paddle shaft as you push against it.

Are you holding the paddle so that you can easily insert the blade into the water? Hold your paddle out in front of you, horizontally. Look at the knuckles on your control hand. The upper edge of your paddle blade next to your control hand should line up with your knuckles at the base of your fingers. Are you the kind of person, like many of us, who is likely to relax your control hand and forget the most efficient position?

The knuckles of your control hand should line up with the upper edge of the paddle blade.

Not to worry. Many paddles will give your muscles and your fingers a quick clue if your positioning changes. Many paddle shafts are oval, not round, and they will feel different if they shift within your hand. If that isn't enough, try taping a matchstick to the paddle shaft right next to your top knuckle line. You can feel the matchstick, and this will let you position your control hand easily.

If you are using an ergonomically bent-shaft paddle you'll discover that the paddle will insist on the best place to hold it. The angled hand-grip areas of the shaft define how you hold it.

If you've chosen an unfeathered paddle, both hands work as control hands. You'll line up the upper edges of your blades with the row of knuckles across the base of your fingers.

Most cruising kayak paddles, as we talked about in chapter 6, can be adjusted from unfeathered to sharply feathered by adjusting a ferrule or lock at the center of the paddle shaft.

We'll start off with an unfeathered paddle—but don't skip ahead, because feathered-paddle techniques grow out of an unfeathered blade. We'll begin with a stroke on the right side. Extend your right arm so that your elbow is straight and your right hand is about at the same level as the peak of your deck. As you do this, at the same time, bring your left hand back almost as if you were going to put a shot—that is, right to the front of your left shoulder. I like to keep the midpoint of my paddle just a bit higher than the lower edge of my sternum. Many paddlers keep their paddles a couple of inches lower. In time you'll figure out which is more comfortable for you. The difference? I think by keeping the center of my paddle shaft higher than my solar plexus, it gives me a more-efficient paddle stroke. The submerged blade is closer to the centerline of my kayak and is more vertical in the water, a combo that gives me more go-ahead power with each stroke. I use more energy lifting the paddle higher, and I probably paddle at a slighter higher cadence.

Holding your paddle shaft higher, above your solar plexus, allows you to keep your paddle closer to the side of your kayak and puts the paddle blade closer to vertical in the water.

If you keep your paddle shaft closer to your deck, around your navel, your stroke will sweep out farther from the side of your kayak and the blade will be less perpendicular in the water. You'll save some energy by not lifting your paddle higher. You'll also probably paddle at a slightly lower cadence.

You'll insert your paddle blade into the water pretty close to where your feet are braced against the foot pegs.

If you lower the center point of your paddle shaft, down toward your navel, it results in a paddle stroke that sweeps out more into a broader "C." The first part of the stroke pushes your bow away from the paddle blade; the mid-part of the stroke moves you forward; and the last part of the stroke pulls your stern toward the blade. This ongoing wiggle won't be very noticeable, but it will be real. You'll use a bit more energy keeping your boat moving in a straight line. At the same time you'll use less energy lifting your paddle higher. You'll most likely be comfortable paddling at a slightly lower cadence.

In time your body will tell you which is more comfortable.

Insert your paddle blade in the water as far forward as you can comfortably reach without slouching your torso forward. You're getting that blade forward with a combination of upper body rotation and arm extension. The blade will enter the water pretty much alongside your foot resting on its peg. You don't have to check this distance exactly—it's just what happens. Don't bang at the water; don't pretend you're a beaver and the paddle blade

is your tail. Just slip the paddle in, silently, as if you're starting to cut frosting on a cake.

How deep should the blade go? If only part of the blade is in the water, you can't develop much power. If you plunge it deeper than the throat of the blade, beyond where the blade joins the shaft, you're just using up leverage without gaining any paddle face. You'd also be rocking back and forth just to reach that deep. Without being too particular, try to just submerge the blade.

With your blade in the water, let your right arm begin to draw the paddle back. Simultaneously, push forward with your left hand, palm forward and fingers relaxed, as if you were aiming that hand right at the bow. Create an imaginary line right down the center of your deck, and don't let your pushing hand cross over that line. You won't lose marks for doing so, but you will over-rotate your torso, tire sooner, and lose power. Don't lift your left hand too high, either. I've watched people lift their left hand in this paddle stroke much higher than their eyes; there is no benefit gained from doing so. If you keep your left hand at shoulder (or perhaps chin) height, you're less likely

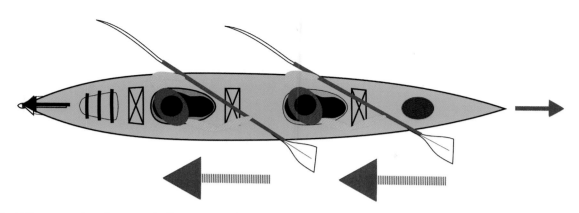

Paddling a tandem is very similar to paddling a solo kayak, with one significant difference: The bow paddler sets the cadence (the number of paddle strokes per minute), and since the bow paddler has a much better view ahead, also decides where to go. The stern paddler has to keep time with the bow paddler's strokes, and must use the rudder to maintain the course established by the bow.

to drip water on yourself, and the power from the blade in the water will actually serve to stabilize your boat. Keep the blade as close to vertical as you comfortably can, because that position gives you the maximum power face. Also, keep the paddle blade as close as you can to perpendicular to the keel line of your kayak. If you angle the blade forward or backward, it will want to either climb out of the water or dive deeper, and the energy you use to correct this would be better spent in moving the kayak. If you let the blade angle into or away from the perpendicular position, it will want to

drift away from the side of your kayak or sheer into it—again, correcting this will be a waste of energy.

The power portion of your stroke should kick in as the paddle passes from your knees to your hips. Once the blade is past your hips, all you're doing is prying up on the water, simply because of the angle of your hands. You no longer are pushing your kayak forward, but instead you are trying to pull your stern deeper in the water. Avoid this by lifting your blade from the water, and, as you do so, continue until your right hand is up by your right shoulder and

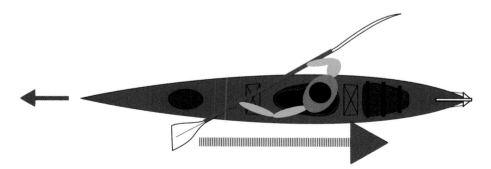

Forward Stroke: With the forward stroke, you insert your paddle blade into the water near your foot or ankle, and then you pull yourself up to your paddle blade. It looks as if you're moving your paddle through the water, as shown by the broad red arrow, but that's an illusion.

You've reached the end of your effective forward stroke when your paddle blade passes your hip. Once the blade is behind your hip, you're merely attempting to lift a whole paddleful of water and not giving yourself any forward movement. You're better off retracting the blade from the water and moving into the stroke on the other side.

your left arm is fully extended. You're now in a mirror-image position of the first stage of the stroke you just completed. Insert the blade and keep paddling!

That segment of the stroke, from when you lift your hand (and paddle) from your hip to your shoulder, is usually called *the recovery.* The recovery from one stroke positions your arms and your torso for the start of the next stroke. There is no pause, no break, dividing the recovery from the next stroke. It's all a seamless flow of motion.

Amazing, isn't it? When you rotate and use your powerful torso muscles, it becomes easier to paddle, you move faster, and you go straighter.

About eight out of ten paddlers choose feathered paddles, and of those eight, it seems as if most use a right-hand-control paddle. So, let's use that same stroke we just practiced, that basic forward stroke, only this time we'll

do it with a feathered (right-hand-control) paddle.

Pick up your paddle and hold it, in both hands, horizontally in front of you. This won't take but a moment; all we'll do is see how your control hand works. Rotate your right hand until the row of knuckles at the base of your fingers is on top of the shaft, pointing at the sky. Relax your right-hand grip and rotate the shaft until the top edge of the right-hand blade is in line with your right-hand knuckles, and the power face of the blade is pointed behind you.

The other blade of your paddle, the non-control-hand one, over on your left, has its power face pointed kind of down (depending on the amount of "feather," or the angle between the two blades).

Since you're sitting in your kayak, rotate your torso counterclockwise, and while doing so, extend your right arm forward and down a bit. At the same time bring your left arm back,

not to send my hand in a great arc before I could learn to keep my pushing hand level. Paddling suddenly got a lot more fun for me. I was working less and getting better.

Adding in the Power Muscles

You've made good progress controlling your arm muscles. Now let's throw in the big guys and see what happens. Step one is to check that you're seated firmly in your boat. Your feet are on the pegs and your back is comfortably pressed against the seat back. Your legs are up against the underside of the deck, but you're not so constricted that you can't relax your legs and lower your thighs. Your hips fit snugly in the seat—you've padded the seat for a perfect fit. You are one with the boat from the waist down, while your torso can rotate freely. Remember, you're not in a chaise lounge. You want to be sitting erect. Fuss with this until you're comfortable, because you're not going to paddle with the least effort and best result until the boat is an extension of yourself.

Now you're going to learn to add in the power of your power muscles. When you have to pick something up, you squat because that brings your major thigh muscles into lifting, rather than your out-of-position back muscles. When you lift something heavy from a tabletop, you use your biceps rather than your little finger. And when you paddle, you'll use the big muscles of your torso and back rather than the smaller muscles of your arms to scoot yourself along.

The next step is to start your stroke, just like you've been doing, extending one hand ahead to plant your blade. Take a mental snapshot of what you're doing right now. Your shoulders point directly out to the sides of your boat, perpendicular to the keel line. If your boat is perfectly aligned north and south, you have one shoulder pointing due west and the other east. All your drive is coming from your arms. Now, reach farther. Don't lean forward. Rotate your torso. Don't try to twist yourself up like a towel you're trying to squeeze the last dribble of water from, but just swing a comfortable distance. You will likely rotate your paddle-side shoulder forward about 45 degrees, or one-eighth of a circle.

It's all too easy to think you are rotating when in fact you're just pumping your elbows in and out. Look down at your PFD zipper. If the zipper continuously points at the bow, you're riding on your biceps. If the zipper moves back and forth, through an arc of 4 inches or more, you're rotating your torso.

So, what have you done?

First, by rotating your torso while keeping your back vertical, you've increased your reach forward. This is good, because you've increased the length of your effective, vertical stroke. Even more important, you've wound yourself up like a spring and you're all set to uncoil with the big muscles of your back and belly. As you start the pulling portion of your stroke, not only will your arm come back, but your shoulder will also rotate back, adding power to your stroke. Your shoulders will rotate from about 45 degrees ahead of amidships to 45 degrees aft of amidships, or through an arc of a quarter circle. This is not a precise measurement. One person will rotate easily, and another will be tight. You have to stay within your comfort envelope.

As your pulling shoulder comes back, your pushing shoulder goes forward, accelerating the pushing motion of your top hand. Both sides of the paddle stroke gain power.

You may find this hard to measure, but in the primary power zone from your knees to your hips, most of the power will come from the uncoiling muscles in your back. The smallest amount of energy will come from your upper pushing hand, with your lower pulling hand providing the middle ground of energy. Think of what you're doing as moving a spring smoothly back and forth, sort of like a Slinky marching across the surface of the water. Your arms will not be straight as an arrow, but will be bent just a tad at the elbow to keep the paddle shaft away from your chest.

Now you'll see why it's important that your feet be firmly on the pegs and your hips be snugged into the seat. When you're driving ahead with your right paddle blade, you'll feel your right foot push on the right peg. When you drive ahead with your left paddle blade, you'll push on the left peg. If your kayak seat were too wide and you hadn't filled it in with hip pads, you'd slide from side to side with each stroke. Each slippage represents energy that could have moved your boat ahead.

How powerful are your back and abdominal muscles? Let's find out. Turn your elbows off, with no pulling or pushing with your arms. Start with your kayak dead in the water, and concentrate on using just your torso twist to drive your paddle. Sure, this is counterproductive, but we're isolating your power and not practicing paddling for a few strokes. You'll feel the big muscle down the front of your stomach tense and stand out, and the top of your thighs will grow warm from shoving your feet.

Right away I know what you're thinking: "If I really twist, I'll go really fast!" Sorry—it doesn't work that way. Kayaking is a way of becoming one with the water and the environment, not a way of overcoming it. Be gentle, move with calm deliberation, and concentrate on the grace of what you are doing. What we're looking for is an elegance of movement.

The worst thing you can do is to think of each movement as a separate act. Cock a wrist. Extend an arm. Twist. All your moves should flow together in a current of motion, indivisible. There are no absolute rules in the art of paddling.

Changing Speed by Changing Gears

So far you've been power paddling. The way you grip your paddle allows you to transform a lot of arm and torso motion into the maximum power you can apply to the face of your paddle. Think of this as driving your car in low gear. It generates a huge amount of power—listen to that motor roar—but it doesn't offer a comfortable and efficient freeway speed. Let's shift your paddling out of "low" into a comfortable cruising "drive." We'll do that by moving your hands.

Grasp your paddle shaft comfortably with both hands. Tuck your elbows to your sides and bring your hands up so that the big knuckle at the base of the index finger of each hand is in line with the little bone that pokes up at the top outside rear of your shoulders. The midpoint of your paddle should be around the little vee where your collarbones connect to your sternum. You're now holding your paddle in the high-gear slot, where you will get the maximum paddle-blade movement with the minimum of hand and arm movement. It will take more muscle to move the paddle, but you'll be able to keep up a higher paddle cadence more comfortably, and for a longer distance and a longer time.

Some paddlers, liking a visual and tactile reminder of where high gear lies on the paddle shaft, will place a strip of tape just inside of each thumb position. You won't need this for long, if at all, because your muscles will tell you if you're trying to paddle in too high of a gear.

Think of a teeter-totter with a small child on one end. If you hold the other end, it doesn't take much effort to lift and lower the board. However, you'll twist through a long arc to sweep the child up and down. Now move in about halfway between the end of the board and the center point or fulcrum. Now it takes a lot more force to raise and lower your playmate, but you only move through a smallish arc while sweeping the child through a great distance.

Your paddle works the same way. Slide your hand out toward your paddle blade and increase your leverage, translating into greater power on the other blade and paid for by moving your hands and torso through a longer

Sliding your hands in on the paddle shaft until they are about as far apart as your shoulders are wide positions you to conserve energy and still keep up an efficient paddling cadence. It balances the leverage (how far you move the paddle blade as you move your hands) with how much energy you have to move that blade.

distance. Slide your hand toward the middle of the shaft and you decrease your leverage and mechanical advantage; you'll need more muscle power to move your paddle shaft, but you'll need less arm and torso motion to apply power to the blade in the water.

You can put your hands anywhere between the tapes marking your "high" and "low" gears, depending on the amount of power you want to apply to the paddle. Your forearms, upper arms, and shoulder width are probably not the same as mine, so you shouldn't measure my hand positions and apply them precisely to your paddling. That said, I'll move each of my hands in or out through about 23 centimeters—9 inches—on a 220 cm (86-inch-long) paddle.

Stopping

Let's try something different. Aim the bow of your kayak at the beach over there and make a half-dozen or so strokes with your hands out in the power position. Put some grunt into

it. Then rest your paddle across your cockpit with both blades out of the water.

You're right. Three things happened: First, you realized that your kayak will glide, or coast, for a good distance after you stop paddling. That's what a touring kayak does—it efficiently and gracefully slips through the water. Second—and from the look on your face, unexpectedly—it curved to the side. And third, you just realized a kayak doesn't have a brake pedal down by your feet.

Well, they are all connected. When your kayak is moving through the water, the wind pushes on every above-waterline surface. Waves, sometimes no more than ripples, will slap against your hull. These, working in conjunction or opposition, can and will slew your kayak from your expected direction. At the same time you'll feel the effects of the wind and waves and will shift your weight to one side or the other to counteract them. Heck, you do that when you're walking, as you lean

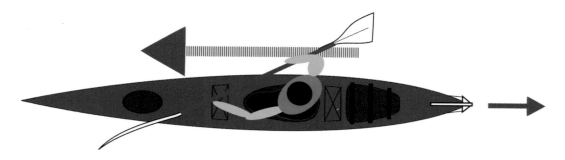

Rotate your torso so that you are turned a bit toward your paddle side, and insert your paddle blade so that it's perpendicular to your kayak's keel line, and as close to vertical as comfortable. Push forward, as shown by the large red arrow. The inertia of your kayak gliding forward means you won't move the blade far forward, but you will feel the boat rapidly slow. If you were just sitting in the water when you made this stroke, you'd back up.

into a wind, or when you teeter along, walking a line. As you shift your weight to the side, that side of your kayak sinks deeper into the water (perhaps even imperceptibly) and the other side lifts a corresponding amount. This changes the shape of your kayak in the water from symmetrical to asymmetrical, and the kayak will carve a neat turn.

Your kayak may not have a foot brake, but it does have a hand brake. Remember the recovery part of your paddle stroke, with one hand over the midpoint of your foredeck, one hand down by your hip, and your paddle blade almost skidding over the water as it is angled toward the stern? Wiggle around into that position, with your torso torqued around toward the wet paddle blade. Don't force the torque; just be comfortable.

Insert your paddle blade into the water. Be careful, because the water is going to put a lot of pressure on the *back* of your paddle blade. Your kayak wants to keep gliding forward—that's a matter of physics—and your paddle blade is grabbing the water and stopping all that forward rush. To increase the braking, push the paddle blade forward so that it becomes more vertical. The paddle will push you back into your seat and you'll feel the force against the back of your kayak seat.

Remember how your kayak turned as you shifted your weight and in doing so made its underwater shape asymmetrical? Well, you've just crammed a big, water-grabbing paddle blade into the wet 20 inches or so out from your kayak's keel line, and that is majorly asymmetrical! Your bow will slew toward the submerged paddle blade, and even if you had a rudder, you couldn't stop it.

What do you do? Your paddle has a blade on each end. As soon as you feel resistance, swap paddle ends and insert the other blade—but only for a very brief time. Your bow will slew back, turning toward the blade in the water. Switch sides a few times—probably three or four—and you'll come to a complete stop.

Backing

You stopped your kayak, and that was good. But you stopped in a narrow chunk of water bounded on both sides by finger piers and blocked ahead by a main dock. There's not enough room to turn about. Fortunately, kayaks can go backward. Remember when we started paddling forward, and you found that your kayak moved ahead because you pulled with your paddle and pushed your kayak along with your feet? We're going to build on that, but turn it all around. Keep your feet on the pegs, exerting enough pressure to keep your knees up against the bottom of your deck and your rump securely braced against the back of your seat. You remember the position. But now you're going to push yourself along by pushing your back against your kayak.

In stopping your kayak you probably shifted your hands out to the outer tape mark, to the low-gear slot, when you put on the brakes. You needed power to resist the forces shimmering up your paddle blade. Leave your hands in this position, because you're going to need a little power to get going. Just like backing up a car, you're not going to need speed to get you out of this situation.

You might lean back toward the stern just slightly, or you might try to keep your back straight and vertical. Both positions work; do whichever is more comfortable. But if you lean forward, you'll lose the ability to rotate your torso. Keep your paddle in its standard paddling position, with the power face aimed aft toward the stern and the upper edge of the control-hand side aligned with the row of knuckles at the base of your control-hand fingers. Some people will try to flop their paddle and put the power side toward the bow. If you do this, you'll lose the control of blade angle you've been trying so hard to master, and you won't gain any power. Really, you already have more power and speed than you'll need here. It's just like in the stopping maneuver, only the back side of your paddle blade will be used.

Either side will work for your first backward stroke. It feels natural to start on your control side, same as with the forward stroke. If you have a right-hand control, rotate your torso clockwise until your shoulders point about 45 degrees from straight out abeam, or just about as far around as you learned to coil in the forward stroke—remembering, of course, that in the forward stroke you rotated your shoulder blades forward and now you're rotating your

shoulders back. Both arms should be comfortably bent, with your elbows fairly close to your body. Insert the paddle blade as close to vertical as is comfortable, with the blade perpendicular to the keel line and the point of insertion about 2 feet behind your hips. Obviously, you're going to be lowering your hand next to the blade, and in doing so you'll raise your opposing hand. There's no reason to lift that hand above shoulder or chin level, and there's equally no reason to push that hand well forward. You may find that you're dropping your shoulder on the paddling side and raising your shoulder on the other side, and as long as you're not skewing yourself into some odd corkscrew shape, that's perfectly normal. Don't be concerned. You'll know if you're doing it right because you'll be comfortable. If it doesn't feel right, it probably isn't.

Uncoil, rotating your paddle-side shoulder forward, and as you rotate you'll apply pressure to the paddle blade stuck in the water. Since the blade is relatively immobile, what you're doing is pushing yourself in the opposite direction—and if you shove yourself toward the stern of your boat, your back and rump will shove your kayak in the same direction. As you push against the paddle, you'll find yourself leaning just a tad toward the stern of your boat. That's natural, and just a matter of the physics of muscle movement and leverage. All the power won't come from your unwinding torso. Apply pressure with your relaxed palm as you extend your arm toward the bow, and use this pressure to guide your paddle. As your hips move back past your paddle (the first time you do this, you'll swear the paddle is moving forward, but what you're really seeing is something analogous to sitting on a rear-facing seat on a train and watching the telephone poles appear at your shoulder and rapidly recede in the distance), turn up your throttle and apply maximum thrust until your knees reach your paddle blade. Retract the blade just after your knees pass.

The closer to vertical (and the closer to perpendicular to the keel line) you keep the back of your paddle blade, the more surface you will have to grip the water, and the more power you'll be able to generate. For a moment, let's flop out of the kayak and float in the water, stomach down, with your shoulder touching the bow and your eyes just below the surface. We'll let someone else get in the cockpit. Put on some goggles so you can see better. For easy measurements (these numbers bear no relationship to the real shape of a blade, but I can't do complicated sums in my head), we'll assume that the paddle blade you're looking at is 12 inches long and 12 inches wide. So you have 1 square foot of blade surface. If the blade is absolutely vertical and at a perfect right angle to the keel line, every bit of that surface will press against the water.

Now, the paddler is getting a little lazy. His or her top hand has moved far forward of the hand next to the blade in the water, so that the paddle shaft and thus the blade is at a 45-degree angle to the water. From where you're watching, up at the bow, the apparent height of the blade is now only 6 inches. Sure, the real length is 12 inches, but the column of water pressing against it is only half that. Now, the paddler's arm is still lazy, and the blade cants off 45 degrees from perpendicular to the keel line. From your viewpoint, the blade that had appeared to be 12 inches wide is now only 6 inches wide. The apparent surface has just been reduced by half again, so we're down to one-quarter of a square foot of blade surface. Just by not taking full advantage of the paddle stroke, our paddler has lost three-quarters of the paddle surface.

Let's allow our substitute paddler to go off and practice somewhere while you get back in the boat and avoid the mistakes you just observed. For maximum power, keep the paddle close to the side of the boat, with a little power used to keep the blade down and most

of your power spent in keeping a straight line parallel to the keel line.

As you lift the paddle blade from the water, your shoulders will be rotated and your hands will be moving in the proper position to begin the next stroke on the opposite side.

Nothing, though, is simple. What you have is a powerful stroke, one that will move your kayak backward—but your boat was designed to track in a straight line going forward. Backing up can be a challenge, with the stern of your boat darting unexpectedly sideways. Think of your kayak as a weather vane—it wants to point into the wind. If you twirl the back end of a weather vane around, or attempt to fling an arrow feathered-end first, the resulting action will be at best erratic.

Try inserting the lower outside corner of your paddle blade into the water first, a foot or more off that imaginary point a couple of feet back from your hips. The apparent movement of the blade toward the bow will be in an arc, something like one side of an arch, until you retract the blade as it passes your knees. This is an unbalanced stroke, but it will work! You'll start by going straight astern, but the last part of the stroke will really pull the bow toward the paddle side. The alternating stroke on the other side will pull your bow to that side, and you'll glide backward in a wiggling line.

You're right. This is not the most efficient way to move astern, compared to a straight line. What this does do, though, is present you with a whole series of potentially correcting strokes. If your kayak begins to turn to the right, put a little more muscle on your next stroke on the right side. You could also reach out a bit farther to the right and exaggerate the arc of the stroke a little more. We're not talking about major corrections here, just little nudges that will keep you going in one direction. Backing up (or in nautical terms, "backing down") is a compromise between the two extremes of this stroke.

The faster you paddle, the more likely you are to shift your weight, and the more likely you are to let your boat swing widely out of alignment. Keep it slow, keep it easy. If you back up slowly, you'll need smaller corrections, and you'll actually go faster than if you paddled very quickly and burned off all your energy and speed with abrupt course corrections.

You'll also find that peering back over your shoulder is inconvenient and uncomfortable at best, and one of the reasons that you'll veer off course. Line up the point of your bow with an object on the shore, and keep those two marks in line for three or four strokes before you crane your neck around.

That's all there is to backing. You can plant your paddle blade in the water and pull yourself up to it, or you can plant your paddle blade in the water and push yourself away from it. Every variation of these two strokes involves either a change of direction in the force exerted or a combination of the two forces. I think most paddlers know this, at least in their muscles, even though many will articulate the names of all sorts of variations. My friend Steve pointed the two-stroke truth out to me while teaching a basic canoeing class, and it's made my time on the water easier.

Turns

We've managed to board our kayak, paddle in a straight line, stop, and back up. What's next? There's a whole world off to our left and right. We need to learn how to turn our kayak, at the speed and angle we wish, in order to explore the world passing alongside.

Sweeps

To turn, think about going straight. When you inserted the paddle blade into the water close to the gunwale (the outside edge of the kayak), with the blade close to vertical in the water, and pulled yourself right past it, you went straight. If you held your paddle shaft closer to the deck while you inserted the blade in the water next to your knee, it would be much harder to keep the apparent path of the paddle exactly parallel with the keel line. You had planned on moving straight ahead, but the apparent path of the paddle looked like a "C," with the open mouth of the letter wrapping around the cockpit. You were actually inserting the paddle ahead of the center balance point of the kayak and shoving the bow of the boat sideways during the first part of the stroke—until the paddle stuck straight out sideways from the cockpit—and then pulling the stern of the boat over to the blade in the last half of the stroke. Your kayak moved ahead in a series of sinuous curves.

And good that you did! Why? The straight-ahead, right-down-the-keel-line stroke applies power—and thus, speed—to the boat. But when you "sweep" the paddle around in an arc, you enacted the "sweep" stroke, one of the basic steering strokes.

Let's back up a step. No one can make an absolutely vertical, straight-ahead stroke. To do so, you'd have to insert your paddle through the bottom of your boat and pull yourself right up and over the shaft. Anytime you put the blade in the water, even as close as you can to the gunwale, the center of your paddling effort is going to be off the center of the boat, and there will be a tendency for the power to turn your kayak to the side, away from the paddle. At the same time, you're instinctively going to resist splashing your paddle in up around your bow and twirling the blade in an enormous half-circle from bow to stern. It violates all the things you've learned about pushing, pulling, and direction. You may or may not articulate this, but you know it.

Back in the boat, and now you are cruising down the bay. Something catches your attention over to starboard, and you'd like to swing over that way to investigate. What do you do?

You could try putting more force on each stroke on the left side of your boat. Remember, every forward stroke is unbalanced just a bit off center, and a few hard strokes might push your bow around. For that matter, if you're really forcing one side, you might just as well ease up on the other to make the paddling even more unbalanced and the turn easier. The next logical step would be to paddle on the left side only, with no strokes on the right. You can't get more unbalanced than that.

This may not turn you in time, however. Big, lazy arcs will eventually get you around, but we have a few other tricks in our bag. When you plant that paddle blade in the water on the left side of your boat, slightly change the angle of the blade. Don't aim the power face of the paddle straight back, but rotate the blade so that the power face is aimed just slightly away from your kayak. As you pull yourself up to the blade, you'll push your bow to the right. You'll feel this turning motion through the first

The power face of your paddle should be pointing out and away from your kayak as you initiate your sweep stroke. You'll push your bow away from the paddle and begin your turn.

half of the stroke. As the paddle passes perpendicular to the keel line, or straight out from you, start pulling the stern toward the blade, which increases your right turn. It's natural to attempt to rotate the blade in the water, with the lower edge ahead of the paddle shaft. If you do that, however, it will seem as if you're lifting the entire ocean (even though you're really lifting only a few gallons). In addition to making your stroke less effective, you're wasting a lot of energy.

To make this stroke as comfortable and natural as possible, keep your paddle shaft fairly low and as close to horizontal as you can while keeping your hands off the deck and the blade fully in the water. You don't even have to be moving ahead in order to make it work. You can—and you should know how to—pivot your boat in a circle just by a series of sweep strokes.

You can exaggerate this stroke by shifting your hands so that the hand near the immersed blade is at the midpoint or so of your paddle, and the other hand is at the throat of the upper blade. This gives you a much longer reach and increases the sweeping motion. But this move is risky; you can lose the muscle memory in your hands of the orientation of the blades, and, in the worst case, could send a flat blade hydroplaning along the surface. Better to just extend your arms while doing this stroke. You could, if you wish, lean forward a bit to plant the blade as far ahead as possible, which actually increases the effective length of your paddle and also increases the power of the sweep.

The first third or so of a typical sweep stroke gives you both forward power and starts your turn. The middle third moves you ahead, while the ending third really cranks your boat around. Okay, you saw this for yourself about the third time you tried a sweep, but it's the kind of thing you want to keep in mind when you start to plot a change in direction.

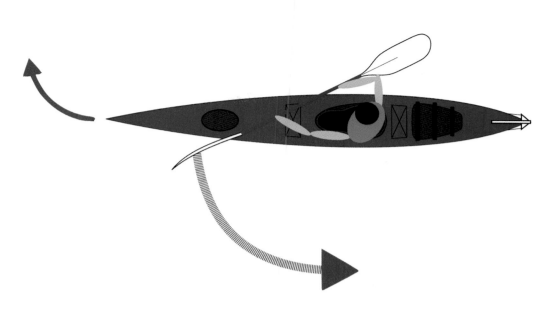

In a bow sweep stroke, your paddle stroke will push your bow to the side in the first part of the stroke, and then add some forward momentum as you bring your paddle straight out to the side of your cockpit.

You don't really have to sweep from bow to stern. Just use what you need.

So far, we've been concentrating mainly on the strength of your arms (with some assistance from your torso), and while that works, it also means you're working too hard. You have other muscles that you can bring into play! The total amount of work being done will be the same, but you've already seen the advantages of letting more muscles share the effort.

Press ahead with your foot on the stroke side, as if you were attempting to scoot the kayak along just with the power in your leg. At the same time, press upward with your stroke-side knee. When you do this, you will almost naturally shift your weight toward that lifted knee.

Think about what's happening to your boat as you shift your weight. Even though you're more comfortable in your kayak now, having paddled a bit, it still wobbles from side to side underneath you. Your kayak has a long, straight keel line with vertical flat surfaces at the bow

and stern. Every time you try to turn while sitting flat on the water, you shove these great kayak walls sideways through the water. Now, think of the "footprint" your kayak leaves when viewed from below. Each side is a smooth arc, and each side is the mirror image of the other. When you shift your weight to the stroke side, to the outside of the turn, you cause your boat to heel, and in doing so you create a new underbody—or underwater—shape. You no longer have a long, straight keel line with symmetrical sides supporting your weight. The stroke side, where you've shifted your weight, is now shaped like a much wider and shorter arc, and the side from which you've shifted your weight is a very narrow arc. By shifting your weight and leaning your kayak partway over on its side, to a certain degree you've lifted your bow and stern out of the water.

It's unlikely that you're paddling in a mirror-smooth pond. Odds are that waves are reverberating about, and they probably are big enough to move you up and down. Do you want to attempt a turn when you're in a trough and your bow and stern are deep in the waves ahead and behind you? This doesn't make much sense to me. When you're in a trough and your ends are deep in the water, your boat is pretty well stuck in one direction. Wait until the crest of the wave is under your cockpit and the ends of your boat are dripping water in the air. You'll dramatically reduce the lateral resistance on the ends of your kayak, and turning will be much easier. You probably won't have both ends of your boat out of the water, at least not in your beginning days, but any reduction in wet surface out on the ends will help.

How much muscle should you put into the sweep? A properly designed cruising kayak is going to resist your attempts to send it off in a new direction. After all, some designer spent a lot of hours and brain power in figuring out how to keep it from turning. The key is to watch your blade. If you're skidding it through the water you may have the musculature of an ox, but you're merely plowing the water and losing the efficiency of the stroke. Ease up. You should see little eddy swirls peeling away from the edges of the blade, but you shouldn't see turbulence and aeration in the wake of the blade.

Every kayak paddle, by definition, has two blades—one on each end of the shaft. With one blade you can sweep-stroke your boat around to a new course. But you have another blade just hanging out on the other end and ready to work. Let's say you want to make an abrupt change in course and perhaps even slow down a tad. That neat thing you spied earlier is still off to starboard, but unless you really crank a corner, you'll glide right on past the

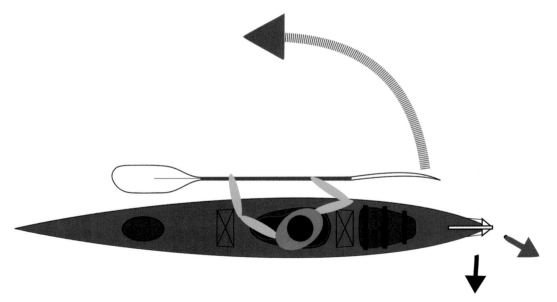

Reverse Sweep Stroke: Remember the back stroke that you used to stop your kayak? You'll take that same stroke and tweak it into a sharply turning stroke. Start the reverse sweep stroke the same way, with your torso rotated to your paddle side. Insert the blade into the water, but this time, a bit farther behind your hip—whatever is comfortable. The back face of the blade should point away from your kayak. Push the blade out and away from your kayak in a broad arc, like the broad red arrow. The initial movement is shown by the black arrow, but by the time the stroke is completed straight out from your cockpit, the final movement is shown by the small red arrow.

only narrow little channel you can follow to it. To turn sharply and abruptly, turn your sweep stroke around and make it a reverse sweep stroke.

Keeping your back vertical, rotate your torso to the right, with your right shoulder back a comfortable 45 degrees or so. Keep your right arm mostly straight and as far behind you as is comfortable, while your crooked left arm comes around until your left hand is right off your solar plexus. Plunge your right paddle blade into the water vertically, close to the stern of your boat, with the power face aimed aft and the back of the blade toward the front of your kayak. That's the normal paddle position.

Keep your paddle shaft low, just off your deck, and your blade completely immersed. Drive the blade, back side forward, toward the bow of your boat in a great C-shaped arc. Let your uncoiling torso drive the paddle, and use your sweep-side arm to guide it and maybe add just a bit of power.

The first third of this stroke will really snap your boat around and could startle you—and rightly so. This stroke is going to seem unstable. You're going to be perched right on top of the paddle when you start the move, and you'll notice that you're taller in the boat and that you won't seem as totally connected to your kayak. On the other hand, you're getting a major amount of support because of the weight and pressure you have on the paddle blade. I started serious paddling in the stern of a slalom C2, a decked two-person canoe designed to turn and twist in white water, and it wasn't long before I could almost lift the stern of the boat out of the water as I snapped it around with a reverse sweep.

The second third of the stroke continues the turn, but also quashes much of your forward motion. The last third is the weakest part of the whole, in which you pull your bow over to the paddle blade, but you can dial in a few extra ergs of energy by leaning a bit forward in the last few degrees of arc. Withdraw the blade before you slam your boat into it. (This isn't a joke; it can happen.)

I said earlier to keep the blade as close to vertical as you can while swinging through the arc. If you tip the top edge of the blade a bit forward as you apply forward pressure, the blade will almost want to hydroplane up and out of the water. If you cant the lower edge forward, the blade will want to dive. If it dives, you just might follow it down.

If you have any *way on,* which is a nautical way of saying you're moving, the first third of a stern sweep is a powerful steering tool. It comes at a price. It washes away the forward speed you've worked so hard to build. The forward sweep and lean conserves your forward speed, and that's a good thing in most cases. That said, you should practice a reverse sweep turn for those times you really need it.

Sweeps in a Double

So far, you've been practicing your sweep strokes in a solo boat (or a K1, if you prefer). "K," of course, for kayak, and "1" for the fact that you're the only person in it. What about a K2—or what we sometimes call a tandem, and sometimes a double? If you're paddling in the bow of a two-person kayak, the area of an effective sweep is the arc from ahead to perpendicular to your hip, or the front half of a sweep. Any attempt to sweep from abeam aft will just stir the water about, as you have a lot of boat sitting behind you.

If you're in the stern, however, just the reverse is true. Your sweeping arc of power is from a point perpendicular to your cockpit aft toward your stern. If you were so bold as to swing your paddle through the first half of the arc—say, from just off your knees to straight out abeam—you wouldn't be sweeping your boat into a turn, but would be *prying,* or shoving your boat sideways.

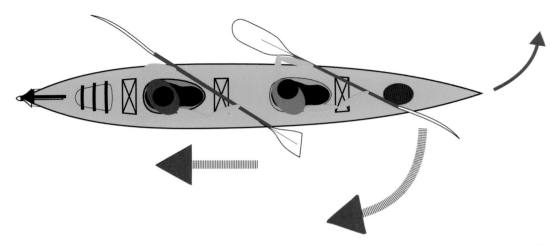

A bow sweep in a tandem works just like in a single kayak, but all that boat behind the bow paddler results in a slower turn. The effective power in the stroke comes from just off the bow to straight out from the cockpit. Anything behind that is thwarted by the length of the tandem.

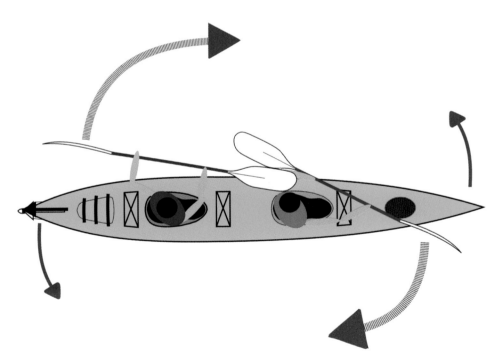

If both the bow and stern paddlers in a tandem kayak execute a sweep stroke, the kayak will pivot about its middle with no forward or backward progress. If the kayak is moving forward and only the bow paddler executes a sweep stroke, the kayak will turn to the side, away from the stroke, with no loss of forward speed. If the kayak is moving forward and the stern paddler executes a sweep stroke (really, a reverse sweep stroke), the kayak will turn to the side of the stroke, but the stroke will act as a brake and slow the forward movement.

The Stern Rudder: Precise Steering with a Twist of the Paddle

The stern rudder is one of the most versatile strokes in your bag of skills. You're going to want to use it to keep your boat heading where you want to go, whether conditions call for subtle course corrections without scrubbing speed away or keeping your stern under control in heavy winds and resulting seas. Think of it when threading rock gardens, with the wind shoving at your back, or when you're riding the waves.

Like most things in a kayak, the stern rudder is all about preparation. Imagine that you're gliding smoothly ahead and you've paused about three-quarters of the way through a forward stroke on the left side of your kayak. Your torso has rotated with the stroke so that you're facing the working (in the water) paddle side. Your power-side hand is near your hip and your right arm is extended over the deck so that your paddle shaft is close to parallel with the keel of your boat. You've probably extended your paddle-side leg a bit to increase your rotation.

At this point your wet paddle blade is trailing behind your hip and the leading edge is slicing cleanly through the water like a knife through soft butter. If you were looking at the blade rather than where you're going, the blade would be disturbing the water as little as possible.

You're all set to alter your course. Now subtly rotate your paddle shaft to let the water push against the power face of the blade. If your left blade is in the water, that's clockwise; on the right, it would be counterclockwise. What you're doing is rotating the front or leading edge of the blade away from your boat. Angled as it is now and moving forward through the water, the paddle will attempt to pull out from the boat's side. But you're holding onto it. The result is that the paddle blade will pull the boat's stern to the left and pivot the bow to the right.

Do you want to increase the speed of the turn? Draw the blade toward the stern of the boat, a draw stroke, while shifting your weight to the left side of the boat.

It's almost instinctive to reverse that stroke, to twist the leading edge of your paddle toward your boat and to pry the stern away from the blade. While it does turn your boat toward your paddle side, it's a barn door hanging out into the water flow, burning off your speed. It doesn't add to your stability, either. Just remember that you have a blade on each end of your paddle and you can draw from either side.

That said, the rudder/stern-pry combo is an effective tool for countering *weather-cocking*. That's the tendency of some boats to turn bow into the wind, much like a weather vane.

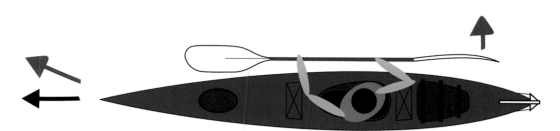

Stern Rudder Stroke: The stern rudder stroke is a dynamic stroke, which is another way of saying that it only works when you're gliding through the water. If you weren't moving relative to the water, it wouldn't work. The flow of water pressing on your paddle blade allows you to make the subtle adjustments in angle that result in precise turns.

Put Your Strokes Together

Few paddlers use the rudder stroke by itself. Come to think of it, few paddlers use any stroke by itself. All strokes flow into one another as paddlers attempt to gain the greatest results with the least energy expenditure. Most stroke techniques spring from common families: The rudder, the reverse sweep, and the sweeping low brace (you'll learn about braces in chapter 10) all build from a common foundation. Discover the common elements and move from one stroke in sequence to the next, and you'll find an amazing wholeness in your paddling. You won't be restricted to stammering over one paddling word, mentally translating it, and then flailing about for a second and then a third word. You'll think in kayaking sentences with a fluent patter rolling off your blade.

Sorry, but there's no magic formula to make it all work so easily. You'll have to learn by rote, until you reach that surprising point when you're no longer thinking but merely doing.

How can we help that happen? Stretch out before you clamber into your boat. Touch your toes, windmill your arms, and do the light exercises that should be part of the tune-up of your body every day. And relax.

Don't put your fingerprints into the paddle shaft. All you really need to do is lightly push with the pads of your palms. Support your paddle in the circle of your thumb and index finger, but don't worry about imprisoning it.

Speed comes slowly. Paddle slowly, and the speed will come. If you paddle at a cadence of twenty or so strokes a minute, you'll feel how the strokes fit together. Triple the stroke rate, and you'll splash about and veer wildly from left to right. If you stroke with a feather-light touch, your correction strokes will also be light and smooth. Pull hard on that shaft, and you'll have to correct just as hard as you would if you'd made a major error.

If you have access to a good gym, test your arm strength. If you're like most people, one arm is stronger than the other. (That's positive thinking. I just heard another paddler make the same bet, saying that one arm was weaker than the other. If you think negative, you'll paddle negative.) Don't let one arm overpower the other. The easiest way to do that is to keep your strokes light and easy as you learn. For that matter, don't let your paddle shaft creep through your hands until one hand is up against the throat of a blade and the other is around the shaft's midpoint. It's very difficult to go straight with that as your driving tool.

The last tip is hard to do. Don't look at your paddle, don't look at your bow, don't focus on your compass, and don't close your eyes to concentrate. Pick out a bright mark on the far shore and paddle toward it. You'll soon paddle straight and smoothly toward your goal.

CHAPTER 9

Draw Strokes

Look at the little inlet over there, way back in the cove where we've been playing. It's the mouth of a stream, and just a bit upstream on the north bank there's a small, T-shaped floating dock. You know, because it's a stream, that there is a current flowing down it. And on one particular day the wind was blowing—not strong—from the north. That was across the beach and over the floating dock. The tide had been ebbing for a while, which meant as the water level in our cove dropped, the force of the current in the stream mouth increased. A rising tide would have, in effect, plugged the mouth of the stream and decreased the water flow.

Unfortunately, I knew all these things at the time.

I figured out precisely just how hard I'd have to paddle to breast that current, where I'd ease up to glide to the dock (and come to a halt without banging into it), and I even had the bow line from my kayak at hand to secure the boat when I got there. It almost worked perfectly.

It was easy paddling up against the current; I judged just where I'd ease up, and glided to a halt right alongside the dock. Alongside the dock, but about 4 feet away from it. Just outside of grabbing range. A puff of that darned wind caught my bow, the kayak turned out into the current, and after a graceful and totally unprepared-for pinwheel, I was carried back down current.

With a little forethought I could have frantically splashed through a bow sweep stroke, just like you've been practicing, which would have swung my bow over to the dock. Probably with a healthy *bang*. I may not have had room for a forward stroke on the side between me and the dock, and I would've had to have taken

care not to trap my paddle between the kayak and the dock—but I would've gotten there.

What were my options?

You're right. I could have powered ahead, staying in control with my paddle strokes, and making a big circle back downstream and then up at the dock again for a second and better-executed approach. I could have gone upstream, made a tight little circle, and drifted down on the dock from above. You caught the challenge of that. The current would have carried me along, and I would've had to have back-paddled with vigor to stop the kayak next to the dock. If I'd cleated my bow line to the dock (that's the sole line I had ready), the current would have pivoted my stern around.

Fortunately, there is an easy and elegant answer. We call it the *draw stroke,* and it allows you to precisely scoot your kayak sideways.

Good news! You already know how to do most of this maneuver.

This time, we'll slide over to your left. The stroke works the same both ways.

Sitting in the cockpit, your shoulders are square to your keel line. Start by rotating your torso counterclockwise, so that your left shoulder moves toward the stern and your right shoulder toward the bow. Staying within your comfort zone, your shoulders now will be about 45 degrees from your kayak's keel line.

Reach straight out from the side of your kayak and, while keeping the paddle as close to vertical as you can, plant your blade in the water. This is one of the few strokes in which you can raise your top hand—in this case, your right hand—higher than your chin, and it might be convenient to do so as you strive for that vertical plant. It's my suspicion that most kayaking shoulder injuries are caused as paddlers force their hands up above their shoulders and apply stress at an awkward angle.

You're not going to reach out 9 feet and drive the blade throat deep into the brine. Few paddlers can, when keeping their weight centered, reach out 36 inches; 30 inches might be a good working goal. If you're a small person in a beamy boat, don't be discouraged if you can't reach past 24 inches. With the blade in the water, your left arm will be straight and your right arm will be cocked somewhere around a right angle at the elbow. Remember that all the dimensions and angles given in this book are no more than hints. If they work for you, great; if another way proves more comfortable, that's okay.

You want to keep your paddle blade as vertical in the water as possible. To do this, you're going to bring your right hand—that's the one

up in the air holding the dry end of the paddle—to more or less in front of your face. At least at first, when you're learning how to draw.

How come? It's a matter of balance. If you cross your upper hand too far across, you'll shift your weight past the left gunwale of the kayak, and you'll scare yourself because the boat will wiggle.

Besides startling yourself, unbalancing yourself to the left in this example will cause the left side of your kayak to dip. As you pull yourself to the paddle blade, a boat leaning toward the stationary blade in the water can trip. Since you are careful about your balance and with your strokes, this is unlikely, but an unwary paddler can get their hair very wet.

Now, let's say you're leaning over the left side of the boat and you're skidding the boat sideways to the left. Friction is grasping at your hull, and the combination of your weight and the drag all along the bottom as you slide across the water is going to dip your port gunwale. Bad news. No, you're not going to see your hull trip and suddenly spill over. But you are causing more drag and thus making more work for yourself than need be. Push your left knee up against the deck—remember, we're still moving left—and the torque will rotate the boat back level. I sometimes think I overdo this and actually lift up the leading gunwale so that the kayak's flat bottom attempts to slide up on the water, but I think this is more illusion than reality.

So now you've stuck the blade in the water. The stroke itself is simplicity in action. Pull in with your lower left arm. You might want to push with your top hand a smidgen, but this is only going to be 5 percent of the paddle force. You'll scoot your boat right over to your paddle. Stop the stroke when the blade is 6 inches or so from your boat's side.

You don't want to bang into your paddle. Elegance and coolness aside, if you slide into your paddle, that darned stick can work just like a lever. The wet blade will move under the edge of your kayak, and that will jarring-quick shove the upper end in a speed arc into the water. If you have a good grip on the paddle shaft you just might follow it over.

We haven't said anything about using your rudder or skeg, and I hope that you have it neatly tucked up in the air like the tail of a proud rooster. That broad blade is an anchor on your pivot, and will keep your stern nailed right to the water.

Whoops! You are kind of slipping sideways, but if your bow and stern were in a race, the bow would surely win. What happened?

Think about it. You're attempting to drag a long, skinny object sideways with all your force focused on one spot. By the way your face just lit up, I guess you figured it out. You have to insert your paddle blade straight out from the center of lateral resistance. That's overly fancy talk for straight out from the middle of your boat. Fortunately, there's an easily identifiable mark that shows the point we're talking about: your hip. Stick the paddle in the water straight out from your hip.

If you draw your paddle back toward your knee, or thereabouts, you'll pull the bow faster (or, with more effort/leverage). If you bring the paddle back behind your cockpit, you'll pull the stern faster. The magic line is to insert the paddle blade straight out from your hip and pull your hip right toward the blade.

When you're around 6 inches (or a spread hand's breadth) from the paddle, change the direction of motion but *not* the angle of the blade. Slice the blade, like a knife, aft (okay, backward), and cleanly up and out of the water.

Some folks like to rotate the paddle shaft 90 degrees and slice the paddle blade back out to the distance you originally inserted the blade into the water. They rotate the blade again so that it's parallel to your keel line, and again draw the blade in. This does keep your paddle

blade in the water, and no doubt could offer a bit more stability, or at least the potential of such. It's really not that hard to withdraw your paddle from the water and re-insert it.

Other folks prefer—as the paddle blade comes to within inches of the hull—to smartly rotate their control hand through 90 degrees and then slice the paddle edge first back out and up from the water. This prepares you to insert the blade for another draw stroke, or apply forward pressure in the last of a forward stroke.

Some folks may think the draw stroke is a less-than-balanced stroke, and in those fractions of a moment when the blade is in the air, they may have a point. But think of a ladder, or a person standing with his or her legs apart and plenty of weight on each foot. It's hard to rock them. You can put a great weight on your draw stroke, and that paddle will be as steady as if it were set into concrete. During the drawing motion of the stroke, you effectively extend the width of your kayak by the distance the blade is from your hull.

Learn to Scull

Is there a way to keep the effectiveness and power of the draw stroke without that momentary pause as you lift the blade from the water? Sure. You can start sculling when you're balanced out there in the first stage of a draw stroke. The sculling draw stroke is a logical extension of the draw itself, just as the draw is an extension of the forward stroke.

Now, before we get involved in the mechanics of the sculling stroke, let's go for a car ride. I'll drive, and you play just like a kid in the passenger seat. Remember how you used to be an airplane in the car? You'd make a blade of your hand, and as long as your hand was horizontal, it would just float in the wind outside the window. If you tilted your hand up a bit, your arm would swoop up toward the sky like the wing of a plane. That's just what we're going to do, once we get back into the kayak. But first we're going to stop by the river and play with your paddle. Go ahead; step out there on the rock so you can reach to where the current is swift.

Plant your paddle firmly in the water, so that both edges are precisely aligned with the flow of the current and the water passes smoothly across the power face and the back of the blade. It would help if the paddle shaft were more or less vertical, but this is not imperative. Set your arms so that you can rotate the paddle shaft but the shaft cannot pull away from you. Now—this is the tricky spot, and if you aren't ready, you may be surprised off your rock—rotate the paddle so that the upstream blade edge turns away from you into the current. That paddle is pulling away from you! Just like your hand rising in the onrushing air past your car window. If you were holding the paddle firmly and the rock were slippery, you'd be pulled directly toward the paddle and into the water.

You've just learned all you need to know about sculling. From here on out we need only talk about refinements. What do you mean, you don't understand? Your muscles do—trust me.

Back to your kayak. Get into your cockpit and start your draw stroke. Once your paddle blade is immersed, though, I'm going to freeze the action. It's okay, I'm bracing you. Your paddle blade isn't all that smart; it acts the same whether moving water is striking its power face or the moving blade is exerting force on still water. It knows its own angle and the feel of the water deflected off the blade.

Back to real time. When you did your first draw stroke, you set your power face so that it aimed directly at your boat, at your hips. That's where we'll start now. Your lower arm is bent just a bit and is poised to put all the power into the stroke. Your upper arm is arched, and your hand is all set to be the solid fulcrum around which your paddle will twist. If you don't think

I'm watching, you might attempt to move that upper hand around so that you're gripping the paddle shaft from underneath—perhaps you think the angle you've made is uncomfortable, awkward, and certainly not very effective. This would not be a wise move. When you keep your hands in the normal paddling position, you're ready for any surprises that may be poised just out of eyesight, waiting to catch you unaware. I don't know exactly what is waiting to catch you off guard. If I did, I could warn you. But I do know that Loki (the mischief-making Norse god) or Coyote (the trickster from the desert in Native American legends) is just quivering with anticipation. One time I saw a totally distracted paddler shift his weight out of balance and at that precise minute get blindsided by a duck. He flailed about, which worked out fine because he got his arms moving just before he turned into a swimmer. You can't plan for a duck attack, but if you're alert as you paddle, you'll be better prepared to deal with one.

Rotate the paddle shaft so that the bow edge of the blade is canted out 20 or 30 degrees from the keel line of the kayak. Too small an angle and you won't get any bite on the water; too big an angle and your blade will stall instead of slice. You'll be able to feel the pressure on the power face and experiment a bit until you get the correct angle.

Now, using just the power from your lower arm, push the paddle toward the bow of your boat on a path parallel to your keel line. You may have seen all kinds of diagrams showing figure-eight patterns, lazy-S patterns, and even jagged lightning-bolt or interlocked-Z patterns. These are all right, but they each focus on the aggregate motion of your boat and paddle, and not on the way in which you do the stroke.

Move the blade from just behind your hips to just ahead of your knees—the normal 4-foot-or-so sweep of your blade. As you move the blade, you'll feel the paddle tug away from you. Don't let it go! Hold the paddle shaft (and it will not appreciate your efforts at control) so that the paddle blade stays the same distance from the keel line of your kayak throughout the entire length of the stroke. The paddle is going to climb away from its location in the water, by a few inches, but as it attempts to move away from you and is restrained from doing so, it's going to drag you along. Think of the paddle as a horse, yourself as the harness, and the kayak as the cart. The horse moves the harness, and the harness moves the cart. All together.

The scull works as a series of little motions. Somewhere around your knee, stop the blade, reverse the angle so that the stern edge of the blade is now angled out at a 20- to 30-degree angle, and bring the blade smartly and in a straight line parallel to your keel line, back to just past your hips.

You think, "Hey, this can't work. I'm starting around midships and working toward the bow, so I'm going to pull my bow around but leave the stern wallowing back there." If you were doing just one stroke, sure. But you're working first one end and then the other, and the inertia of your hull will dampen out abrupt swings. You might find that either the bow or the stern does advance faster, and that's because for one reason or another you're a bit unbalanced. If your stern is lagging, either move the paddle motion farther astern or put a little more *oomph* in the stroke toward the stern.

You'll set up the blade angle with your control hand, be that the top or bottom hand when you're moving your boat. Change the angle with the same little twist of your wrist that you used with a feathered paddle. (See, I told you all these strokes connect.)

The sculling draw is a long series of continuous motions. What you don't do is move the blade . . . stop . . . change the angle . . . stop . . . move the blade . . . stop. Instead, strive for a constant, uniform flow, without a discernible break in the motion. The first time you do this, your motion will be jerky. That's fine; you'll smooth out as you practice.

You'll find that, just as with the draw stroke, the combination of your weight on the stroke side of your kayak and the friction along the keel line will tip your stroke-side gunwale down. This means you're putting more boat in the water, and in doing so you're increasing the friction. If you ski, your feet and knees know all about sideslipping with skis flat on the snow; edge, and you'll stop. Push your stroke-side knee up against the thigh pad and deck and scoot your hip toward the paddle to keep the boat as flat as possible and to let it sideslip as easily as possible.

A draw stroke has more quick power. A scull provides constant power, plus it offers you an apparently wider base and more stability.

For the fun of it, set the blade angles backward and with each scull have the paddle push the boat. This is slow, inefficient, and could be better done with a regular scull or draw on the other side (why else does a kayak paddle have two identical ends?). But the reverse scull is a beautifully precise way of moving a boat a few inches without switching sculling sides, and it's a powerful learning tool as to how and why the stroke works. Give it a shot.

CHAPTER 10

A Bracing Experience

When you're sitting in the low cockpit of a cruising kayak, the sea is an in-your-face experience. Spray washing over the deck is very personal, waves that lift and drop you echo in the pit of your stomach, and the wind curls and eddies around your ears. Grow comfortable with it, because when you venture out on exposed waters, you will get wet and you will teeter up on edge. Unless you learn to be comfortable within the arms of the sea, you will find these experiences to be upsetting in every sense of the word.

Am I trying to scare you off the water? Nope. You're already putting together the skills to paddle happily for an afternoon's picnic or a long journey into the wilderness. Today we're going to add a couple of strokes to your paddling repertoire, for those rare occasions when you exceed the nominal boundaries of stability. You have a couple of great things going for you. First, you know your body position as you're sitting in your kayak; this lets you keep centered in a changing world. Second, you have the absolute support of that which at first would appear to be the most fluid—the water upon which you float.

Your eyebrows are kind of creeping up in disbelief. How are you going to use a fluid like water to balance yourself? Climb aboard, and let's take a look.

Our kayaks are bilaterally symmetrical. That's a fancy way of saying that the right and left halves of your boat (divided right down the keel line) are mirror images of each other.

Buoyancy, then, is the same if measured an equal distance out on each side, perpendicular to the same spot on the keel line. The net effect is that the boat is perfectly balanced at the keel line. Don't believe it? Just look at a kayak floating in the water. It doesn't sag to one side or the other.

You and I are symmetrically balanced, too. Imagine drawing a line, or better yet, a plane, vertically down through your spine and sternum; the left and right halves would weigh about the same. Keep that line centered vertically right over the keel of your kayak and you and your boat would be tranquilly in balance. If you were sitting in your cockpit and

we started measuring the combined weight of you and your boat in horizontal layers, from the bottom of the keel to the top of your head, as if you were made of cakelike layers or sedimentary bands, the center of your total weight would be somewhere around your navel.

Think of that point, that concentration of weight, as the focal point of all the forces pushing downward, or the center of gravity. There's another point that is the focus of all the forces that are supporting you and your boat. The forces that keep you afloat are concentrated in a point called the *center of buoyancy*. If you are sitting level, just like you are, it's going to be right over the keel of your kayak and pretty

Photo courtesy Ocean Kayak

Flying across the face of a wave can be an exhilarating ride, with a bit of experience and gear. There's a whole school of paddlers who take to waves just like snow skiers take to moguls, and for the same exciting rush. This paddler is leaning slightly into the wave, which gives him a more stable ride, and is reaching over the top of the wave with his paddle if he needs to high brace in the less-aerated water behind the foaming and unstable crest. He's also wearing a helmet, mandatory for playing in the surf, and a paddle leash secures his paddle to his boat. You can see his knees hooked under straps, securing him on the boat. In a conventional kayak, the paddler would brace his knees and thighs against pads mounted under the deck on each side of the front of the kayak.

close to your waterline. If you tilt your kayak to the side, part of the hull will go deeper in the water and part will lift up a bit. The part of the hull that is now deeper in the water will provide more lift or buoyancy, and the center of buoyancy is going to shift a bit over to that side. That's a good thing. It's your boat's way of increasing support when it is leaned to the side. It changes with each degree of tilt or list as different parts of your kayak hull are immersed in, or lifted from, the water.

If your kayak is absolutely level, your center of gravity, center of buoyancy, and keel line are all in a vertical line. If you shift your weight to one side, the center of gravity will thus be to one side of the center of buoyancy, and your kayak will tilt to that side. If your center of buoyancy didn't move, you'd just continue right on over. As your boat begins to tilt, however, it puts more of the widest beam into the water. This alters the center of buoyancy and moves it in the direction of the added support—and, in effect, moves the center of buoyancy back under the center of gravity.

The center of buoyancy, despite our occasional hope and wish, is not indefinitely movable. If you move your center of gravity past the furthest adjustment to the center of buoyancy, you'll capsize. That's as true for a kayak as it is for an aircraft carrier. Kayaks, however, come with a built-in device that manipulates the center of gravity—you. That's right. You can shift your weight, you can tilt your torso, and in doing so, you can preserve the balance of your boat.

To see how this works, we'll start by locking your body into a rigid whole. Now, start to topple your body to one side. All too quickly, you'll pass the point of no return where your center of gravity overturns your buoyancy and you capsize.

Now, suppose your boat is tilting to one side. Instead of keeping your body rigid and perpendicular to the keel line, twist at your hips to keep your upper body vertical. This keeps your belly button and your center of gravity balanced over your center of buoyancy, keeping you upright. What could have rocked you up on edge? Perhaps you're gliding sideways on the face or the back of a wave, and because the surface of the ocean is tilted at that point, you're also tilted. Perhaps you're thrown about in the wake of a careless powerboater. The why doesn't matter; what does matter is that you were able to twist your body to keep your weight and buoyancy in line.

The Hip Flick

Was this a fluke? Hardly. Come and sit in the placid bay and let's play a bit. With your paddle in the basic forward-stroke position, and horizontal, wiggle your boat a bit just using your hips. To do this, make your torso vertical and let your rear be the pendulum of a clock, with your hips the pivot point. If the left side of your boat is low, press down with your right cheek and at the same time, push up against the deck with your left knee. Your boat will rotate under you, from up on its beam end to a horizontal position. With any balance whatsoever, you can snap your kayak back to level with what will become an instinctive move. When talking to a bunch of experienced kayakers, just nod knowingly when they mention *hip flicks*. Those are what you've just been doing.

The hip flick works when you're just rocking back and forth in less than extreme angles, extreme being as often as not a state of mind. But what do you do when your kayak is apparently thrown up on its beam ends—way over on its edge—and you feel that you need to take more-aggressive measures?

You're going to do the same thing you did in your garden when you thought you were going to lose your balance. You're going to put your hand down for support.

Now, it's going to seem not only very strange but also downright backward to lean out over something as soft and unsupportive as water when every muscle in your body is screaming that you're falling abruptly in that same direction. The first brace you use will seem a fluke, the second a coincidence. With just a bit of practice, though, your muscles will come to rely on the brace.

If you think about it, the sweep stroke that you are already pretty good at works because the paddle blade exerts tremendous resistance on the water. You stick the paddle in the water and, with the blade as a fulcrum, scoot your kayak around it. You and I are going to take what you've already learned and twist it around with a few modifications in technique and direction, to brace a tipping kayak and rotate it back upright.

Just as with every other paddle maneuver you've learned, you have two ways to support yourself above the sea. We can use the power face of your paddle or the back face of your paddle blade. Both methods work well, depending on your position and need.

The Low Brace

We'll start with a *low brace*. Low is a simple concept. The paddle is held below, or lower than, your wrists. Start in the basic forward-stroke position and assume that you're toppling to your right. Hold your paddle so that it is at right angles to the keel line and horizontal to the water surface. Right angle? Figure that as straight out from the side of your kayak, just in front of your hip. With your control hand, rotate the paddle shaft so that the back face of the paddle blade is toward the surface of the water. Don't shift your grip, but if you have to, cock your wrists in order to bring the blade flat. Extend your right hand so that your elbow is about straight and keep your left hand more or less in front of your left hip. You do not have to rotate your body. Firmly and briskly, slap the surface of the water with the flat of your paddle. If you really smash down with a report like

We call it a low brace because the paddle shaft is lower than your wrists.

that of a terrified beaver, you've slapped a little too vigorously. If you can't hear the paddle hit the water, you've slapped too weakly.

Once the paddle blade is on the water, push down on it hard with your right hand. It takes a lot of force to push the blade down into the water, and what you'll end up doing is pushing yourself back up. You're using the palm of your hand against the top of the paddle shaft in a one-handed push-up. Since you and your kayak are one, the kayak will come with you. You're not going to be able to hang out on that blade all day. This is a momentary support, and so you'll have to help it along with a hip flick to rotate the hull back under you.

Push the back face, not the power face, down against the water to rotate yourself back upright—just like a push-up.

You just did this with your right paddle blade on the water and your right hand pushing down. It works just the same, and just as well, if you use your left paddle blade on the left side of your kayak, pushing down with your left hand.

Remember—and this is important: Your paddle blade should be horizontal—close to flat—when you put the blade on the water and your weight on the blade. If you do as I have done in the past and forget to rotate the blade from vertical to flat, the edge of your paddle will slice downward like a knife in soup, and in the blink of an eye, you'll be in the soup, too.

To be a tool in your paddling repertoire, the low brace has to be an instinctive reflex—as automatic as putting a hand out to catch yourself when you stumble. And that's all it is. A quick little whack on the water that keeps you high and dry.

The Skimming Low Brace

Hey, this is kind of fun. After a bit of practice you're getting good. You can lean your kayak way over and with a bit of a slap and a hip flick, just bring her back level as sweet as can be. You also pointed out that the low brace gave you plenty of righting momentum, but that you could only apply this power for a relatively brief time. We're going to extend that time, using the motions you've practiced so far in learning the strokes.

Start to slap the water in a low brace, but instead of whacking straight out from your hips, bring the paddle back with a little torso rotation and arm flex so that it's about 45 degrees or so from the keel line. Just like rotating to begin a reverse sweep stroke or unwinding your rotation at the end of a forward stroke—one stroke leads right into another.

Just before you bang the blade on the water (remembering to keep the back side of the paddle toward the water and the power face up), cant the front edge, the edge toward

the bow, upward about 20 or 30 degrees. This is a good starting zone, and you'll instinctively find your own best angle after attempting this stroke a few times. We played in the river with the current to see how a blade reacted to moving water, and then we translated that to the back-and-forth swoops of a scull. We'll be working with the same concept now, with a few significant variations. You can see that you're in almost the same body position as you were in a reverse sweep.

Now, whack the water! As you do so, push down on the shaft with your outboard hand (the one next to the wet blade), just as you did in the first low brace. As you do this—and it should be in a smoothly combined movement, and not first one and then the other—move your body and arms as if you were in a sweep stroke. The blade, canted up as it is, will skim across the top of the water through the arc of the sweep. Think of a racing speedboat, skimming across the top of the water. You're putting plenty of downward pressure on the shaft, for sure, but this is being countered by the climbing force you created with the canted blade and the forward motion of the blade. The upward force lasts much longer and can be more precisely controlled than the simple push of a blade straight down into the water.

There is a danger, however. What if the blade trips during the arc, and its front edge dips? Unfortunately, the blade will then dive—just like your hand did when you were flying it outside the car window. If you keep the downward angle and keep your weight on the shaft, you're going to do a face plant on Father Neptune's roof. Odds are, you'll also do a deck plant.

The skimming low brace works when you are sitting still, but the forward motion of your kayak under way dramatically increases the lift during the sweep. The skimming blade, though, creates resistance, which does two things: It turns you to the paddle side, and it slows the boat. In fact, it will slow the boat until the forward motion is not enough to support your weight. By then, you should have flicked your boat back underneath you. If not, go ahead and start a sculling brace with the back side of your blade—no one said you can't. You've already practiced a sculling draw; the sculling brace is executed with the same motion, but your hands are above the paddle shaft and you apply power to the back face of your paddle blade. How much forward speed do you need, and how much sweeping motion from your paddle? It's a balancing act. With a lot of forward speed, you don't need to sweep at all. With no forward speed, you need a powerful sweep. Balance out the two, judging how much lift and stability you need in your particular situation.

The skimming low brace is a super tool for moving your kayak around. Want to take a look? Let's head on down the bay, just a few hundred meters in order to pick up speed, and we'll curve around behind that little skerry. As you and I approach the rock knob with its somewhat disgruntled-looking great blue heron staring at us, you notice that I let my paddle trail back into a stern rudder. You do the same, but you wonder why I've left the turn so late. It looks as if we're going to turn in an arc far beyond the skerry, and instead of catching the eddy made by the ebbing tide, we're going to have to paddle back against the tidal current. As you watch, I rotate the top of my ruddering blade out away from the boat, increasing the angle of the turn, and then, to your surprise, actually shift my weight out onto the paddle shaft. What I've done is to combine the stern rudder with a sweeping low brace, and in doing so, put enough of my weight on the shaft to really crank my kayak around. As I sit, bobbing, in the eddy behind the skerry, you duplicate each movement and glide in beside me. We didn't practice anything new. We did, however, link together the strokes we've been practicing, and in doing so we've demonstrated the skimming low brace.

The skimming low brace is good for more than turning, valuable as that skill becomes. If you find yourself swooping down the face of a wave (at this part of your paddling career, let's hope it's a small one) and you have little faith in your ability to twitch your balance (hey, on your first ride your bottom is going to be clenching the kayak seat with muscles you'd forgotten you had), just reach over the top of the wave and rest your weight on your skimming blade, sliding just a tad behind the top of the wave. You might be sliding sideways, but your paddle will keep you upright as you slip along.

The low brace, especially when linked to the sweeping motion that sends your blade skimming over the water, is your bomb shelter. When in doubt, even experts fall back to the reliable, incredibly stable, and remarkably easy-to-do low brace. Learn it, and learn to love it.

The low brace works best when applied in the arc from your hips (perpendicular to the keel line at the cockpit) aft. It's difficult to apply the needed downward push when the blade is in front of the cockpit. This isn't so bad, once you realize that the low brace is done with the back face of your paddle. Remember, you have a whole other face, which is prime for the bracing you want to do ahead of yourself.

The High Brace

There are no all-purpose, one-stroke-for-everything techniques in a kayak. The low brace is a great stabilizing tool; the skimming low brace is super for stabilizing yourself and for turning. We're going to find situations where the strengths of the low brace don't match up with the challenges.

That's why there are two faces to your paddle blade, and a blade at each end of the paddle shaft. When one approach isn't as effective as you'd like, you almost always have another.

You don't have to always push on your paddle shaft. Pulling can work just as well, and

Your paddle shaft is higher than your wrists and—you're right—it's a high brace.

in some cases, even better. When you want to stabilize your kayak by pulling against the power face of your paddle blade, you'll use one of the most misnamed and often mistakenly executed strokes in kayaking. The latter is unfortunate, because the high brace—that's what we call it—is also one of the most useful tools you'll learn.

A high brace is high neither because it is favored by high society nor because its

With a high brace you insert your blade in the water and pull yourself up. If a low brace is a push-up, then the high brace is a pull-up. If you're crossing from one current to another across an eddy line, you can reach forward with a high brace into the new current and both stabilize yourself and turn into the new flow.

practitioners belong to a high church. It isn't even high up in the air. It's called that because the paddle shaft is higher than, or above, your wrists. A properly performed high brace is actually as low to the kayak as possible; in fact, for health and safety's sake, never lift the paddle shaft so high that you can't see over it.

There's a popular perception of a kayaker with arms extended far over his head, just planting his paddle into an incredible brace as his boat smashes through a wall of foam. But what this picture doesn't show is the fierce strain rippling through that kayaker's shoulders, which, with luck, won't result in the ripping sound of a shoulder dislocation.

With the low brace, you applied power by pushing down on the shaft and building resistance with the back side of the blade. With the high brace, you apply power by pulling down on the paddle shaft and building resistance with the power face of the blade.

Don't move your hands from their normal paddling position. You'll set the angle of the blade used in the stroke by rotating your control-hand wrist and, if needed, cocking up your forearm. You'll be tempted to cheat and shift your hand, but if you try it a few times, you'll find that the upper-hand position becomes viable. Not strong, and I don't think comfortable, but as long as you keep your upper hand close to your body, it will be sufficient.

Remember, the high brace works best in that broad arc from ahead of, to perpendicular to, your hips. Once your boat moves your hips ahead of the blade, the potential power and stability erode rapidly. I know what you're smiling about. That low brace you've been working on works best from straight out to the side of your kayak and back toward the stern.

Let's set up an example: You're paddling ahead, and you stumble off balance—the reason why doesn't really matter. Reach out with the paddle on the side toward which you think you're toppling and whack the water hard with the power face of your blade. With a "normal" paddle of around 220 or 230 centimeters and an "average" kayak beam of 24 inches, you're going to reach out around 30 to 42 inches. You're not aiming at a precise target—you want to reach out as far as is comfortable to give you the best leverage. You should make a good bang with it, much like a beaver passing the word. If you forget to rotate your paddle and slam it into the water edge first . . . well, experience in this case is a very wet teacher. Your bracing-side arm is extended almost straight, and your upper hand is tucked in fairly close to your shoulder. Go ahead and do a one-handed pull-up with your bracing hand while your upper hand is locked into a fulcrum around which the paddle rotates. Don't punch out or up with your upper hand, despite an almost-instinctive inclination to do so. You need the strength of that locked-in hand with its contracted biceps.

Go ahead and try it. You discover that the first few inches, perhaps as much as a foot or so, of paddle-blade travel from the surface down into the water give you the most righting motion. You can hang off the shaft and really twitch your boat back underneath you. As the blade goes deeper, you'll pull your boat toward the paddle shaft, but it will be more difficult to rotate your boat under the shaft. By the time you pull your boat right to the blade, you can either rotate the blade and convert your motion into a forward stroke, or you can retract the paddle by pulling the blade aft—edge first—until it rotates up and out of the water.

Photo courtesy Ocean Kayak

This guy is poised and ready! He's set to go into a high brace on either side, or he can jam a blade in the water for a powerful forward stroke. If he rolls his wrists he's primed for a low brace or a back stroke. And he's probably smiling, too.

Right again! The high brace is a kissing cousin to the draw stroke you already know. When you did a draw stroke, you concentrated on pulling your kayak sideways to the paddle blade. With the high brace, you concentrate on rotating your kayak back under you, combining the dynamic support of the blade pushing down into the water with a bit of a hip flick—that same hip flick you practiced just a bit ago.

This stroke works just as well off the right side as off the left side of your kayak. Some people fall into the evil habit of only practicing this stroke on one side. As a result they have a bombproof monster high brace on one side, but if they're bounced on the other . . . well, call it a learning experience.

Just about everyone I know (me, too) falls into the trap of practicing or relying upon those things we do well. Are you really good at bracing on the right side? Then, to become really comfortable paddling in the wilderness, put more time in practicing on the left. Your weight—yours, and your kayak's—is bilaterally symmetrical, as is your boat and your body. To fill out the picture, your skills should be the same as a kayak's.

A few pages back you were sliding down the face of a wave; you calmly reached over the top of it and planted your low brace on the back side of the wave. That works quite nicely . . . up to the point when you can no longer reach over the wave. You could just close your eyes and toss your paddle away—a technique I've attempted on more than one river. While your kayak has the inherent stability to ride through some pretty amazing water, however, I wouldn't suggest this abject surrender to natural forces. If you can't push, then pull. Bend both your elbows until your paddle shaft is about shoulder height and then firmly stick your blade into the face of the wave next to your shoulder. You want to reach into the upper portions of the wave in order for this to work, but you can find quite a bit of support by attempting a chin-up off this shaft. Your kayak will be moving faster than the motion of the energy coil inside the wave, and you're balancing on a dynamic high brace.

A high brace doesn't have to be a static stroke, however. Remember how you sculled, or swished, your paddle blade at an angle through the water, to move your kayak sideways? That sculling draw stroke translates perfectly into a sculling high brace. You already nailed the basics. Begin with a forward stroke mixed with just a bit of a sweep stroke on the side to which you feel unbalanced. You won't be as fully extended as you were with a sweep stroke, but the blade will arc out in a curve rather than paralleling the straight line of your kayak's keel.

Instead of keeping the paddle blade vertical in the water, angle the top edge of the blade back toward your stern. As you pull on this angled blade, two things happen: You pull your kayak forward, and as you apply pressure to the angled blade, the paddle attempts to lift out of the water. Don't let the blade rise. Instead, use the upward force as a bar you can hold on to and stabilize your kayak. The effective end of this stroke will be at your hip, or just behind it, and well off the side. There is no need to get involved in a long discussion of how much angle to dial into the stroke, or even at what point and speed the lift from the angled blade becomes effective. Practice the stroke a few times in placid water and change the blade angle with each stroke. You'll learn more in a few minutes than we could discuss during a long day on the water.

The Sculling High Brace

Super job on that last high brace. You nailed it. But I saw a bit of panic there in your eyes, just for a moment, when you feared you'd need a longer period of support than what was offered in a high brace. No need to worry; you can scoot your boat directly sideways. You already know how to do it! You learned how when you combined a draw stroke with a sculling motion. All we have to do now is change the angle, so that you're pulling down on the paddle shaft rather than using the paddle shaft to pull your kayak toward the paddle.

Sit square in your kayak, with your back erect. Bring your paddle up to a line just below your shoulders, horizontally, with the midpoint of the paddle right at your PFD's zipper. Extend your hand on the bracing side so that your elbow is about straight and your hand is underneath the paddle shaft. Your paddle should be about perpendicular to your kayak's keel line. Think of holding the paddle shaft as if you were going to do a chin-up. Your upper hand should be in front of your shoulder, and the zipper of your PFD should line up with the bow of your kayak. In other words, don't rotate your torso. Thump the water with your paddle blade, power face toward the water.

If you were starting a normal high brace, you'd pull down on the shaft and let the paddle blade sink into the water. But you need more support. Cant the front edge of your blade up, and sweep the blade forward. Once the blade is up around your knees, reverse the angle so that the stern edge is canted up and then sweep the blade aft. The stroke ends at, or just a bit behind, your hip. Switch the angle with your control hand, but don't shift your basic paddling grip. You want to rotate the *lower* edge of the paddle blade forward until

it's a bit above horizontal. Push the blade forward so that it again wants to climb up out of the water. The motion should be smooth and continuous—no starting and stopping. You create a righting effort by pulling down on the shaft with your brace-side hand (the other hand at your shoulder is a fulcrum). At the same time, you keep the blade at the surface with its angle and the back-and-forth sweeping motion. If you're just rocked over a little, you'll use long, back-and-forth sweeps. If you're well over on your beam ends, your strokes will be shorter and faster.

How long can you keep this up? That depends on your attention span and your physical condition. If you're up to it, you can let your boat rock over until you're almost kissing the water and just hold your boat there all day.

The skimming low brace is a rock-solid brace, and one you need, but it works well only when your kayak is close to horizontal. When the world really starts turning sideways and the angle of lean gets scary, scull out of a high brace. You might be battered by a wind, tossed about by waves, or even washing-machined in the wake of a hot-rodding powerboater—it makes no difference. When you're on your beam ends and nothing else will help, you can scull your way out of trouble.

And if you never need this support? You'll still be a way better paddler, because you'll be confident and relaxed in a wider variety of paddling environments.

CHAPTER 11

Linking Strokes: Making Your Paddle Work for You

Okay, I understand that you're a little frustrated. Everyone (me, too) says that you should link all your paddle strokes into a smooth, fluid flow. And everyone (me, too) seems to offer up little packages that each contain a separate paddle stroke. So how's a new paddler supposed to learn how to turn all these separate and distinct strokes into some sort of seamless flow?

Let's solve this on the water right now. See that mooring buoy over there, the white one with a blue stripe around it? That's where we'll start.

Stop so that the buoy is straight out from your side, about two boat lengths away. That's between 30 and 40 feet. Lift your skeg or rudder from the water. Paddle in a circle around the buoy, keeping the same distance from it. You'll have to shift your weight to lean your kayak, and you'll have to apply more force on one side of your paddle stroke than the other.

You might even have to use a little stern rudder to keep your bow swinging in a smooth arc.

You already know how to do this. Now you have to put the lean and the strokes into one package.

The first time I tried this I spoke in ungentlemanly terms. And splashed. A lot. It's far easier to describe than it is to do.

I don't know that I'd call the first path you followed a circle, but you did get the whole way around. I told you it was harder than it looked, and your laugh just before you started said you didn't believe me.

We'll raise the ante. A few minutes from now we're going to paddle an English gate, which is an exercise in concentration. And fun. But we can use the same gadget and course that we'll use in the English gate for the next step. Two-gallon plastic bleach bottles are moored about 4 feet apart. Your job will be to paddle a

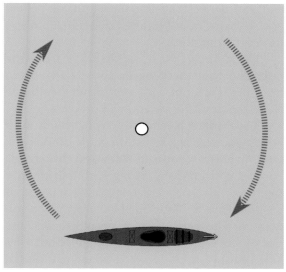

Paddling a precise and smooth circle is challenging. It's great practice for learning to carve turns.

figure-eight course, with the crossover in the middle of the eight right between the jugs. The first time around, do it at any speed you want.

The second time and the third, try to pick up a little speed. As you grow more comfortable, see how close you can stay to the jug buoys as you swirl around.

When you start to get cocky, we'll reverse it. No, you shouldn't turn around and paddle forward the other way around the buoys; go backward around them.

Despite what you're thinking this very minute, our exercise is not a lesson in humility. You are learning how your kayak feels while it is turning, and how to help it turn where and how sharply you want. You can use it to hone your skills, to warm up your muscles before a day on the water, and, if you have the urge to show off a bit . . . well, you earned it.

See that floating dock up the inlet? I'll follow you over to it. Get up to a comfortable cruising speed and head just off to one side of the dock. When you think the time is right, I want you to make a sharp turn and glide up alongside the front of the dock, close enough to catch hold. The first time I tried this I was

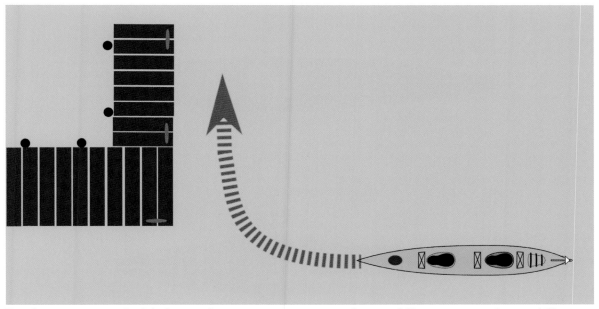

Turning to stop at a dock helps you learn to gauge your speed, your ability to turn, and your ability to stop at a precise spot.

the perfect distance away from the dock, but I had enough speed so I coasted right on by. On my second attempt I stopped gracefully immediately in front of the middle of that darned dock. If I hadn't been 5 feet away from it, it would have been perfect.

We're using the dock because it has plenty of water under it, there are no sharp underwater objects poised to grab you, and we're not faced with sneaky currents. In the real world it could be a dock, another boat, a rock, even a big log—simply the place you want to stop. Airplane pilots practice touch-and-go landings for the same reason. Why don't you try a few?

You're really getting the hang of it. So let's add a high-value twist. This time, do on purpose what I did by accident: Come parallel to the front face of the dock and stop right in the middle of the dock, but 5 or 6 feet away from it. You know how to do a draw stroke

and you understand the sculling draw. When you're ready, move yourself sideways until you can reach the dock.

Good show! Now paddle away from the dock and come back, again, about 6 feet or so from the dock, but with your other side parallel to the dock. Draw yourself on over.

You had to paddle in a straight line, turn where you wanted, adjust the angle of the turn, stop, and draw yourself sideways. Best of all, you did it seamlessly, linking each motion into the next.

I do have a minor quibble, and it's one you noticed. The bow of your kayak reached the dock before the stern. You're right about why. You reached a bit forward when you placed your paddle blade in the water for the draw stroke, and you pulled yourself at a bit of an angle. Move out from the dock and bring yourself back so that your bow points at the dock face and you are straight out from the dock,

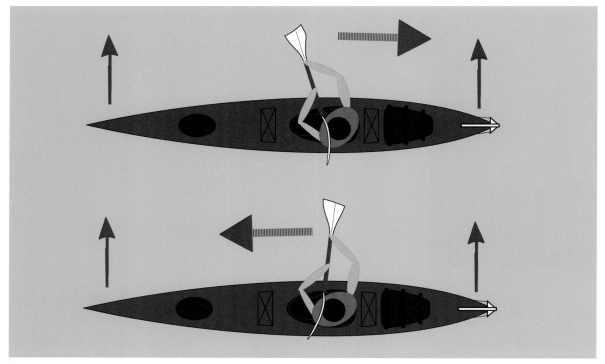

Practice moving your kayak sideways, using draw strokes and sculling draws.

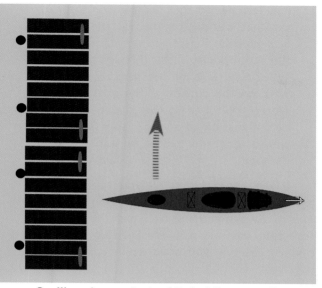

Sculling along a dock while holding your distance off the dock requires concentration and precise strokes.

with around 3 feet of water between your bow and the dock.

Use your draw stroke to pull yourself sideways down the entire face of the dock while keeping your bow that same 3 feet away. Within a few minutes you'll be able to keep your kayak moving directly sideways while holding the same distance from the dock.

Do you think you have it down pat? Let's both draw ourselves along the dock, the same path we've been doing, but this time with the stern pointed at the dock.

You're catching the feeling of where you are in the water. You're also becoming more sensitive, because of the sideways motion, as to your balance (it wiggles), and how flat or level you're keeping your kayak. If you let the leading side of your kayak dip and dig deeper in the water, it becomes harder to paddle and noticeably less stable.

We're both getting a bit tired, so let's break for lunch and then we'll play with the English gate.

Most of the times we've been out on the water we've been one person to a kayak. K for Kayak, 1 for the number of people, and that is abbreviated as a K1; with two paddlers, it's a K2. The vast majority of touring kayaks are K1 or K2 boats. Some specialized kayaks, such as Olympic-style flatwater race boats, might have four paddlers.

If you're going to paddle with a two-person boat, take some time and run through these same exercises. You need the same skill sets for either.

Playing in an English Gate

To really put all your skills together, and for a fun afternoon in a quiet bay with some friends, zip through an English gate. I learned it from our whitewater cousins, and it doubles as a training tool and a low-tech and way-fun competition as you race yourself against a clock. Slalom drivers use English gates as a way of honing their turning and balance skills, and the gates work just as well for quiet-water paddlers.

The gate is simplicity itself. All you need is two marks and a little water. Slalom drivers use poles suspended from an overhead line. If you don't have anything to dangle a pole from, consider a pair of bleach jugs anchored about 4 feet apart. If you're in the mood for craftsmanship, start with a 4-foot length of plastic pipe for your pole. Tie a 3-foot line from one end of the pole to the handle of a bleach jug. Tie another 3-foot line from the other end of the pipe to a second jug. Fill two more jugs with gravel. Tie a line equal to the depth of the water less 2 feet from one end of the pipe to one gravel-filled jug and a similar line from the other end of the pipe to the other jug. Drop one anchor jug, and then paddle out a bit and drop the other. The jugs will stay in line and 4 feet apart, despite your wake. The plastic pipe should—if you measured correctly—be a couple of feet underwater and out of your way.

How do you use your gate? Here are a few routines that will hone your paddling (and because of the sharp turns and changes in directions, your bracing) skills.

1. The simplest path I know starts with you on one side of the gate. Paddle through the gate, make a left turn and return through the gate, and then make a right turn and pass through the gate again.

2. The second exercise starts with you just outside the gate with your stern toward the gate. Back past the gate without passing through it. Scull sideways until you are lined up with the gate. Paddle forward through the gate. Once through the gate, back down past the gate on the opposite side from your initial course and do not go through the gate. Once past the gate, scull sideways until you are again lined up with the gate and paddle through the gate opening.

3. A third exercise starts with you just outside the opening of the gate and with your stern toward the gate. Back past the gate but don't pass through it. Continue backward and make a left turn, which sets you in position to back through the gate. Make another left turn and back through the gate.

4. The fourth exercise starts with your bow pointed toward the opening of the gate.

Paddle forward past the gate on the outside, without passing through the opening. Scull sideways until you are lined up with the gate opening. Back through the opening. Once clear of the gate, paddle forward on the outside of the gate until you are completely past the gate. Stop. With a combination of sweeps, spin your boat end-for-end and paddle forward through the gate.

If you can Eskimo-roll your boat, that's great. Find a convenient point—say in the third exercise, when you first back past the gate and scull sideways until you are lined up with the opening. Before you start sculling, roll your boat.

If you are not ready for an Eskimo roll, try the reentry as a team event. Dump your boat, and then do an assisted reentry/rescue. Getting back in your kayak from the water can be hard work, and this gives you a controlled and safe environment in which to practice.

Paddle through each of the exercises a few times, looking for preciseness rather than speed. You want to be smooth, and you want to put your boat exactly where it should be each time. Once you have each and every exercise in your mind, combine them into one smooth whole. Speed and dexterity will come with practice, and as you practice, your muscles will learn the proper linking of each maneuver.

CHAPTER 12

Keeping It Straight

The first kayak you paddled with me had a rudder hanging off the stern. Within minutes of first snugging down into your cockpit, you discovered that with a quick push of a rudder pedal you could turn your kayak. With alternating pushes on each rudder pedal you managed to correct imperfections in your paddle strokes to keep your kayak moving in a relatively straight line.

That's why we swapped your kayak that afternoon for one without a rudder, or its close cousin, the skeg.

What you did that morning was to paddle into one of the longest ongoing and unresolved arguments in paddle sports. One side says that a kayak should be designed so that it slips smoothly, gracefully, and in a straight line through the water without need of a conglomeration of levers and fins dragging off the stern. Paddlers should learn to control the direction of their boat with the precision and elegance of their paddle strokes. The other camp maintains that changing conditions demand flexibility of the total hull form, and that rudders and skegs are significant control and safety factors that are vital to the sport.

Before you take sides—or maybe it's just me who leaps to conclusions—you should realize that both sides are absolutely right, and both sides are using deceptively similar words to discuss really different concepts.

Rudders and their close cousins, skegs, aren't hanging off the stern of your kayak to help you turn. Quite the opposite. They're

The rudder on this kayak is retracted up and out of the water. Considering the way its load is positioned and the way the wind and waves are at this time, it is balanced, which is a more detailed way of saying it will glide in a straight line.

back there to help you go straight. Either one is simply a fin. The rudder is hinged so that it can turn from side to side. The skeg is held in a rigid frame so that it cannot turn from side to side but holds perfectly parallel to your keel line. Almost all skegs can be adjusted by how much of the blade is inserted into the water.

Let's get basic. Wind blowing on the side of your kayak tries to push your boat downwind. The underwater shape of your kayak attempts to keep your kayak from being pushed sideways. What happens if you have a high bow and a low stern, while the underwater shape is the same from end to end? With more surface to

grab, the wind will shove the bow with more power and the boat will turn downwind. If you have a lot of gear (and a big paddler) sticking up near the stern, the back end of the kayak may be forced downwind more quickly than the bow, and the kayak will turn into the wind. The paddler may have loaded all of the heavy gear into the bow, and the lighter stern will be pushed downwind. If all the heavy gear is in the stern . . . well, you see that there are a host of variables. The wind may not be blowing straight against the side of your kayak, but might be coming from an angle. Wind creates waves which slap against the hull of your kayak and attempt to batter it off course. Any of these may be so minor as to be almost unnoticeable, or might be so strong that only a determined action can counteract them.

Why, you ask, can't the kayak builder just build a boat that will go straight? The simple answer is that they do. That is, they can and do design kayaks that will glide effortlessly straight under one particular set of wind and water conditions. They design kayaks equally well that will hold a course over a broader range of conditions, but with a little trade-off between conditions, handling, and performance. Equally important, they design kayaks that will turn upon demand.

The rudder or the skeg improve the sea-keeping characteristics when you paddle outside the optimum conditions for the boat's design. That's a good thing.

What can we do?

If a breeze is pushing your bow off course, you might just paddle a little harder with your downwind blade. You could paddle harder on one side than the other, you could take two strokes on one side for each one on the other, or you could start throwing in a few sweep

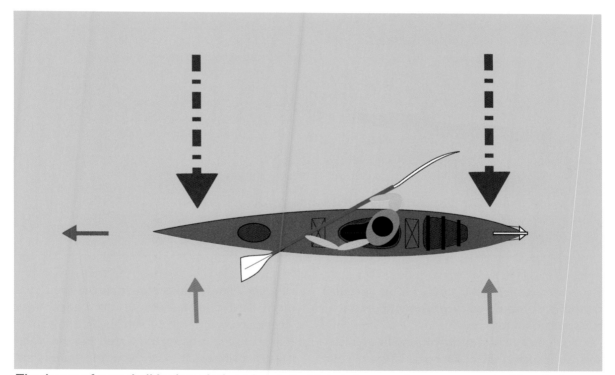

The dream of every builder is to design a kayak that is in balance under every conceivable set of circumstances—another way of saying a kayak that will hold a straight course, neither turning into or away from the wind, no matter what the direction or force of the wind. Lateral resistance as shown by the green arrows—not wanting to skid sideways—would be the same at the bow as at the stern. Sorry, folks, it ain't happened yet, and it probably won't happen. At some point the stern of your kayak will be forced downwind more rapidly than the bow, and you'll think your kayak is turning into the wind. In boat talk, that's weather helm, because you're turning toward the weather (the wind). As conditions change, your bow will slip sideways faster than the stern, and you'll think your kayak is turning downwind. That's because you're turning to the lee, or downwind, side of your kayak.

The Way You Pack Affects Your Steering

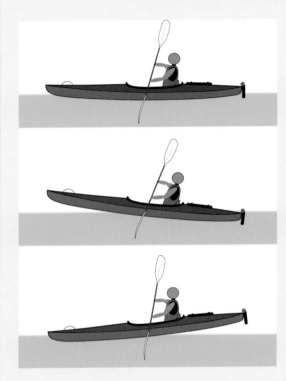

The top kayak has its load balanced equally so that the boat sits flat on the water. A wind directly from the side would most likely just blow the kayak sideways, with the bow not swinging into or away from the wind.

The middle kayak had all the heavy gear jammed into the stern, forcing the back end deep into the water and leaving the bow up in the air. A wind from the side would have a heck of a time blowing the stern sideways. However, there would be no resistance whatsoever up on the bow, and the wind could easily force the bow quickly downwind.

The bottom kayak is carrying all its weight way up in the bow, which has forced the bow deep in the water and left the stern high in the air. Wind could have little sideways effect on the bow, but could just whip the stern around. A heavily laden bow often makes a kayak more difficult to paddle in a straight line, no matter what the wind.

The wind doesn't have to come directly from the side of your kayak to affect its ability to glide in a straight line. While the net effect might be more pronounced when the wind is at certain angles, it can and will affect your kayak coming from any direction.

strokes to correct your course. This irregular rhythm will make you weary in a short time, but you can do it.

You could lean your kayak, and let the lean and the change in the underwater shape of your kayak counteract the wind. Again, that works.

One of the easiest solutions is to just turn your rudder a slight bit, just enough to counteract the wind. On the negative side, keeping your rudder at a slight angle *does* increase drag, which means you'll have to put in a little more paddling effort. However, a big percentage of K1s—single-paddler kayaks—don't have

rudders. Many paddlers feel that the additional mechanical complexities of the rudder—its "hinge" connecting it to the kayak, the cables that change its angle in the water, and the lifting lines that remove it from the water—are more bother than benefit (not to mention an additional cost). They prefer paddling technique over technology. Paddlers that prefer rudders do so with all the passion and good arguments of those who don't. It really boils down to what you like.

This doesn't hold true for the touring doubles, the K2s. For two-paddler kayaks,

A short-term solution to curb a kayak's inclination to wander off the straight and narrow is to slightly lean the kayak. You do it the same way as in initiating a turn, with a little hip rotation and knee pressure. If you lower the right side of your kayak you'll turn to the left, and vice versa. You want to do this subtly, so that the turn you've initiated is balanced exactly with the opposing turning force of the wind. If you were out in really crappy slop, I'd be more concerned about balancing the kayak than tilting it.

with their larger size, greater windage, and the challenges of balancing paddler sizes and gear stowage, rudders are a definite plus.

A skeg is a far simpler gadget. It is a blade or fin in a rigid frame that can be inserted in whole, or in part, into the water. You are sitting in your kayak with the breeze blowing directly against your side. With the way your kayak is loaded today, the breeze is pushing your stern downwind just a bit faster than your bow. From your perspective in the cockpit your kayak is "weathercocking," or turning bow first into the wind like a weather vane or weather cock.

What can you do? Right! You remembered lateral resistance, and you increased the lateral resistance at the stern of your kayak by

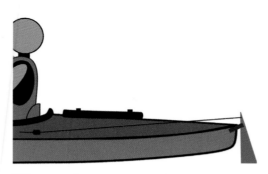

When you immerse your skeg completely in the water, you increase the lateral resistance at the stern and curb your kayak's inclination to weathercock, or turn its bow into the wind.

lowering your skeg into the water. Now the wind can't push your stern around.

What if, after lowering the skeg, it appears that the breeze is now skewing your course too much by pushing your bow downwind? Right again! Just lift the skeg a bit out of the water. Not the whole way, just a bit. You are adjusting the lateral resistance and in doing so are looking for a neutral balance. Think of it as adding or removing small amounts of weight to one end of a teeter-totter so that it will balance level.

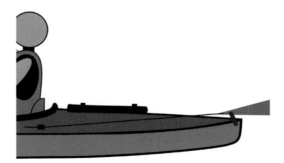

If you are fighting a lot of lee helm and your skeg is completely in the water, the tendency of your kayak is to point its bow downwind. Retract your skeg and you'll lose much if not all of the lee helm. You control the depth of the skeg by a cord from the top of the skeg to a cleat by your cockpit. You can fuss and tweak just how much of the skeg is in the water—it's not an all-or-nothing affair—until you balance your kayak.

A cautionary note: See the rudder retracted out of the water and onto the rear deck of this kayak. The stern of the kayak is in the water. When coming into land, remember to retract your rudder or skeg into the air or onto your rear deck. The noise of that fin banging and bending on the rocks is annoying.

Trimming Your Course with a Rudder

The most common way to adjust the angle of a rudder is by pressing on foot controls, which are in turn connected to the rudder by cables. Push ahead with your left foot, and the blade of the rudder is pulled to the left side of your boat. This makes your boat arc to the left. If you looked at the boat from overhead, you'd see that the angle of the rudder actually pushes the stern of your boat to the right, and that your boat pivots at a point somewhere around the cockpit. Just like on a teeter-totter, when one end goes one way, the other goes in the opposite direction; that's why the bow swings to the left.

Foot pedals, though, are not the only control mechanism. An alternative system, which works quite well for paddlers with limited leg mobility, controls the rudder angle with a line that is snugged through a jam cleat. When the control line is totally slack, elastics pull the rudder over to one side. A little tension on the control line brings the rudder to a neutral (amidships) position, allowing the kayak to glide in a straight line. More tension on the line will bring the rudder to the other side, again turning the kayak.

Trimming Your Course with a Skeg

Most skegs will have a single line that is attached to the top of the skeg and which leads forward to a cleat just behind and to the side of your cockpit. Pull the line, and the skeg rotates out of the water. Relax the line, and the skeg plunges deeper. The cleat holds the line and the skeg at the angle you choose.

Most kayaks with rudders have a similar line that either completely lifts the rudder from the water or completely immerses it; it's an all-or-none adjustment. Rudders are designed to work in the fully immersed position.

I've been talking about wind as the principal reason for these controls, because wind is the principal variable in the cruising kayak environment. But lots of other factors can come into play. If you're tired, if your boat is unevenly loaded, if you're towing another boat and the effort swings you about—use your rudder or your skeg as a tool to keep you on the straight and narrow.

For that matter, don't be afraid to use your rudder or skeg when maneuvering is tight and you feel the need.

Rudders and skegs cannot be the only answer; you also have to learn the strokes and how to balance in order to keep your boat on a straight line. Any mechanical device will fail, and the unfortunate rule of the world is that it will fail at the most inconvenient moment. Sand or grit will jam a blade, corrosion will eat away at a connector, and elastics will lose their snap. If you can paddle well without these aids, you'll be a better paddler, able to venture forth safely and with confidence.

CHAPTER 13

Wearing Your Kayak

You have a case of the bleak miseries. "This kayak," you say, "just barely moves no matter how hard I paddle. It won't turn when I want it to, and it swerves all over the place when I want to go straight. And my back hurts. Even my feet go to sleep!"

"Come on down to the beach," I offer, "and we'll make it right."

Heck, you have a good kayak, and a better-than-average paddle. Your PFD fits. And the sun is shining. So what's the problem?

Kayaks don't come out of the mold in a one-size-fits-all configuration. You have a whole passel of adjustments at your fingertips, and with a little tweaking you'll be delighted at just how efficient and responsive your kayak becomes. Adjustments? In order for you to paddle efficiently and with pleasure, your boat has to fit snugly and give you support at your feet, knees, hips, rear, and back.

You didn't complain about a tired and tender rump, twinges on the insides and backs of your knees, a stiff neck, and sore shoulders. I guess that either you didn't want to sound all whiney, or you needed to spend a few more minutes in the kayak. It doesn't have to be like that. Let's see what we can do to get you a good fit.

Let's turn the clock back before we start, if you don't mind. It's possible to find a kayak that's completely unsuitable for you and your paddling dreams. Some boats are designed for relatively small people, others for bigger people. If you weigh 325 pounds and have size 14 feet, you're not going to be comfortable in an extremely low-decked, low-volume kayak. Likewise, if you're over 7 feet tall, you probably won't be happy (nor can you cram into) an extremely short boat. If you're tiny you'll find a very high-volume kayak with a cavernous

Igor Shootov; licensed by Shutterstock.com

interior and cockpit so deep that your armpits will rest on the coaming uncomfortable. I'm belaboring the obvious, of course, but it's often the obvious that we don't see.

On the plus side, I know that you've found a middle-of-the-road touring kayak from a darned good builder. We don't have to confront an inappropriate kayak—just one that's not ready for you.

Get back into your PFD, grab your paddle, and scramble back into your kayak here on the beach. Sit in your boat, with your rump fully on the seat (most seats are form-fitting, so you're really *in* them) and your back up against the back-band of the seat. Adjust your back support so that you're sitting comfortably erect. As your mother used to say, don't slouch. To use your total body to paddle, you're going to have to sit up.

Are the balls of your feet pressing lightly against your foot pegs? What do I mean by *foot pegs*? The places you rest your feet. If you could see up and under your foredeck while you're sitting there, you'd see two long metal tracks fastened to the outer walls of your kayak. Each has a cushioned wedge that can be moved fore and aft, along the track. Some will have a spring-mounted peg in the wedge, with the peg locking into one of a series of holes in the track. The wedges on yours have the same row of little holes, with a bolt and wing nut locking them into place. There are probably a dozen other adjustable locking mechanisms, including ones that can be slid back and forth while you are sitting in your kayak. These footrests should be adjusted so that your feet are on the rests, your knees are on the underside of your deck (usually, like yours, against pads), and your back is resting against the back support.

Some kayaks are equipped with rudders, and you rest your feet on the control pedals. You can adjust the pedals fore and aft, sometimes as a single unit and sometimes as two separate units. Most likely you'll have to adjust the cables from the rudder pedals to the rudder at the same time. That's no big deal.

You have the balls of your feet on the pegs, your heels are angled in toward each other, and your feet are at a right angle to your lower legs—all is right with the world except that your heels aren't resting on anything. Your feet are just dangling off the pegs. Take a couple of squares of closed-cell foam and tape them to the deck where your heels should rest. (We haven't opened the glue can yet—and don't. Use some of that duct tape and tack the foam into position.) A couple of thin pieces may

be easier to place than one thicker pad, but that's going to depend on what size of foam you acquired. My feet are long enough to reach the pegs when my heels are on the hull, and I think that a square of foam feels better than the fiberglass of my boat.

You might find a kayak with fixed or non-adjustable footrests. One design might have your feet resting against a bulkhead, another might have solid wedges glued or 'glassed to the inside of the kayak's hill, and a third could be a tube placed transversely across your kayak and held in place with a series of notches or holes in supporting structures, glued or 'glassed to the inside of the hull. The first two are not nonadjustable; it's just that making adjustments is a pain. You will have to figure out how much padding you think you'll need on the solid wedges or against the bulkhead. (I did this way back in the past and am not interested in doing it again.) Then you'll have to crawl up under the foredeck and tape the padding in place. Crawl out and clamber back into the cockpit, right side up, to see how close you were; you'll probably have to go through the whole thing several more times as you fine-tune the thickness of the padding. When all is perfect, remove the tape and glue the padding to the footrest.

If I had a tube-type footrest, rare as they are, I'd take it out and throw it away. I'd buy a set of adjustable foot pegs and mount them. That's easy. I imagine sticking my foot under the tube and wedging it in place, which would not be a good (or a safe) thing to do.

Are your legs the same length? If not (and it's not all that uncommon), adjust each side to a comfortable length. Nowhere does it say these must be the same.

Most cruising kayaks, but certainly not all, have a seat dangling from the coaming, and most of these seats are form-fitting. In other words, if you sit on the seat, you'll slide into the right spot. Your behind will give you comfort clues

Think of your kayak as a superb shoe: It supports and protects you, and when it fits properly, you barely notice that you're wearing it.

on that. What if your back support doesn't support your back when you're sitting there?

Look at the back part of your kayak seat and at the back-band that comfortably supports your back as well as providing a strong surface upon which you can brace yourself. On your kayak, and this is pretty common, you have a wide piece of padded and molded plastic held in place by a pair of straps. You might have a buckle or a jam cleat adjusting the length of these straps, which allows you to move the back support forward or backward. Some kayaks will have a molded back support hinged at the bottom edge, with a single strap adjusting the fore-and-aft motion, and thus, the angle of the back

You seem to think this a bit fussy, sitting so erect. If you are not sitting up, the only power you have to paddle comes from your arms, and arm muscles just aren't that strong. You need the big muscles of your torso to move your kayak. If you slouch, sure as shooting you'll quickly have sore arms as your muscles tire, and you'll probably compensate by gripping your paddle more tightly. Squeezing on the paddle means sore wrists, and sometimes

a tight neck, and a tight neck usually converts into a headache. Also, if you're slouched down, you aren't supporting your back, and you'll soon feel this in a tender band across your lumbar region, from hip to hip.

Slumped posture affects your steering. As you already learned, you turn your kayak just by leaning it to one side or the other while moving forward. You lean by pressing down with one cheek while raising the other knee up against the inside of your deck. If you're slumping, that's biomechanically challenging.

If you're scrunched down low in your seat, your paddle will be lower to your deck. That results in a forward paddle stroke more in the shape of a C. The first part of the stroke forces your bow to the side, the middle part gives you some forward motion, and the back part of the stroke pulls your stern to the side. The result after a few strokes is a zigzag course. You're wasting a lot of energy continually forcing your kayak to turn, and you're limiting the amount of stroke that moves you ahead.

Why don't you slide your fingers vertically down your hips until your fingertips reach the

Wearing Your Kayak 125

bottom of the kayak seat? You fit in your seat well, and there is little room for side-to-side motion. Not everyone fits so well.

Imagine a case where there was as much as a couple of inches between the paddler's hips and the seat side. With each stroke the paddler would slide from one side to the other. Pushing your weight from one side of the kayak to the other is hard work. The constant weight shifts also result in a long series of subtle turns. Fortunately, there's a good solution: hip pads. They have nothing to do with bustles. Hip pads are molded blocks of closed-cell foam that fit against the vertical sides of your kayak seat and keep you from sliding back and forth. If you need them, I recommend just taping them in place at first, until you've shaped them to just the right size for you. That's when you glue them in place.

Whether you buy a set of pads and strap them in or carve your own from foam and place them yourself, don't add so much that you are wedged in like a cork in a bottle. You should be able to slide your fingers down each hip and touch the seat when you're sitting in place. That means at least a half-inch, but not more than an inch, of free space off each hip.

You talked about your feet going all tingly and going to sleep. Most likely the front lip of your seat is pressing against your sciatic nerve, causing that tingly discomfort, and, in some cases, even a momentary paralysis. A lot of guys have discovered this feeling by driving long distances with a fat wallet crammed into their rear pocket.

To avoid this, the fore-and-aft angle of your kayak seat should match the angle of your thighs. If your foot pegs are set way too far forward, you may have been pressing down in the front edge of the seat. Adjusting the foot pegs so that your knees are lightly pressed against the underside of your deck could take care of the issue.

If the bowl of the seat is too low for you and this has put your thighs against the seat edge, you might want to experiment with a thin layer of neoprene—say, 2 millimeters—fabric side up in the lowest part of the seat. This will lift you just a tad and can relieve sciatic pressure. It will also make the seat a little "stickier," and reduce your sliding around.

For comfort, I like a thin square of foam on the underside of the deck where my knees rest. I paddle in shorts much of the year, and I like the extra padding the foam gives me. From limited experience, I think I'd like foam on the inside of a plastic boat as well, and I know I'd want it on wood.

Up to this point everything has been held in place with tape, and you should plan on a fair amount of paddling before you change from tape to glue. Make sure the padding you've added is comfortable, and make sure that you can paddle efficiently before you glue the pads and squares in place. Check with your kayak's manufacturer as to appropriate glues or stickum for your particular kayak. Remember the carpenter's axiom: Measure twice, cut once.

You said, and you were right, that your kayak seems to swerve around even when you're trying to paddle in a straight line. It's not your fault. You wanted a kayak suitable for weeklong adventures, and that means a kayak that can carry a fair amount of camping gear, food, and water. Right now you are the only thing in your kayak, and it's floating very high in the water. Consider sticking a 5-gallon jug (heck, 2½-gallon jugs might work) filled with water up forward and another one in the stern. Ten gallons of water will add about 83.5 pounds to your kayak, and that weight will bring your kayak closer to its designed waterline, making it far less susceptible to breezes. If you think in metric, 38 liters of water weigh about the same as 10 gallons, so try two 20-liter jugs.

A properly fitting boat is a joy to paddle, and you'll be amazed at how many more miles you'll be able to fit into the same day without stretching the seams of your physical conditioning.

CHAPTER 14

Rescues

I hope this doesn't affect the relationship we've built as we've paddled together, but I have a confession to make. I can't Eskimo-roll my Klepper double kayak. My decked canoe is a snap to roll—an open canoe, stuffed with float bags, will slosh right back to sunny side up. But you see, with my Klepper, I fall out. I've been experimenting by seeing how far up on its beam ends I could rock that big kayak, and I keep falling out. The kayak eases back from its edge and bobs right side up as if laughing at me.

That's okay. I have a big, old, comfortable tractor seat in my Klepper, with no hip pads, and my feet are braced against the frame rather than on a set of pegs. My knees aren't pressed on the underside of the deck, marginal

as it is, and I'll squirt out like a wet watermelon seed between two fingers when the kayak is rolled up on its side. It doesn't matter. I still can enjoy puttering around an urban lake while watching the shipyards, the fishing boats, and the houseboats. I'm also comfortable about loading the Klepper and heading out into the remote islands along the fringes of the North Pacific for weeks at a time.

What I'm trying to say is that you don't *have* to learn to Eskimo-roll your boat the first week you go paddling. It's a good thing to know. You'll build up your confidence and become a better paddler because of your increased abilities. Since you know you can rescue yourself, you won't be nearly so nervous about probing the edge of your balance envelope. Who knows; someday you might need that skill. On the other hand, I know people who have logged thousands of miles without once being upset.

What's their secret? They paddle within their own capabilities. They serenely consider their options before paddling ahead. They are in no hurry. Let me back up a step or two before you think I'm inventing these paddling paragons as we glide along. Yes, these perfect paddlers have been in the water. But they upset in controlled conditions, testing the limits of their braces, their boats, and their ability to get themselves out of difficulty.

They were exercising the muscle between their ears.

To get to that point, you're going to have to learn to use some other muscles, and how to link together paddling skills you already know. There's a difference—a big difference—between knowing something and mastering that same thing. Imagine yourself sitting in your kayak, feet against your foot pegs, and your back braced against the back-band. Your knees are against the underside of your deck. That's how you sit while you're paddling. This time is different. That's because your hair is sopping wet and you're hanging upside down.

Your quickest way out of that upset position is to Eskimo-roll your kayak. You extend your paddle straight out to the side with the blade flat against the water surface, and while bracing against the resistance of your paddle blade, you flick your hips—you rotate the kayak—until the kayak is deck side up and you can withdraw your head from the water.

Sounds easy, doesn't it? It is, but it's a lot like learning to ride a bike or tie your shoelaces. Maybe only one out of a thousand, maybe only one out of ten thousand, can learn how to do it from reading words in a book. The rest of us do better (and learn far more quickly) getting wet in the hands of a teacher,

whether in a formal class or in a paddling club training session.

Let's go through that rolling bit again, but a little slower.

You'll start by leaning over the side of your kayak until your center of gravity overwhelms your kayak's innate stability. A moment later you'll discover that a kayak is perfectly happy floating while inverted. I found it easier to wear a mask (or goggles) and a nose clip the first few times I *huli*-ed—*huli* being Hawaiian for "capsize."

Relax for a moment and get comfortable. You have plenty of air in your lungs and you're already good at a wet exit. Besides, I'm in the water next to you. Hold your paddle in both hands, gripping it at about the power position. Swing the paddle until it is right along the seam between your deck and hull, with the blade closest to the stern parallel to the surface of the water. Your knuckles will be bumping up against the surface, and the aft blade will be just below the surface. Let your PFD float you up toward the surface, and as you bend in a C-shape toward that side, swing your paddle easily until the blade that was at the stern of your boat is now sticking straight out from the side of your kayak, still with the blade just under the surface. Your paddle shaft should be closer to the surface than your wrists. You still have lots of air, so don't pop your head above the water. In the real world you can sneak up for a breath, but we won't do it while learning.

You're right! Your hands and paddle are in a high brace. Upside down, but still in that position. Now, use your hips and knees to rotate your kayak until it is beneath you. Remember that hip flick we practiced? This is exactly the same.

Leave your head in the water. Your head is heavy, so let the water cradle it while you're rotating your kayak. Your head should trail your shoulders out of the water as your kayak and body come upright. Now your body will be bent into a C-shape, but a mirror image of that first C. Now you know why they call it a *C-to-C roll*. Those folks who lead with their head usually topple back into the water.

I kind of cheated a bit that time. Just when you extended your paddle out to the side and started your hip flick, I reached over your kayak's hull and gave it a bit of rotational assist. You were also startled when you did pop out of the water, so I caught you before you continued your rotation by flopping back under on the other side. Even without my help you started to get the picture of how this rolling thing works.

You might like to practice this while grabbing the little drain gutter along the edge of a warm swimming pool. You could do the same by holding onto the side of a low dock. I've seen people practice with a big square of flotation. All of 'em work. You're discovering the feeling of when your kayak wants to upset, and the feeling as you rotate the kayak back underneath your balance. You're also doing it in an environment where you are confident and not afraid.

Why don't you practice your hip flick and rotation again? Position your kayak parallel to the side of the pool (or the dock), turn your torso so that you face the side and the pool edge, and just latch your hands onto the edge. You don't need a death grip. Use your hips and your torso to rotate your kayak so that it is tipped up onto its gunwale and you're supporting yourself and your kayak with your hands. Just using your hips and knee, rotate your kayak back so it rests flat on the water. That wasn't hard. Try it again, but this time, see if you can bring your deck closer to vertical. Do it a few more times if you're not tired, and you'll be amazed to find that you'll have your deck in the water, your shoulders wet, and the bottom of your kayak pointed at the sky. Without even thinking about it you'll be able to rotate your kayak back underneath you.

Practice with a club; practice in a class. You'll probably meet some super people, you'll be exposed to new ideas and new destinations, and you'll find friends to share the water with. If the first club doesn't fit you like a glove, take a look around and find another. But join a club. Trust me.

My guess is that no more than two or three cruising kayakers out of a hundred have a bombproof Eskimo roll. That's because no more than two or three kayaks out of a hundred have the hip pads, back braces, and thigh supports needed to lock the kayaker into the boat in order to roll back up. Anyone paddling one of the other ninety-seven or ninety-eight boats is going to do just like I do in my Klepper—when the boat goes over, the paddler is going to fall out.

The Klepper was a red herring. With its knee braces and foot pegs in place, it comes upright easily. My Pygmy Coho, a solo kayak, rolls right side up almost without effort. Fortunately, falling out isn't the end of the world. I'm going to assume that by the second time you topple over, you won't have all sorts of loose gear in the cockpit or resting on the deck.

Back in the boat now. Feel my hand on your shoulder, and feel the quick shove? You're a swimmer!

Now what?

If you had been ready and prepared, you could have come back right side up with the Eskimo roll you learned in class. If your capsize was totally unexpected and you came out of your kayak, you may have had the presence of mind to swim under your kayak, slip yourself back into the cockpit, and roll upright. Now you have a whole bunch of water in your kayak and the roll is more difficult and your stability when upright is questionable. You'd better start bailing and balancing when you do it.

Let's get back to thinking about how we can rescue ourselves from uncomfortable situations.

Rule number one: Save the person. If a swimming paddler is being swept into danger, into surf or rocks or through a channel and out into open water, move them into safety. Abandon their boat and tow them yourself, or, better yet, get them out of the water onto your rear deck and ferry them to shore. If you are the one in the water and you are but 50 yards from shore in thigh-deep water, get up and start walking. If you are wearing shorts and a T-shirt and the water temperature is 50 degrees, you probably can't swim 50 yards. Half of all people in those circumstances can't.

Dress for water temperatures and enjoy air temperatures.

Fortunately for us, there are a number of low-tech rescue techniques to snatch a paddler from the water. Learn them before you need them.

Swimming Aboard

Let's assume I pushed you over again, and toppled you out of a sit-on-top. This is a setup, because it's pretty easy (relatively speaking) to re-board a sit-on-top. You use a paddle leash so you won't have to hunt for your paddle.

If the kayak is upside down, turn it over. The easiest way is to position yourself next to the cockpit (or either cockpit with a tandem). Reach across the boat and grab the scupper holes. Bring your knees up and onto the hull of the kayak, lean back, and the kayak will flop right over.

Face the kayak and swim up to the cockpit. Squirm over the side between the seat and the foot wells, and let your feet and legs float up to the surface. Right now you are belly down. A lot of us will kick with our feet to move over the edge of the kayak. This is not easy, but it's certainly possible for most of us. Roll over onto your backside, rolling toward the seat. You should end up sitting in the seat.

Sit up, swing your feet into the foot wells, grab your paddle, and you're ready to go.

Right the overturned kayak.

Swim aboard, belly down, between the seat and the foot wells.

Roll over onto the seat, swing your legs aboard, grab your paddle. and go.

Photos courtesy Ocean Kayak

Practice this a couple of times and you can be back aboard in just a couple of minutes.

Whoops—got a problem here. You're not paddling a sit-on-top, but one of those dag-nab-it skinny cruising kayaks.

With some broad-ish and big-cockpit-ed kayaks you can swim back aboard the same way. Mostly you can't; not by yourself. This is one of the reasons you paddle with a friend.

Assisted Rescue

It's not a good thing to be accidentally in the water, and it gets worse the longer you're there. Water is cold, and it's going to steadily sap your strength. It will eat away at your resolve and confuse your thoughts. The assisted rescue is the quickest way I know to get a capsized paddler out of the wet.

As soon as she's checked that you are okay and not injured, your paddling partner scoots over to the bow of your capsized kayak. (I'm assuming it went over as you came out. Your boat could have righted itself as you exited.) You swim to the stern of your boat. She comes perpendicular to your kayak, with your bow right at the front of her cockpit. She grabs the handle or loop at your bow.

You put both hands on the bottom of your boat, just a few inches ahead of the end, and when you're both ready, you vault skyward with a mighty push on the bottom of your kayak. She lifts your bow and pulls it up on her deck. Why the mighty effort? You have to release the suction of your cockpit in the water. She rocks your kayak gently from side to side and water gushes from the cockpit. If you have a bulkhead behind your cockpit, this will take care of most of the water in your kayak. If not, you might have to lift the stern and drain more water out.

Flip the kayak over. There's still some water aboard, but you've removed enough to somewhat stabilize your boat.

She brings her kayak alongside yours and grasps the cockpit coaming. Most paddlers think that reversing the position of the kayaks, placing each bow next to the other's stern, works best. While she braces and stabilizes both kayaks, you should slither up on the rear deck of your kayak. This is hard work! You'll probably find it easier to start by hooking a leg into your cockpit for leverage.

So now you're belly down on your rear deck, puffing from the exertion. Carefully roll over, lift your other leg into your cockpit, and

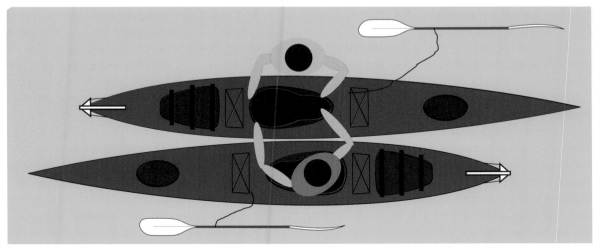

In an assisted rescue, one kayaker stabilizes and braces the rescued kayak as the paddler scrambles back aboard. Easy to say, hard to do without some practice.

slide down onto your seat. If it is flat—the water, that is—have her continue to stabilize your kayak as you pump and sponge the last of the water out. If the water is splashy, snap your spray deck into place to keep from being swamped by a passing wave, and tuck your pump under an edge of your spray deck to remove the water.

Grab your paddle, catch your breath, and proceed.

I have to make three points: First, it's hard scrambling up on a kayak. Some paddlers will use a spare paddle. They hitch a long loop of rope around the paddle shaft and place the paddle perpendicular to both kayaks, under the cockpits. The loop would go over my kayak and would hang down 2 to 3 feet into the water, creating a step for me. If you use a similar loop but drape it around the cockpit, my weight will tend to rotate my kayak.

I've seen some paddlers effectively use this method, but with the paddler in the water coming up between his kayak and the rescuer. It's said to be a much more stable position in which to hold the rescuee's kayak. I can see a wave crunching the two kayaks together at the worst possible time. I'm probably being paranoid.

If you have a choice, you'll find a double kayak is better as a rescue boat. More arms, more strength, more stability.

If you've practiced this a few times, you can have a rescued paddler back in the kayak in two to four minutes.

Paddle-Float Rescue

You have an alternative if you are by yourself (even though good sense says you should be paddling with a partner). It's called a *paddle-float rescue,* and with it you can stabilize your kayak and climb back aboard. It's not easy, but it *is* possible. I shoved you over in a very calm, protected, and warm bay. Even though you didn't notice when we were talking, a third friend drifted up behind us just to add a little moral

support and safety during our demonstration. If this had been cold, open water, wracked by waves and swept by winds, everything would have been a lot more difficult and potentially a lot more dangerous. The little practice we're going to do here is just a taste (rather than the full banquet) of rescue techniques.

Your boat will have to be properly rigged, and you'll need a spare paddle, a paddle float, a pump, and probably a loop of rope to use as a step as you scramble back aboard.

With this gear we're going to build a small outrigger that will stabilize your boat. Splash over to your cockpit (roll the boat right side up if it's capsized) and hook your leg into the cockpit so that you can look at the rear deck. Your foot just keeps you and your kayak together as you rig the float system. You'll see two jam cleats (one off each rear corner of your cockpit, far enough away so neither interferes with your spray deck); two tee cleats with their tees aligned with your cockpit, and set on your flat rear deck, just a couple of inches behind your cockpit and as close to the gunwales as I could fit them; and a pair of eye straps a couple of inches aft of each tee cleat. The eyes work well, but I could have mounted one-horned tee cleats with the horn facing aft instead.

The cleats are not just screwed into your deck. Each is fastened down into a reinforcing metal pad, fiberglassed to the underside of your deck. I've run a quarter-inch line from one jam cleat back to the eye strap, then forward to the tee cleat, where I've wrapped it around the outside of the cleat and across your boat to the matching tee cleat on the other side. The line goes around that cleat, aft to the eye strap, and then forward to the second jam cleat. Because I don't want to lose the line, I tied a stevedore knot into each end, which prevents the line from coming loose and being washed away.

Slide your spare paddle out from under the bungee straps. (If it is a take-apart, as is logical, snap it together in an unfeathered position.

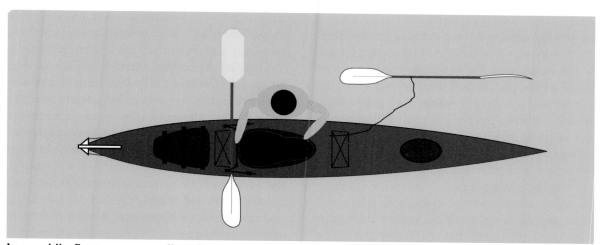

In a paddle-float rescue you literally assemble and mount an outrigger on your kayak, and use that outrigger to balance your kayak as you scramble back aboard. You need to have your kayak equipped with tie-downs to lash the paddle (the arm of the outrigger) in place, and you need a float that can be attached to your paddle. Balance is critical when clambering aboard. It might take fifteen minutes to rig the float and re-board.

If it isn't, or it's only feathered, don't worry.) Reach in behind your seat. I've tucked what looks like a plastic bag there. This bag is really a float, and you'll find it has straps to secure it to your paddle blade. It's kind of like a little life jacket. Some are made with foam flotation, so all you have to do is strap it to your paddle. Others have to be inflated. Ones with foam are quicker and easier to use, while the inflatable versions are easier to store. Slide the float over one blade of your paddle and fasten the straps around the paddle shaft. A big float could have 40 pounds of buoyancy. Earlier versions of the float were a seat cushion (with 18 pounds of flotation) or an empty bleach jug (with about 8 pounds of buoyancy).

Loosen the line on your right-side-up kayak so that it slips off the tee cleats, and lay your paddle across the deck between the tee cleats and eye straps, in much the same position that you would have used to board your kayak off the beach (see how all our kayaking skills fit together?). The blade without the float is just past the edge of your deck. The float is on the outboard blade, now 4 feet or so out from the

side of your kayak. Think of it as an outrigger, because that's really what it is. Tuck the line around the two tee cleats and pull on the end through a jam cleat until the line is tight and the paddle is firmly secured to your deck. You'll need the buoyancy of your PFD, and you'll have to support yourself by hanging onto the boat.

Using the leverage of your foot in the cockpit and the strength of your arms, wiggle your way until most of your body is on the rear deck. Keep a fair amount of weight on the float. If you don't, you might see the float arc through the air over you as you capsize on the unsupported side. It's hard, but doable.

Get both feet into the cockpit. Gingerly roll over onto your back (you're still lying on the rear deck) and slide into your cockpit. Keep some of your weight on the float side. Reel in your paddle leash and retrieve your paddle. If you have a soft plastic bucket, scoop out what water you can. You don't have a lot of room in the cockpit. This might be a good time to reattach your spray deck. As full of water as your kayak is, it's floating low in the water, and a small wave can wash aboard. Stick your pump into your cockpit by lifting just a bit of the side of your spray deck and start working the handle.

Some folks find it difficult to squirm up out of the water onto the kayak, starting from just ahead of the paddle and putting weight on the paddle shaft and the float as they first slither up onto the rear deck, and then flopping over and wiggling back into the cockpit. If you take a circle of rope that can stretch out to 2½ feet or so and loop that around the shaft, you can use the rope as a step.

Why all this bother over breaking out a spare paddle for your float, rather than your regular paddle? Well, you were the one in the water. Something put you there. In most cases, that would have been a combination of wind and waves. Neither eased up while you were in the water. If they knocked you over once, they can do it again. You have to be able to brace your paddle with both hands while you are pumping, which also takes both hands. If I could, I might want to come up beside you and attempt to stabilize your boat as you pumped. Once your boat is relatively dry, pop the paddle-float line from the jam cleat and retrieve your spare paddle and stow all the components.

A few caveats to using a paddle float: First of all, it's much harder than it sounds. The first time you need one for real, you won't be in a pool or protected bay, so you should practice until you can do it right. Second, although I have not seen it, I understand that some people have managed to bust their spare paddles while re-boarding. My guess is that they had their step loop positioned right about where the ferrule is in a break-apart paddle, so you may want to watch out for that. (The ferrule is the joint between the two paddle halves.) Third, I do know folks who rolled right over again as they put their weight on the wrong side of the kayak and re-dumped. This is an example of good planning, but poor execution. Fourth, if you are in the water and being knocked about by waves as you attempt to right parts on a

ton or more of swamped kayak, you're likely to get crunched. A boat is slippery, huge, and awkward—and will sorely try your patience.

Rigging a paddle float and re-boarding takes time. When the water is cold and the wind is blowing, it seems to take hours. It often takes fifteen to twenty minutes to get back in a kayak, and it could take longer. That's plenty of time for the first stages of hypothermia to kick in. You're going to be cold, you are shivering, and you lose a little muscle strength with that much time in the water.

Some people claim that a paddle float is inherently dangerous. While I believe they have a point, it still is the best way for a solo paddler to re-board a kayak unassisted. You should use caution and practice to minimize the risks.

Sponsons

You might also consider sponsons as a rescue device. Sponsons are a pair of fabric pontoons, about 6 inches in diameter and 3 feet long, that strap on either side of your kayak. Straps go underneath the boat from sponson to sponson and then over the deck, fore and aft of the cockpit buckle, from one sponson to the other.

In place and inflated, sponsons stabilize your boat to the point where you can get up and stand in the cockpit. I have friends who use them when fishing or while photographing—folks who paddle narrow kayaks and delight in the additional stability. I have never attempted to strap sponsons onto my kayak while I'm out on open water with waves kicking up, nor while in the water, but I don't want to hang around a swamped boat when it's being tossed in the waves. Given that, sponsons work almost like the side air chambers in my Klepper and some other folding kayaks, and provide a lot of stability. One of my fishing friends leaves his deflated most of the time, with only the stern strap attached and the deflated sponsons tucked under rear bungee cords. With the second strap passed under his hull and then snapped

The More the Merrier

Always paddle with a buddy or, even better, in a group. First of all, there's a safety factor. If one paddler encounters a problem—a broken paddle, a lack of sunscreen, an inadvertent swim, or whatever—others in the group can be there to lend a helping hand. Second, it's a great learning experience. You'll share techniques and tips, and watch how others respond to every paddling situation. Third, it will keep you paddling. The group will inspire you and sweep you along in their enthusiasm. You'll share drives to the water's edge, group equipment, the muscle power of carrying boats and gear, and the efforts in planning your trips. Lastly, it's simply major fun to paddle with friends. It makes the day brighter and the water warmer.

into place, he can inflate the two air chambers in mere moments. He says he can squirm back aboard without the need for an outrigger float.

Eskimo Rescue

In an Eskimo rescue, the capsized paddler stays in his boat and raises a hand out of the water. The rescuer comes up perpendicular to the capsized kayak and allows the paddler in the water to grab the rescuer's bow. With the bow in hand for support, the capsized paddler lifts, and with a hip flick, rotates his boat upright. Just like you did off the wall in the pool. It's hard to get to the right point in time; it's hard for the inverted paddler to find and grasp the rescue bow; it's hard to keep the boats from thumping together; and most often, the paddler in the water runs the risk of shoulder injury because of the angle of the lift.

Another suggested plan is for you to stay in your inverted boat with your head underwater until I paddle up alongside you, bow to bow, about 2 feet off your side. I place my paddle between my deck and your hull, you reach up from the depths between our boats and grasp the paddle, and with that as a lever, you pull yourself and your boat right side up with a hip flick. Before you say, "Okay, this sounds like a snap," think of this: What prevents my boat and yours from crunching together as you roll up? You also run the risk of shoulder injury.

I can't recommend either of these rescues, but you'll probably be exposed to someone who advocates them sometime in the future.

I've seen folks work together in a swamped double, with one of the partners stabilizing the boat with his or her own weight and paddle while the other squirms aboard. With one aboard and the boat pumped, a firm brace will support the boat while the other climbs in. Maybe. This is very difficult, and demands super teamwork.

Has all of this discouraged you? I hope not. I simply wanted to keep you from building up false expectations. In a couple of decades of kayak cruising on salt water, I have not had to roll my boat nor use the other rescue techniques mentioned in this chapter. None of my friends and paddling companions has needed to use any of these methods. We have practiced them against the day that something goes wrong, and we have huddled on the beach waiting for the weather to blow through. You don't have to paddle in the wind and surf. That's not in the contract.

There should be at least two separate rescue packages with each kayaking party; what if the sole rescue package you have is aboard the boat on its way into the depths? You should have a spare paddle, a stirrup loop, a portable bilge pump, and a floating towline at least 20 meters long.

Use a big dollop of common sense in any rescue situation.

Imagine a paddler capsizing and coming out of his boat. It happens. If you're 50 feet off the beach in waist-deep water and with no wave action, just go ashore. It's easier to pump out your boat there, plus get some dry, warm clothes.

What if the capsized paddler is drifting into danger? What if the current is sweeping him into a reef, or out away from land? If land is nearby, in time if not in distance, consider having the paddler in the water clamber up on the rear deck of a kayak to catch a ride to the beach. It would be relatively quick, compared to other rescue methods, and the paddler/swimmer would have access to dry clothes, warmth, and shelter while others in the party attempted to tow the overturned kayak back to shore. For that matter, if it comes to choosing, it's a lot more important to bring a paddler ashore than a boat.

Towing

First of all, if possible, right an overturned craft. It will tow more easily. To outfit a boat for towing, hook a carabiner into one end of the towline and snap the carabiner into the bow loop of the disabled boat. Run the other end of the towing line through a strap eye on the rear deck of the towing kayak, and secure the line in one of the jam cleats within easy reach of the cockpit.

Some folks believe in running the towline through the bow loop and back to the cockpit, where it can be secured to a deck fitting. Forget about tying a big loop into one end and passing it over your shoulder. There will be a surge and snub every time the two kayaks are out of phase in the waves, not to mention a side-to-side yawing of the towed boat. Your back doesn't need that whiplash crack! I suppose you might be able to run the towed boat tight under your quarter and tie its bow loop to your jam cleat, but this doesn't strike me as suitable.

Two kayaks can tow one, with a line going from one rescuer through the bow loop of the towed kayak and on to a cleat on the second rescuer. The rescuers would form a vee, with the towed boat at the point of the vee. Take care with this, because the tow rope will tend to pull the two towing kayaks together.

It's also possible to have two towing kayaks, if they use significantly different-length towlines. The towline from the lead kayak may somewhat impede the strokes of the following rescue boat.

You can make use of the advantages of having a double kayak along. The bow paddler in the double can transfer to the empty single and paddle it to the shoreside rendezvous. If the paddler in the rescued boat is ill or injured, that paddler can swap places with the double's bow paddler. Switching places is a skill that you ought to practice before you need it.

I've heard of systems where the disabled boat is rigged in front of the rescue boat, with the bow loop snubbed to the other boat's jam cleat and the rescue boat pushing the rescued craft, but I fear this would be like pushing a rope.

> ## Learn It, Know It, Live It
>
> You can prepare for a rescue at sea in any number of ways. There's a possibility that just as you flop over you'll hear a helicopter, and as you bob to the surface you'll see Johnny Depp reaching out his hand to pull you aboard. Moments later you could be on his yacht, enjoying a gourmet dinner. While that is possible, I don't think it's likely. Learning self-rescue and assisted-rescue techniques seems like a better long-term bet.

CHAPTER 15

Tools of the Piloting Trade

Navigation is a rigorous science, steeped in mathematics and requiring that you learn precise skills. If you're going to paddle across the Atlantic or Pacific—it's been done—it's a skill you should master. On the other hand, two centuries ago twelve-year-old boys shipping out on British men-of-war were required to master the navigator's art without calculators or stopwatches, so there is hope for us.

Me? I poke about from landmark to landmark, checking road signs as I amble along. Works for me. If you want a more-formal term, this is called *piloting,* and it has worked quite well for thousands of years.

What will you need? Start with a chart, which is a different cat than its cousin, the map. It helps to have a way to determine North, and a magnetic compass is perfectly adequate. You need a pencil and a straightedge of some sort to draw the route you wish to follow, and you need a way of measuring the angle of that proposed course, or heading against the "north" of your chart. You'll also need some sort of

Mark Carroll; licensed by Shutterstock.com

This little navigation deck clamps to either of our cruising doubles, holding a Magellan GPS and a compass. The chart is enclosed in a clear waterproof bag, with the courses and distances already plotted.

measuring stick to determine just how long a course line you drew on your chart.

If you're paddling on salt water, a little booklet showing the times of high and low tide each day will make your life a little easier.

Are you a gadget freak? You can weigh down your kayak with thousands of dollars' worth of high-tech positioning devices, speedometers, and radio direction finders. They won't make your paddling life much harder, other than for the weight and the batteries you'll lug about.

A map shows a predetermined route, or a choice of routes, that you may follow to go from

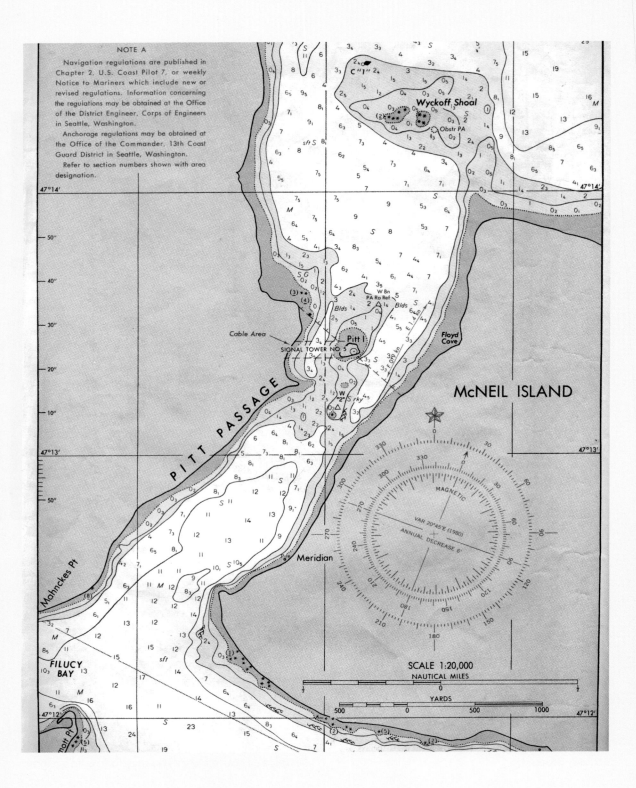

47°14'

Wyckoff Shoal

C "1"

Obstr PA

47°14'

50"

40"

30"

M

Cable Area

Pitt I

SIGNAL TOWER NO

W Bn
PA Ro Ref

Bids

Bids

Floyd
Cove

McNEIL ISLAND

W
"2"

47°13'

PITT PASSAGE

330

330

30

60

300

MAGNETIC

VAR 20°45'E (1980)

ANNUAL DECREASE 6'

270

90

Meridian

240

120

210

150

180

Mahnckes Pt

FILUCY
BAY

47°12'

47°12'

SCALE 1:20,000

NAUTICAL MILES

YARDS

500   0   500   1000

Reading Your Chart like a Book

A nautical chart is, to the patient eye, a wonderfully detailed book guiding you across the water. How detailed? Let's go for a quick cruise around a portion of Chart 18445. Mind you, this is only a portion of a chart, so it does not include a lot of the information you'll find on the whole thing.

Down at the bottom it says SCALE 1:20,000, which means that 1 inch on the chart represents 20,000 inches on the ground. That's a more formal way of saying 1 inch on the chart equals just over a half-mile on the water. Below that is a visual representation of the scale, in nautical miles and in yards. Right above the scale is a compass rose, showing true north, and at this location magnetic north. Just above the compass rose is a name, McNeil Island, giving the location. Look over to the left and you'll see Pitt Passage, the name of the channel. Up above you'll see Wyckoff Shoal, a shallows of significant interest to boaters passing through. See those lines running horizontally just above and below Pitt Island? They are marked 47°14" and 47°13", and mark out 1 minute of longitude. That's 1 nautical mile. The six numbers in between are nautical seconds (60 seconds to the minute, just like a clock) and 1" equals about 101 feet, or 31 meters. I'm rounding the numbers off.

Land areas are kind of a beigey tan with a black outline that is an accurate representation of the shoreline at high tide. Next to the land you see a band of grungy-green, with a dotted border on the outside rather than a solid line. This is the intertidal zone, with the dotted line showing the approximate shoreline at *mean lower low water,* which is the average of the lowest tides. Outside of the intertidal zone is a band of blue, which shows shallow waters. On this particular chart the outer edge of the blue shallows is 3 fathoms, or 18 feet. The first black line you see wandering up through the blue area (again on this chart, because this varies with the scale of the chart) marks a depth of at least 1 fathom. That's the line, and the depth will decrease as you move closer to the intertidal area.

Beyond the blue is the white, and the white indicates deep water.

There are numbers all over the water area. That's the depth of the water in fathoms. In the first part of the blue band you see numbers such as 0^3, which means the water depth at that point is 0 fathoms plus 3 feet. That kind of number is common when marking shallower waters—on this chart, up to 10 fathoms.

Let's go a little deeper.

"Deeper?" I see your eyebrows shoot up.

Look just to the right of little Pitt Island in Pitt Passage. See the capital S? There's another S a bit south of Pitt. That indicates the bottom there is sandy. Just to the right of the second S you saw is *rky.* You're right. That means rocky. Northwest of Pitt is a G for gravel. Extending west of Pitt are two purple dashed lines identified as a cable area. There is an electrical cable there, and if you lowered an anchor you might snag it. This would be a bad thing.

On Pitt Island itself is a circle with a dot in the middle, which is identified as SIGNAL TOWER NO. 5. Yeah, it's a radio tower, and a clearly visible landmark.

Look due south of Pitt Island, right in the middle of the 1-fathom blue patch. There is a triangle marked W "2." It's a white triangle sign mounted on a pole. This is a traffic sign. The little wiggly lines just to the right (east) of the daymark indicate kelp.

There are two little intertidal patches on each side of the daymark. To the north it indicates a mound that is exposed as a low tide. South of the daymark is a similar intertidal patch, but this one has what looks like an asterisk on it. That's a rock that is uncovered at low tide. There are a lot of similar rocks along the intertidal zone on the southwest edge of McNeil Island. When you see a number inside a pair of parentheses next to a rock, that tells you how much rock is exposed at low lower water.

Look just to the east of Pitt Island. See those purple numbers next to arrows? F 0.9 kn means that the maximum current flow during a flood or rising tide is 0.9 knots, and the arrow points in the direction it is flowing. Then the E 1.4 kn makes sense. It's the maximum current flow during the ebb or falling tide, and the arrow points the way it is flowing.

On the west side of McNeil Island, near the compass rose, is where the village of Meridian used to be. Right off the name, in the intertidal zone, is a small circle marked *piling*. That's a big pole sticking up out of the beach.

Take a look on the west side of Wyckoff Shoal. See the flopped-over black triangle? That's a black buoy shaped like a can, with no light, and marked with a "1." If you were paddling west around the top of Wyckoff Shoal and turned south around that buoy, it would be on your left. That's because the ocean would be behind you and the head of the waterway would be well ahead, over your bow.

What's the value of all this? When I go ambling along, paddling my kayak, I go from landmark to landmark. There's no magic involved.

a starting point to a destination. Maps rarely provide a representation of relief, and almost never describe road surfaces or conditions.

A chart describes the conditions of an area, starting with a detailed and accurate representation of a coastline, water depths, bottom conditions, wrecks and obstructions, and potential tidal currents. It provides all the information a navigator needs to determine a safe route from a starting point to a destination.

Charts are drawn to various scales, as needed. There will be a note somewhere on the chart indicating its scale. One scale may be 1 to 80,000, usually written as 1:80,000. That means 1 inch on the chart represents 80,000 inches in the real world—which translates out to 1 inch on the chart measuring just about 1.1 nautical miles in real distance. A 1:40,000 scale means 1 inch on the chart equals 40,000 inches in the world, or 1 inch represents just a tad over a half-mile. The scale on your chart should be a reasonable one. It would be absurd to make a 1:40,000 chart of the sea surface between Los Angeles and Hawaii—not to mention a waste of trees to produce all that paper. At the same time, it wouldn't be useful to produce a chart scaled to 1:800,000—or 1 inch equaling about 11 miles—of a terribly convoluted harbor with many small points and obstructions. Since charts are made for people in boats, it stands to reason that more detail is given to the water than the land. Some important land fixtures should be shown, of course, such as towns and harbors, as well as easily identifiable objects like church spires or petroleum tank farms.

Usually, land will be depicted in a beigey-yellow color, shallow water close to the land will be blue, and deep water will be white. The division between blue and white will vary with the scale of the chart.

You point at my chart, eyebrow raised. Yup. There is a band of grungy green clinging to the land's coastline. The shoreside is a solid line, while the water side of this color is usually dotted. This is the intertidal zone, and uncovers at mean lower low water, which is the mean average of the lower low water tides. In other words, all of the intertidal zone is not uncovered during every tidal cycle.

Water depths may be shown in fathoms and/or feet (1 fathom is equal to 6 feet), or may be stated in meters; that will be identified on the chart.

All the "road signs" of the sea will be marked on the chart. On the water, cone-shaped buoys, called *nuns,* and can-shaped buoys, called *cans,* mark out channels; these buoys are color-coded as well as numbered or lettered. When coming from the sea, buoys on your right are red (remember that with Red Right Returning), while green or black buoys are on the left. There's a twist on the Intracoastal Waterway, which more or less parallels the coastline from the upper Atlantic to Texas. There, the memory aid is Red Right Returning to Texas. Some buoys have lights (occasionally flashing), while others have horns or bells. There may be lights mounted ashore, or large signs called range markers that may be lined up so that one appears directly above the other to signal you are right in the middle of a channel. Most of these signals are depicted on a nautical chart as little symbols that look just like what they're supposed to be.

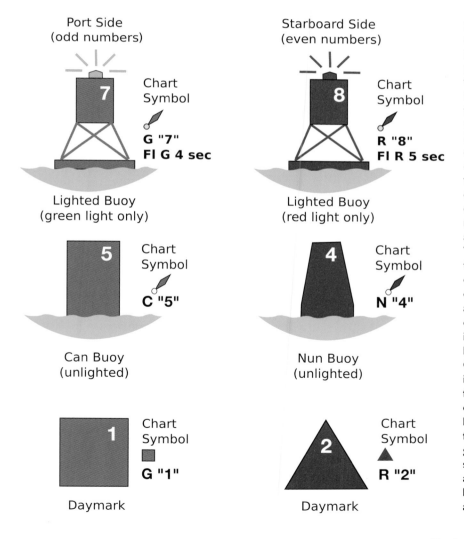

Port Side
(odd numbers)

Chart Symbol

G "7"
Fl G 4 sec

Lighted Buoy
(green light only)

Chart Symbol

C "5"

Can Buoy
(unlighted)

Chart Symbol

G "1"

Daymark

Starboard Side
(even numbers)

Chart Symbol

R "8"
Fl R 5 sec

Lighted Buoy
(red light only)

Chart Symbol

N "4"

Nun Buoy
(unlighted)

Chart Symbol

R "2"

Daymark

Buoys are just road signs. Green or black buoys mark the left or port side of a channel or waterway when returning from the open ocean toward the land. They may be either color. Red buoys mark the right or starboard side of a channel or waterway when coming from the ocean to land. The green or black buoys are odd-numbered; red buoys are even-numbered. Those numbers are on the buoys and identified on your chart. The green or black buoys may have a green light, and your chart describes the flashing pattern of a particular light. One marked Fl G 2.5 sec. means that it has a green light that flashes every 2.5 seconds. Some buoys also have bells and are identified on the chart. Unlit green or black buoys are shaped like barrels and are called cans. Unlit red buoys are cone-shaped and are called nuns.

Safe water markers are white with red vertical stripes and mark mid-channels or fairways. They indicate unobstructed water on all sides and may be passed on either side. They may be lit or unlit, or may be daymarks.

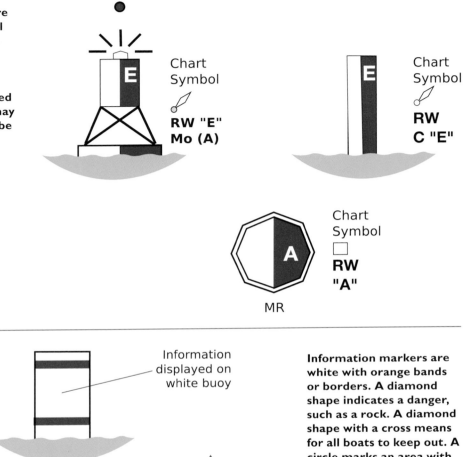

Chart Symbol

RW "E"
Mo (A)

Chart Symbol

RW
C "E"

Chart Symbol

RW
"A"

MR

Information displayed on white buoy

ROCK

Diamond Shape warns of danger

Diamond Shape with cross means boats keep out

Information markers are white with orange bands or borders. A diamond shape indicates a danger, such as a rock. A diamond shape with a cross means for all boats to keep out. A circle marks an area with specific controls, such as a speed limit, a no-wake zone, or other indicated rules. A rectangle displays information such as directions, distances, locations, etc.

5
MPH

Circle marks area controlled "as indicated"

BLACK LAKE

For displaying information such as directions, distances, locations, etc.

The vessel lanes for commercial ships are also marked, and just as the high-speed lanes of freeways aren't places for Sunday drivers, these aren't good spots for small craft such as kayaks to dawdle.

If you fall in love with charts (it's easy; they're seductive, with the promise of mysteries unfolding), you might want to download *US Chart No. 1: Nautical Chart Symbols, Abbreviations, and Terms* (published by the National Oceanic and Atmospheric Administration), a great little booklet that clearly illustrates every symbol on a chart (www.nauticalcharts.noaa.gov/mcd/chartno1.htm).

In most (but not all) cases, the top of a chart is north, the left west, the bottom south, and the right east. There are strip charts, made for small boats, which extend along waterways rather than being oriented to the north. All charts have at least one drawing of a compass face from which you can align yourself with the world.

Compasses

Take a good look at the drawing on this page. It's called, in boat talk, a *compass rose,* and it really has two sets of degree markings on it. The outer set of numbers refers to true north, which is the way mapmakers see things. The only problem with this concept is that the little magnet in a compass points to the big magnet up near the top of the world, which unfortunately isn't at the North Pole. There are all kinds of neat little tricks and mnemonics to let you convert from the direction your compass thinks is north to the direction of the North Pole, but you don't need to know any of them. All we're going to do is figure our directions using our magnetic compass and simply use that inner ring of degrees on the compass rose.

So you're going to need a compass. Probably the easiest type to use is a deck-mounted dome firmly attached a bit ahead of your cockpit. This type has a line down the clear dome of

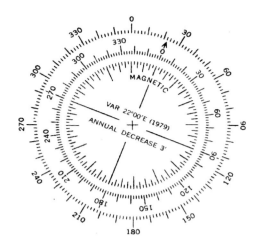

There are two circles in a compass rose, each marked in 360 degrees and noted with the cardinal directions of north (N), west (W), south (S), and east (E). The outer ring is oriented toward true north, or the North Pole. The inner ring is oriented toward magnetic north, as on a magnetic compass. At the center you'll see a note on the variance between the two, which is different in almost every location in North America, so use the rose shown on every chart rather than relying on memory. On many compass roses there will be a third ring, divided into quadrants but not marked with numbers. This reflects a bit of navigation history, when sailors steered by points (as in "north by northeast" or "west by southwest") rather than degrees.

the compass (called a *lubber line*), showing the direction of travel; the compass turns underneath this line. You read your direction from the numbers under the lubber line. If you want to talk nautical, the stand that holds the compass is called a binnacle.

When we're paddling our solo kayaks, we use two different models of surface-mounted compasses. Neither are permanently mounted, but use shock cord and snaps to hook into eyes mounted just ahead of our cockpits. (A permanently mounted compass is less likely to disappear from an unwatched boat; a removable compass is less likely to get banged around when you're transporting your kayak).

A permanently mounted compass such as this Suunto Pioneer, bolted through the deck of a fiberglass kayak, is far less likely to be lost—either dropped overboard or lifted by sneak thieves. On the other hand, it is more likely to be banged about when the kayak is being transported.

A removable compass such as this Suunto Orca clips to the deck hardware on your kayak. It can be removed for safekeeping or when not in use. On the other hand, it can be dropped overboard, misplaced, or stolen.

Some paddlers prefer to use an orienteering compass. Think of a rectangle of clear plastic, usually with an arrow carved into the plastic, with a rotating dish or bowl mounted on the plastic rectangle. The outside of the bowl is marked off in 360 degrees. Within the bowl is the compass needle, swinging so that it always points to magnetic north. Keep the plastic rectangle and its arrow parallel with the keel of your kayak, rotate the outer body of the compass so that the needle points to the 0-degree mark (north; usually, there is another arrow inside the body of the compass, and you can align the compass needle with this arrow), and you can read your course where the number on the compass body crosses the direction arrow on the plastic rectangle.

When possible, take a bearing at an object on your course and look at that object while you paddle. Despite claims to the contrary, I know few kayakers who can hold a course within an arc of 10 degrees once the waves get a little sloppy. And so what? You're going to a place, not attempting to carve a razor-straight line on the sea.

There are little round compasses without base plates; there are great big, huge machines that have a circle floating in a thick liquid, with degrees marked clearly; and there are electronic compasses that read beeps and chirps from satellites or distant radio transmitters. But there are no best models. You'll probably find one that is simple to use, without batteries or gadgets, and that's the one you'll stick with. Remember, kayaks are a low-tech, keep-it-simple way of traveling. You don't need to clutter up your mind (or your boat) with modern inconveniences. But whatever type you select, remember that compasses sink. Tie the compass lanyard to your boat against the day you will drop it—and believe me, someday you *will* drop it.

If you want to use your GPS for your compass, that's cool. They are great tools. Keep two things in mind, however: One, the batteries will go dead at the worst possible moment. You'll probably even drop the fresh batteries over the side when you're trying to replace them (well, I did). Second, with my GPS, the compass indicates which way I'm moving, and

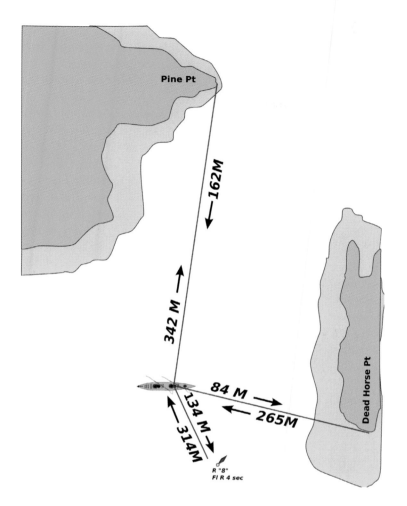

Pine Pt

162M

342 M

84 M

134 M

265M

314M

Dead Horse Pt

R "8"
Fl R 4 sec

Finding your position on the water is easy—well, easy on paper—but you need some practice to do it from the cockpit of a kayak. Take a bearing (aim your compass and note the direction) on an easily identifiable object. This could be a point of land, a buoy, a building marked on your chart, or any other prominent landmark. Determine the reciprocal of that bearing, which is exactly the opposite of your first bearing. If the bearing is more than 180 degrees, subtract 180 from that number. If the first bearing is less than 180 degrees, then add 180 to it. Draw a line from the landmark you selected at the same heading as the reciprocal you determined. You're somewhere along that line. Repeat this whole process on a second landmark. You are where those two lines cross. To be sure, try it with a third landmark. Take your time and practice onshore a few times, and you'll be surprised by how easy and accurate this method is.

that can be sideways or even backward. A magnetic compass indicates which way I'm pointing, despite which way I may be moving at any given moment. Neither one is better, but you should keep the difference in mind.

Measuring Directions

You'll need a pencil to draw your course, and you'll need a tool to "move" the course line so that it passes through the center of the compass rose.

If I had a table to work on I'd probably use parallel rules, which look like a pair of rulers hooked together. With practice you can "walk" them across a chart from your course

line to a compass rose. That's simply what I learned with, so I fall back on them. You might use a rolling ruler, which looks like just one ruler with a long roller hitched to one side. Put the straightedge on your course line and then roll the ruler over to the nearest compass rose to determine the heading. Heck, I've seen boatmen simply roll a round pencil over the chart to accomplish the same thing. Some folks like a single-armed protractor, which is a square of clear plastic holding a rotating clear circle marked out in 360 degrees, as well as a long, clear arm that reaches well across your chart. To use the single-armed protractor, put the clear arm right along your course and rest

A square of plastic with a circle marked off in degrees and a hank of string—that's about as simple and accurate a set of piloting tools as you'll need. Mark your course on your chart with a pencil. Extend the string along your course, stretching it so that the protector (the circle gizmo) is aligned on a line either of latitude or longitude. Read the degrees from the protractor. Stretch the string along the straight line of your course. Pinch both ends of the course. Move the string over to the left or right side of your chart, and read the distance right off the longitude line.

the center of the plastic square on one of the printed edges of the chart. Rotate the degree-circle until it's oriented to the north, and you can read your course right where the arm crosses the circle.

All of these require a good-size, flat working surface, which I don't have in my kayak.

You might get a sheet of clear, flexible plastic about the size of the clear plastic bag you're going to get to hold your chart on the deck of your kayak, and scribe a whole series of parallel lines about a half-inch apart from one side of the sheet to the other. Hold one of these lines right on your course, and you'll probably be able to reach a compass rose with another line on this sheet. The line passing through the center of the compass rose will show you your course.

In my chart bag I carry a square of thin, flexible clear plastic—about 4 inches on a side—with a circle marked out in 360 degrees on its face. A 2-foot-long black string dangles from a hole at the center. Stretch the string along the course you penciled on your chart, place the center of the plastic and the 360-degree mark on the right- or left-hand edge of your chart, and read the course right off the protractor. Yup, there's one slight problem. You might be reading the correct course, or the reciprocal, but that's an easy challenge to overcome.

Measuring Distances

A pair of dividers is handy to measure distances. Dividers look like a drawing compass, but have two pointy ends rather than one pointy end and a pencil. If you don't have dividers, just use a scrap of paper, marking the two ends of the distance to be measured and then holding the scrap up to the right or left side of the chart. Each of the 1-minute divisions on the sides of your chart equals 1 nautical mile, which means you can read the distance marked by the ticks you penciled on the paper scrap. Look around the chart and you'll find a scale, usually in miles and in yards, which can also be used to translate your measured distance into miles.

When you're paddling, you'll be happier knowing your cruising speed. A watch will come in handy, too. Sure, without one you'll still be able to tell day from dark, and your stomach will tell you when it's time to eat, but if you know about how fast you're traveling and for how long, you'll be able to make an educated guess as to how far you went.

Laying Out a Course

Let's put all these ingredients into the pot. We know where we are, because we drove to our launch site, and even as we're standing here talking, we're under a sign that clearly says BEDFORD TOWN DOCK. And Bedford is clearly marked on our chart, even to the finger of the dock. We know where we're going, because we've already made plans to camp at Deer Island State Park.

With the edge of our ruler, we'll draw a straight line on the chart from Bedford to the bay at Deer Island. That's going to be our course. We might use rulers, or we might use that sheet of lined plastic. It doesn't matter. Then, using our rulers or the lines on the plastic sheet, we'll create an imaginary line parallel to our course, right through the middle of the nearest compass rose. We'll read the course off the inner ring of degrees.

When we start paddling, we'll line up the lubber line of the compass with the degree we just read from the compass, and that's the way we'll head.

The imaginary course line will cross the compass rose at two points. One will give us the compass reading from Bedford to Deer Island, and the other will give us the course from Deer Island back to Bedford. We'll write these readings down on the course line. Then we'll put one point of our dividers at Bedford and the other at Deer Island. We'll move over to the scale, or to the minute marks that are part of the left and right sides of our chart, and count off the distance in nautical miles. It's 6 miles, and we paddle at 3 nautical miles per hour (or 3 knots, if we feel nautical). We'll arrive at Deer Island two hours after we leave Bedford.

What if we want to go to Muggelspell Island, but Deer Island is in the way?

Just like with a lot of other things in life, the route is simple if we take it one step at a time. We'll start by drawing a course from Bedford to the point at the south end of Deer Island. Then, just like we did before, we'll copy an imaginary line through the nearest compass rose to find our compass heading. We'll write it down. With our dividers or scrap of paper, we can figure out the distance. "Hey," you say, "one simple course . . . I can remember that."

But we're not talking about one course. One course, or, more properly, one leg of the course, only got us to the south point of Deer Island. With our ruler we can draw a second course from Deer Island to Muggelspell Island. We'll go through the steps we've already mastered, and now we have a two-legged course that will lead us from Bedford right to our camping spot.

"Why do we have to bother," you ask, "with all those numbers and lines and rules? All we're doing is messing up the nice chart I spent a few bucks on, and besides, I can see Deer Island. It's right over there. And I can see Muggelspell just beyond it."

You're absolutely right—if (and only if) you plan on paddling in a small bay in good weather with excellent visibility. What we're doing now is playing scales against the day we get to play a whole song.

I played a trick on you. Take another look at the course from Deer Island to Muggelspell, right in the channel between Deer and Eizus. That's right, it shows the green of the intertidal

Laying out a course is not complicated. A course, as far as we're concerned, is always a straight line. Using a ruler or other straightedge, draw a line from where we'll start in Bedford to the point off the bay on Deer Island. I used red on this map, but I usually just use a regular pencil. With one of our measuring tools (parallel rules, rolling ruler, or protractor and string), measure the compass heading for that course. If you're using a conventional compass, all you need is the magnetic heading (the inside circle on the compass rose, right off Eizus Island), or if you use a GPS/electronic compass, you can use either the magnetic or true heading. I wrote down both. Measure the length of the course you drew. You can use dividers; you can hold the string from the protractor tautly along the course with your fingers, pinching the string at each end of the drawn line; or you can place the straight edge of a piece of paper along the course and make a little tick on your paper at each end of the course. All of these methods work. You may place this measurement against the mileage scale you'll find on charts (I didn't draw one here) and read the distance off the scale. You could, and this is easier, place your measurement against the north-south edges of your chart. Each minute (minutes are shown as 22', degrees as 37°) is 1 nautical mile. Now you know the direction you want to go, the compass heading, and the distance you will cover. If you need to go around a corner or bend, just draw a second straight line and repeat this process.

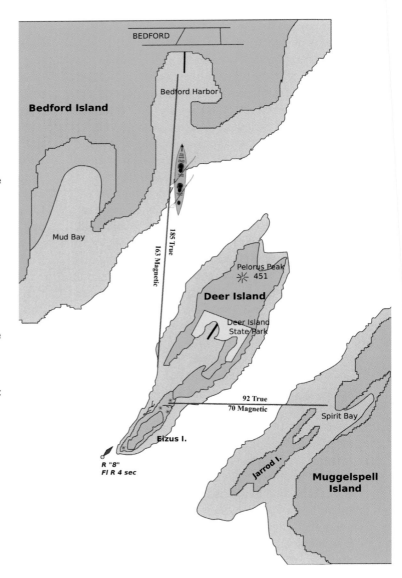

zone that uncovers at part of the tidal cycle. We'll have to check tide tables to make sure we can cross there. Otherwise, it's around the south end of Eizus.

Now that you've laid out a simple course, does it mean you know all there is to know about piloting and navigation? Only if you've just learned how to open up the wrapping on a bandage and you think you're ready to perform brain surgery. The art of finding your way in the liquid world is one in which there is no final examination, no diploma on the wall certifying that you know all there is to know about it. It's a constant aggregation of little skills. Later in this book you'll get a few hints on how to find your way across currents, through winds, and amid fog and darkness.

Use Your Senses

We were paddling home late in the afternoon one day when the sea draped us in a low haze, and within seconds I was totally turned around. My paddling partner canted his head back, took a deep breath, and altered course 15 degrees to starboard. "Beach is right over there," he said, pointing into the haze.

"How do you know?"

"Open your nose. We just came downwind from the pulp mill."

You'll learn, in time, to trust your senses. Shallow water feels different from deep. You'll hear, and you'll see, more than you realize. You'll feel the wind, and—just as important—you'll feel the lack of wind. You'll have confidence that you can read your compass and paddle in a straight line.

To move confidently on the water, you have to know only a few things: where you started from, where you're going, the direction in which you have to go, and your speed.

Speed

If you know how fast you're going, you'll know how long it takes to get where you're going.

You could, if you were so inclined, install a hot, state-of-the-art speedometer on your kayak. At kayak speed, though, sightseeing and gunkholing along as we do, that hunk of battery-eating electronics is close to useless. All you really need is your chart and a watch. Find two marks that are visible and an easily measurable distance apart. There are measured miles and measured half-miles near many ports, but you can use any distance that can be transformed into a percentage of a nautical mile. To make our numbers easy, let's assume that you locate two buoys not in a direct current that are precisely a half-mile apart. If you want to do this on a lake in town, use your car and measure out the distance between a set of streets. Paddle on down beyond one mark and then come back in a straight line from one of your chosen marks to the other. As you pass the first, note the time to the second. Mark the time you finish the run.

For the sake of convenience, let's assume you took exactly ten minutes to cover that half-mile. (If you took three minutes, trade in your cruising kayak and try out for the US Olympic sprint team.) Ten minutes is 0.1666 hour. We figure speed as:

$$\text{Speed (knots)} = \frac{\text{Distance (nautical miles)}}{\text{Elapsed time (hours)}}$$

$$\text{Speed (knots)} = \frac{0.5}{0.1666}$$

$$\text{Speed (knots)} = 3$$

Sure enough, our speed is 3 knots, or 3 nautical miles per hour. That's two ways of saying the same thing, and knots is a bit shorter. Now paddle back the other way. The odds are your time will be a bit different, depending on the wind and currents. Add your camping gear, and you might go even more slowly. Change your paddle, and you could pick up a little speed. But if you make several readings, you'll come up with a fair approximation of your speed. You'll find that experienced paddlers will return to time themselves under different conditions, with different equipment, or even just to keep an eye on their technique.

There is no right speed. That's one of the flat-out absolute rules. You cannot go too slow, nor do you get points for going faster. All you're doing is putting together a very low-tech speedometer for your boat.

Incidentally, 3 knots is not far off an average cruising speed for many paddlers.

Nautical Mile

"How come your mile is different than mine?" you ask.

Good question, as my old teacher used to say many times a day.

Your mile, the landsman's mile, is the distance covered by a Roman legionnaire stepping off 1,000 paces. That happens to be 5,280 feet.

Get out your pocketknife and let's cut the world in half right at the equator. That newly cut surface looks like a circle, so let's stretch the outer ring of a compass rose on it. (The world really isn't a perfect circle, with its bumps, ridges, and hollows, but we'll pretend it is. Scientists and mathematicians are pretty good at this kind of pretending.) This gives us 360 equal segments about the circumference of our world. Unfortunately for most measurements, each of these covers a fair length of world. You know that we can divide a foot into inches for convenience, so let's do the same to each of our 360 segments. Each degree in math-speak can be divided into 60 minutes, just like an hour. If we measure each of your newly divided minutes, we find that they are 1,852 meters (or 6,076.16 feet). And that's how we came up with the length of a nautical mile.

This makes measuring distance on a nautical chart much simpler. The north-south lines of *longitude* (the ones on the left- and right-hand sides of nautical charts) are divided into degrees and minutes, so you have a constant scale within easy reach. Each of these numbers shows where a line of latitude (the east-west line) crosses the line of longitude (the north-south line). All lines of longitude, from pole to pole, are the same length.

The top and bottom edges of your chart (lines of *latitude*) are also marked in degrees and minutes, but these become more squished together as you move from the equator to the poles.

Imagine the top half of our planet as a wedding cake. You could be more formal and call it the northern hemisphere, but it still looks like a wedding cake. If you measure from any point on the bottom rim of the cake to the peak of the cake, the distance will be the same as that measured from any other point on the bottom outside rim to the peak. Go ahead and slice a piece of cake. Look at the piece you just cut. On the lowest level of the cake, the piece may be 6 inches wide. On the second tier the piece may be 4 inches wide, on the third tier, 2 inches, and at the very top, just a sliver.

Let's measure your cake slice further. With a protractor (or a compass, because the compass also divides a circle into 360 degrees), you'll see that the pieces of cake from each layer all cover the same number of degrees of arc. But of course, they are not the same physical size. The piece from the bottom layer is the biggest. Another way of saying this is that 1 degree of arc at the equator covers more territory than 1 degree of arc at Eugene, Oregon, and far more than 1 degree of arc just a few feet from the North Pole.

Now, back to the longitude scale on your chart. Those degrees and minutes on the top and bottom of your chart work just like the cake—they will differ in size depending on how far you stand from the bottom edge of the cake, or the equator.

So are these measurements useful? You need some more information before you can answer that.

There are 360 degrees in the circle of our planet, and we can draw 360 lines—one for each degree—down from the North Pole to the equator. It takes twenty-four hours for the Earth to make one complete rotation, so it takes the Earth one hour to rotate 15 degrees.

A long time ago, the English arbitrarily decided that the prime meridian (the line from the North Pole to the equator, which was on the 0-degree mark) went smack through the Royal Observatory in Greenwich, not far from London. The French thought it should run through what is now the Green Line in Paris, but the English were seafaring and developed charts while the French had a great army and developed maps. Sailors who needed charts went with the English.

Now, set your clock to the exact same time as at the Royal Observatory. The sun should be directly overhead at noon there. But you're not in England. The sun is directly over your head when your watch, still on Greenwich Mean Time, reads 8:00 p.m. It's taken the Earth eight hours to rotate from the point where the sun is directly overhead in Greenwich to where it is directly over you. We already figured that the Earth rotates 15 degrees each hour. Multiply that eight-hour difference by 15 degrees per hour, and you find that you're standing somewhere on the meridian that is right on the 120-degree mark.

But you still don't know where you are. You could be at the equator or the North Pole and you would still be on this 120-degree mark. As far as you know, you're somewhere on an arc that is 5,400 nautical miles long.

Let's help you pinpoint your location. After dark, get out your angle measurer (sailors use a sextant, if you want to be technical) and measure the angle between the northern horizon and Polaris (the North Star). From where you're standing, it's 48 degrees.

Take your drawing of the Earth and rotate it until you find the 120-degree meridian line.

Then go north until you come to the latitude line on the 48-degree mark. Those two lines cross a bit east of Seattle, Washington, and that's where you're standing.

All the numbers are no big deal when you look at things this way. And even if you never paddle out of your home bay, you'll know why there are lines of latitude and longitude on your chart—besides having a good tidbit of information to drop at your next party. Latitude and longitude create a handy grid by which you may locate a point on a globe, and therefore provide a convenient way to tell others of a precise location.

Distance and Directions in a Moving World

With your pencil and chart, you've already discovered how to find your way from one place to another. Compass bearings are easy to sketch in place and relatively easy to follow. But it's not always so easy to get where you want to go.

There are two vastly different distances in the water world, and because of this, two vastly different perceptions of speed: over-the-water speed versus over-the-bottom speed.

If we paddle with the current, we add our boat speed to the current speed. If we paddle against the current, we subtract the current speed from our boat speed. And if we forget, or do it backward, we're liable to end up miles from home.

Calculating speed is relatively simple. The next level of difficulty comes as we calculate directions. Let's cross a current as we attempt to reach a particular point on the far shore. Should we paddle directly at our destination? No, because we're going to be swept down-current and away from our goal.

Let's put some numbers on the chart. This channel crossing is just 3 nautical miles wide, and we have to cross it at the peak of a 2-knot current. Our compass course is 90 degrees, or due east, while the channel runs exactly north and south. Our cruising speed is 3 knots, and in calm water it should take an hour to make the crossing. But it won't today. We're swept 2 miles away from where we want to go—2 very long miles—and since we'll be paddling against the current as we work our way back to our original goal, it will take us another two hours of paddling.

Let's sit down for a moment and see if we can figure out an easier course. On our chart, draw a line from our launch to our landing. That's the base course, or the line we really hope to follow. But we will be blasted a couple of miles down-current if we follow it. Instead, measure up-current 2 miles from our proposed landing and make a mark on the chart. Draw a line from our launch to that second

mark. Using the same tools we used in figuring our course in calm water, transfer that new heading over to the compass rose and figure out the new course.

What happens next requires an act of faith as much as paddling skill. Let's you and I launch our boats together, for company, and steer a compass course keeping the lubber line on your compass right on that bearing. We're not interested in looking at the point on the other side of the channel, 2 miles up from our landing, and we're not interested in keeping the bows of our kayaks pointing that way. What we're going to do is crab kind of sideways across the channel in what a river paddler would call a *ferry*. We'll glide along the line between our launch and our planned landing, but our bow and stern won't be parallel to that line. It's also

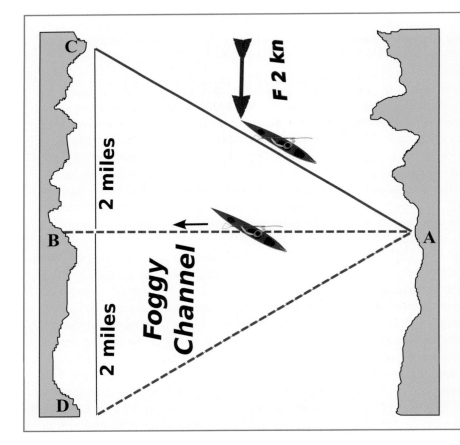

Plotting Your Course in Currents: Paddling the 3 miles across Foggy Channel at our cruising speed of 3 knots sounds simple. It should only take us an hour. That darn 2-knot current flowing down the channel on top of the haze that blurs out our destination on the far shore is going to change that simple paddle. Fortunately, there is an easy solution. If we tried to paddle directly from **A** to **B**, looking only at our compass (remember the haze), during the hour we'd be crossing we'd be swept 2 miles down-channel to **D**. The distance from **A** to **D** is about 3.6 miles, and adding the 2 miles we'd have to paddle from **D** to **B** means a total distance of 5.6 miles. With the current we'd be paddling for around two hours. We could wait for slack water when there would be no tidal current, but that's three hours from now, and it would be getting dark by then.

going to take us a little more than our planned hour to make the crossing. If you measured the line from our launch to that point 2 miles above our landing, it would be close to 3.6 miles long, and at a speed of 3 knots it will take an hour and eighteen minutes to make that distance. That's the distance we're going to make over the water, although we're going to cover just 3 miles over the ground. More importantly, we'll arrive at our original destination.

This is a simple illustration of plotting your course in shifting currents, and it has been simplified even further for your first shot at piloting. In the real world the current will not be constant from one shore to the other, and rarely (if ever) will the distances be so convenient. That's okay; once you realize that high school geometry can be applied to the real world, and you're willing to take your time in applying it, you can find your way anywhere.

Paddling down a Range

One of the basics of kayak piloting is the ability to paddle a reasonably straight line over a distance. Hardly anyone can stare fixedly at a compass and keep paddling (at least not without getting queasy), and lining up on a single reference point and paddling toward it does not take into consideration the effects of wind and current. You may be carried far to the side and only realize it when the point that had been due west of you is now due north. The point didn't move, but you were swept down-current and the relative bearing changed.

One of the best ways—one of the oldest, simplest, and most reliable, and that sounds

---

Time to get out the old chart. Draw a line from A to B. We know A to B is 3 miles and should take us one hour. The current would push us 2 miles in one hour. Let's measure 2 miles up-current from B and mark point C. Draw a line from A to C. Using the compass rose, we figure that the course we want to make good, from A to B, is 258 degrees Magnetic. The heading from A to C is 284 degrees Magnetic.

Now comes the trick: We launch at A, and swing our kayaks so that our bows point at 284 degrees Magnetic. We start paddling, and we keep our heading on that same number. Don't worry about reaching point C. We're "ferrying" across the current, or crabbing sort of sideways, and we're heading right across the channel to point B. We're paddling up-current at the same rate as we're being pushed down-channel by the current, plus we're scooting sideways. As a result we're going to cover more over-the-water distance (the equivalent of the distance from A to D), and the crossing will take us about an hour and twelve minutes.

A note of reality: The current will not flow at the same speed uniformly from one bank to the other, and few (if any) of us can hold a precise compass course while paddling. We start with the science of mathematics, but have to stir in a bit of art and occasionally a guess or two.

like the best—of holding to a particular course over the bottom is *running down a range*. It'll take only a few seconds to learn, requires no fancy equipment, and can be used nearly anywhere. All you do is line up two objects that lie directly on your course. Line up a buoy on the water with a steeple ashore, a smokestack and a fir tree, the edge of an island and a lighthouse. As long as the two objects are lined up, you're on course. If it looks like the nearer of the two objects has moved to the right, what has really happened is that you've drifted a bit to the left. If the nearer object appears to have shifted left, you're to the right of your course.

This works just as well at night, when you can line up two lights. Be a little discriminating, though, when you choose your lights: Headlights from a car, the stern light from a boat, or a star will surely lead you astray.

Bearing Down

Paddling down a range will put you on a line, but it won't give you your location. Kayak touring is mostly preparation, not reaction, and this also holds true with your piloting skills. Using your chart, line up another set of markers that establishes a range that crosses your course. When you look ahead and see your first range marks in line and look to the side and find the second range marks also in line, then you're right where those two lines cross.

A meticulous paddler might want to set up three ranges, to precisely locate a position. Whenever I've tried three lines of position, I've been bouncing around in my kayak, and either I've been off a degree or more in my sighting or the pencil has slipped; in either case the three lines come together in a small triangle rather than at a single point. The good news is that I'm inside that small triangle.

Here's a neat trick that will help you determine your over-the-water speed. As you paddle down your course, look to each side and arbitrarily establish ranges from clearly identifiable landmarks. As you pass each range line, mark it on your chart, along with the elapsed time from your last cross-range line. That will give you an accurate record of time and distance, which translate into your speed.

The Blind Crossing

In the first problem we worked out, we had to paddle across a known current. But what if you don't know the force of the current? Ride along an *azimuth* (compass bearing). With your compass take a bearing on your destination. Just sight over the compass, and see what direction the destination is from your position. Then make a best guess as to the speed of the current, and calculate your kayak's heading based on that guess. Let's assume your destination lies on a bearing of 90 degrees from your launch, and that with a current from the north, you guess you'll have to paddle on a heading of 70 degrees to reach it. Swing your kayak so that the lubber line on your compass is at 70 degrees and start paddling. After ten minutes take another bearing on your destination. If that bearing is still 90 degrees, you're on course. If it is 80 degrees, you're being swept down-current and will have to ferry at a steeper angle (perhaps on a heading of 60 degrees). If the bearing is now 110 degrees, you've overestimated the current and should reduce your heading to 80 degrees.

To complicate things, let's assume it's a foggy morning and you can't see your destination. On your chart, lay out your desired course; this will serve as your azimuth. When you start paddling, though, use the reverse azimuth—the reverse of your course—and sight back at your launch site. The reverse of 90 is 270 degrees on a compass. (If your course is less than 180 degrees, add 180 to find the reverse; if your course is greater than 180, subtract 180 from it to find the reverse.) If the bearing back to the launch is 270 degrees, you're on course. If it's more than 270 degrees, you're being swept down-current. If less, you're paddling too much into the current.

Going Wrong Makes It Right

Hey, you've done great. Let's take what you've reasoned out so far and mix it up with a real-world problem. We've been camping for a few days, and on the last night of the trip, we camped on Little Island, just a couple of miles off the mainland. Come morning, we'll hop across this protected channel to where we left the car. As we look across the channel, though, there are no distinguishing landmarks: The few scattered trees all look the same, and the dominant geographic motif is a series of identical dunes marching along as far as you can see in either direction. It's no help that weather conditions have conspired to form a light haze, further obscuring things, and there's a fluky little wind. Oh, yes, you're pretty sure there is a current along the shore, but you don't know how much of one.

The good news is that we have a chart and a compass, and while a few days of paddling through the islands has dimmed our collective memory of the mainland, the chart shows the spur road where our car is waiting. It's behind a dune, and we can't see it from the water.

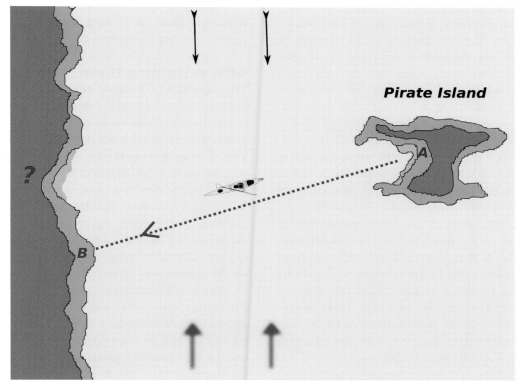

Pirate Island

When Wrong Is Right: We made a simple mistake after paddling off the beach for a weekend exploring Pirate Island. No one looked back to see where we left the car. When we broke camp at A on the island to return, we couldn't see where we had parked. There was a little sea haze to obscure details, and we had a wind from the north that would push us in one direction while a current from the south (fuzzy blue arrows) was shoving us north. The solution was elegant: Instead of paddling for where the car might be (somewhere around the question mark), we paddled off to the south, heading for B. Once landed, we knew we could walk north to find the car.

Now what? If you chart a perfect course to the dune we *think* is in front of the spur road, guess the allowance for the current perfectly (as well as for any windage), and hold that course to the degree, we'll land in front of the car. Scramble a few meters over the sand, and there's the ride home. But what if we're a little off—and with the variables of wind, current, and the ability to hold a course, we probably are. We land, but our car is not there. Which way should we turn? Flip a coin? It comes up heads and we trudge east. After all, there's a 50 percent chance we're right—or wrong. If we landed east of the car, we could trudge for hours through the dunes.

There's an easy solution. Paddle the wrong way. Plot a course deliberately to one side of where you believe the car to be waiting. It won't be the shortest course, and you'll have to take some extra steps, but at least you'll know in which direction your car waits once you land on the beach.

The (Not So) Boundless Sea
It's a fine, fair day, with just enough wind at our backs to push us along and keep us cool, and with the great breast of the tide carrying us toward our destination. We didn't really load up our boats at the same speed, one of us poked along the beach for a few minutes trying for a photo of a fishing eagle, and we don't really paddle at the same rate. One of us wants to gunkhole in and out of the skerries paralleling our course, and the other wants to run right down the compass heading. You can't worry even a little bit, with the beautiful weather and unlimited visibility.

How long is it going to take before we lose track of each other?

Remember, you're paddling on a globe and not a flat surface—despite what your eyes are telling you. With your eyes only about 2 feet above the water, the horizon is only about 1.4 nautical miles from where you're sitting in your kayak. You can barely see the head of a kayaker 2 miles beyond your horizon, with the rest of the paddler hidden behind the curve of the Earth.

A paddle blade may rise 5 feet above the water during a stroke. At 5 feet the horizon is less than 2½ miles away. That 2½ miles, plus the 2 miles from you to the horizon, means you could just see a blade cutting above the edge of the sea at 4½ miles.

Raise a paddle directly above your head, and the top blade will be about 9 feet from the water. From 9 feet the horizon is less than 3½ miles away. That distance, plus the 2 miles to your horizon, means that you could just see the blade held vertically at 5½ nautical miles.

The sea may be boundless, but unlimited visibility comes in a very small circle when you're paddling a kayak.

GPS: A Helping Hand from Space
The first time I crossed these waters it was dark, with just a fragment of a moon tossing little clumps of cream-colored light on the faces of the riffles following the wind from the north. We had a pole mounted on the rear deck and a lantern reeking of kerosene dangling from the pole. We paddled in a cone of our own light, following a compass course down a narrow channel. Somewhere up ahead the sheltering screen of islands to the north broke, and we would slide through the wind and current working their way across our course.

We were heading for a small bay, unlit in those days, more of an indentation in the sandstone walls of the island, with a gravel tongue tucked behind its rocky teeth. We paddled by compass and clock, guessing at our exposure to the push from the north, turning the bow up-current when our estimated speed and our estimated position said we had run from behind the shelter of the islands.

That was then.

Now, when you and I retrace this night crossing, you can key up a screen with the touch of a finger and reach out into space to pluck our position within a few boat lengths along this channel. It's all thanks to a little box, part of the global positioning system. This GPS receiver is easier to use than a microwave oven and costs less than a major trip through a grocery checkout line. Well, make that a very major trip. We're talking under $200 for a basic, battery-powered unit. I paddle with a Magellan SporTrak Pro, a waterproof GPS receiver set up for marine use. I'm not going to go swimming with it (not deliberately), but it's been splashed upon, rained upon, sprayed, and marginally dunked, and it kept right on searching out satellites in the sky. It even displays accurate nautical charts on its small screen.

The concept behind the global positioning system is simple enough. The US government has launched a fleet of satellites that broadcast radio waves. Your GPS receiver listens for those broadcasts, and when it can track at least three satellites, it can locate its position with pinpoint accuracy. If it can see four, it can also tell you your height above sea level.

Why is this so great?

Let's play with it for a moment.

We're camped on one of a host of small islets clumped into a bay on a low coastline. If we worked our way through the channels between the islets and paddled straight offshore, within minutes neither of us would be able to pick out the route back to camp. If we paddled only precise courses and marked each heading and distance down, we could make our way back—but let's face it, we don't paddle that way.

Instead, before we launch, let's ask the GPS to locate our camp and ask it to memorize that location. Then we go paddling, and an hour later, ask the GPS unit where camp is. It will give us a bearing from where we are to camp, tell us how far camp is (in a straight line), and, if we're paddling toward camp at that time, tell us how long at the present speed it will take to

return. Molly (okay, I named it) will also make note of the route we actually paddled, kind of like leaving a trail of breadcrumbs, and is willing to lead us back along it.

That, by itself, is well worth the cost of the unit.

Let's take the next step. All GPS units don't have the same buttons, but this is how I work mine. On our chart I mark out the courses we'll have to paddle from camp to our destination. At every change in course, I make a mark, and, by using the latitude and longitude scales at the top and side of our chart, locate each turn. And I give each point a name.

I put each of those names and locations into the GPS receiver's memory. You can call these locations waypoints, because they are points we'll pass along the way, like street signs. At any time I can ask the GPS to figure out where we are, and in what direction and how far away the next waypoint is. If I take a detour into that little bay over there, the GPS unit won't mind—it'll just chunk along, keeping track of where we are and remembering where we said we wanted to go. If we decide to trim a loop out of the day's paddle, that's all right with it, too. It will just home in on the next waypoint we ask it to find.

When we're paddling along, I can ask the unit to average our speed over the bottom—it doesn't concern itself with our speed through the water—and those numbers will pop up on the screen.

Last, but certainly far from least, it will track our *course made good* (meaning, a composite of our paddle strokes and the drift of the water) rather than limiting itself to merely the direction in which our kayak is heading. We're going to paddle down that same channel I started to tell you about back in the beginning of this chapter. When I'm paddling our Klepper, I have a compass mounted right on the centerline, and the GPS receiver mounted off a bit to the side—far enough away so that when

I turn on the electronics, they don't affect the compass. I ask the GPS to take notice of our course, and it will show the course that we're actually following. When the compass shows us on a heading of 270 degrees, that means we're pointed due west. If the GPS says 270 degrees, we're also moving due west.

"Big deal," you say?

Okay, we move down the channel a little bit. The compass is still rock-solid on 270 degrees, but the GPS says 250 degrees. What happened?

We're still paddling on a heading of due west, but there's a current coming from somewhere off to our right, from the north, and it's pushing us south. Instead of actually moving west, our course made good is a composite of our westerly paddle strokes and the southerly drift of the water mass upon which we're resting.

At this point we have a couple of options: We can ignore the current and be dragged well to the south. Not a good choice. Or we can turn a bit to the north—we'll start by guessing that our compass heading should be 290 degrees—and paddle on that new heading. The GPS doesn't concern itself with which way we're pointed, only which way we're actually moving over the ground. If it says we're making a course of 270 degrees, then we're actually crabbing along on our desired course of due west.

We've paddled enough together, in this kayak with this load, to know we average just a shade under 3 knots. You turn on the GPS receiver and ask it for our speed over the ground. It tells you 3 knots, and all sounds well in the world as we continue on a heading of 270 degrees. An hour later, you check again and it says 1 knot. But we're working just as hard, paddling just as efficiently. We check in another thirty minutes, and the GPS says we're holding a speed of 1 knot, but on a course of 90 degrees. The compass still says we're on a heading of 270 degrees. What happened?

It looks as if we started paddling along this channel at slack tide, making good our average cruising speed of just under 3 knots. The tide, though, is against us. We really didn't tire an hour into the trip, but the current began to build against us. We were still moving at 3 knots through the water, but the body of water was moving in the opposite direction at 2 knots. This gave us a real speed over the ground of 1 knot. As the tidal flow increased, we were actually being carried backward 4 nautical miles for each 3 miles we paddled forward—leaving our speed over the ground 1 nautical mile per hour in the opposite direction we were pointed.

Why do I paddle with a GPS unit? Because it tells me where I am within a relatively small circle; it tells me the direction I want to go to my destination (either a checkpoint along the way, or my final landing); it tells me the direction I'm actually moving rather than the direction in which I am pointing; and it tells me the speed I'm actually making toward that destination. And it will do this despite fog, the fall of dusk, or a horizon curtained with rain.

With a chart, a compass, and tide tables, you and I could figure out each of those factors. They're not hard; they're just common sense applied to a marine environment. The GPS is my warning light, a little alarm that warns me if things in my paddling world are not as I expected.

A GPS receiver is not infallible or indestructible. Batteries will die (my receiver uses four AA batteries, for about twenty hours of use), and the unit will stay alive for about twenty minutes when I'm changing batteries. (This is a common feature that can be found in anything from clock radios to computers.) I could paddle down a narrow fjord where it cannot acquire the satellites it needs for locating our position. I could fail to seat the battery case properly, and water could leak in. Heck, a meteorite could whack it. What I carry is simply one more tool that allows me to paddle with a bit more security.

Is there more to piloting than what we've covered in this chapter? Of course! But these are the basics. In time you'll be able to find your location by the depth of the water and the underwater profile; you'll find your bay by the composition of the bottom materials; and you'll take bearings on distant buoys to triangulate yourself. There are a number of outstanding books on small-boat piloting and navigation, as well as kayak navigation. Consider taking a US Coast Guard Auxiliary small-boat class, or a US Power Squadron class, as part of your kayaking education, and absorb what you can from them. Contact your state's boating law administrator and get a copy of your state's boating education course. Most of these are aimed at powerboaters, but you'll find much to help you in your kayak.

CHAPTER 16

Tides and Currents

Photo courtesy Ocean Kayak

For most of us, the tides and currents sloshing about the edges of the ocean remain something between mystery and magic. Fair enough. Why else would water climb so far up the land only to turn about and rush away? Why does it sometimes come way in upon us, and other times hardly seems to move at all? Why do currents come charging through channels and around headlands in one direction, only to suddenly halt and flow the other way?

Let's clear up most of the mystery by agreeing upon what a few words mean. Tides reflect the vertical movement of water. Currents reflect the horizontal movement of water. The two are closely related, but you and I in our kayaks have to deal with them in different ways. In a lifetime of study, one barely begins to understand the nuances of tides and currents, but in just a little while you can learn more than you'll ever need to know. If you take your kayak out upon salt water, you should have at least a rudimentary understanding of tidal movement, and how you can use tide and current tables in conjunction with your nautical charts.

The moon, with a fair bit of help from the sun, creates our tides. The moon reaches out with its gravitational force and pulls a bulge of the Earth's water toward itself. The sun does the same, but at its distance, isn't as strong. This drags the water in from the sides of the raised bulge and lowers the water levels there.

For most places this means a high tide directly under the moon; low tides 90 degrees of longitude on each side of the high point (it's easy to see, the moon is kissing the horizon); and a second but lower high tide directly on the opposite side from the moon. If the sun, moon, and Earth are in a straight line, at the full moon or new (dark) moon, the high tides will be higher and the low tides lower. If the sun, Earth, and moon form a 90-degree angle (the moon looks like half a circle), the sun's gravitational pull doesn't add its force to the moon's, and the high tides are lower while the low tides are higher.

These tidal bulges don't slosh around the world. The lunar bulge stays right under the moon, and the Earth revolves under it. In most places we have two high tides and two low tides each day, a few minutes over six hours from one to the next. Since the moon revolves around the Earth, the total double tide cycle is about a half-hour longer than a day.

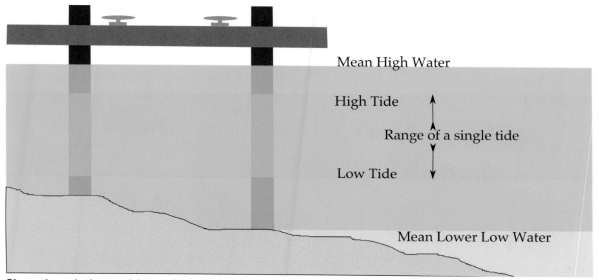

Mean High Water

High Tide

Range of a single tide

Low Tide

Mean Lower Low Water

Since the relative positions of the sun and moon are constantly changing, the range of the tide—from low to high in any cycle—is going to be different. The height of the tide will differ each time the tide rises, and the amount of beach exposed as the tide retreats also changes each time. When you look at a chart you see a band of grungy green surrounding the beige of the land. The line between the green and beige is the shoreline, determined by what cartographers call "mean high water." That's the average of the highest tides. The outer, and usually dotted, line between the green and the blue is called "mean lower low water," and it is the average of the lowest tides. The tide on any given cycle may not reach the highest or the lowest level, but over the year you can expect the water to rise to the highest point and retreat to expose the entire intertidal zone.

The rise and fall of the tide is quite predicable. Tide tables predict the maximum and minimum heights and the times each occurs.

Supplying or draining the water to meet that movement causes currents, the horizontal movement of water.

You should have a few terms at hand. A *rising, or flood, tide* refers to that part of the cycle when the height of the water column is increasing. A *falling, or ebb, tide* refers to that part of the cycle when the height of the water column is decreasing. *Slack tide* is the period of time between the flood and ebb tides, when for a brief moment the water pauses. Scientists and mapmakers invented the 0 mark on the tidal range to use as a benchmark. A *minus tide* occurs when the surface of the water falls lower than this arbitrary level—which is really like 0 degrees Fahrenheit on a thermometer. It

really doesn't mean anything, but it's a handy reference point from which to measure. Expect to hear about spring and neap tides, too, which we'll explain at the end of this chapter.

Yeah, this is astronomy and math and a bit of physics, but what does it have to do with us as paddlers? Lots!

The difference between high and low tides at Charlotte Amalie, St. Thomas, Virgin Islands, is measured in inches. At San Juan, Puerto Rico, it is perhaps a couple of feet. We'll notice it. In Washington's Puget Sound or at Petersburg, Alaska, you'll see a 20-foot difference. Bays, channels, and inlets amplify the range, and the difference between low and high tide can top 40 feet.

Imagine that you're paddling up to a beach. We'll say that it's shallow, with the water only gradually deepening as you work offshore.

Do tides only affect salt water? Nope. Here's an Alaskan river, just a bit upstream of where it flows into the Gulf of Alaska. You have to work your way down through twisting channels at low tide because all the bars and humps are exposed. A few hours later, when the ocean tide is higher and the salt water obstructs the flow of the river water, this will be a deep and wide stream.

At low tide you'd probably have a half-mile of muddy, slippery intertidal zone to slog across before you made it to dry ground. Six hours later, you'd be faced with waves breaking through a logjam at the base of a rocky bluff, with no safe landing. Just supposition? That beach is located just outside of Wrangell, Alaska.

Portage Island in Washington, like Mont St. Michel in France, is a tombolo. *Tombolo* is an Italian word, describing a bar of sand or shingle connecting an island to the mainland. At low tide it's a peninsula, part of the mainland. At high tide, it's an island. If you were caught on one of these beaches as the tide rose from low to high, the water storming over the sand in a

killer froth, you'd be swept off your feet and carried into the depths.

At high tide, Canada's Settler Islands are beautiful—a string of rocky islets, plumed with wind-twisted conifers and featuring dark, rocky sides that stand in stark contrast to the green water, which is great for paddling. Halfway down from high water, currents squirt through the narrow channels, creating huge hydraulic waves and eddy lines that I think stand higher than my head.

We were bobbing off a reef in Canada's British Columbia, looking at fang-like rocks jutting from foam-wracked surf while the tide that day was at its lowest. Five hours later the reef was marked by gentle swells with only a few puckers in the water to show disturbances far below.

The tides may also make you believe in ghosts, as they did the old voyageurs. You paddle across a long set of flats one day, making good time. Another day, you struggle and fight to make the same speed, even though the wind is the same and the current is nearly non-existent. Your kayak displaces a vertical wake as well as a horizontal one, and you may have to fight friction from the bottom while paddling in shallows. You'll use a third more energy maintaining the same speed in water just 1 foot deep than you would in water 10 feet deep.

Does the height of the tide affect us paddlers? I was laying out on a brace rocketing through the Settlers and the question never crossed my mind.

If the world was totally covered to a uniform depth by a single ocean, I suspect the whole question of tide and currents would be a lot simpler. It isn't.

Continents, islands, channels, abyssal depths, and shallows interrupt that implacable progression of the tidal bulge around the world. As a result there are near-constant currents carrying water to or from the maximum tidal heights. Fortunately, these currents are predictable. We can figure out their time, their direction, and their velocity. Current tables are published like tide tables.

Remember that the tide and the current tables are predictions. Weather can skew reality, and you'll be better off observing what is actually happening rather than blindly following what should be happening.

So the tides are important. How can we use them to make our kayaking more enjoyable?

First of all, work *with* the tides rather than against them. Your primary tool is the tide tables produced annually by the National Oceanic and Atmospheric Administration. NOAA publishes time and height predictions of tides, both high and low, for a host of points all around the country. If you're not at one of the tidal stations listed, check the back of the book for height and time corrections at nearby locations. You might have to add or subtract time or adjust the height of the prediction. Before you do that, though, check the cover of the tables to avoid an easily made yet embarrassing mistake—make sure the tables you are reading are for the area you're in. The front cover will tell you. Check your watch, too. Most tables are figured in standard time, which means you have to reset your clock during a daylight savings time cruise.

I can tell by the look on your face that you just caught one of the problems of tide tables. You know the high and the low times, but if you're landing two hours into a flood tide, how high will the tide climb in the next two hours?

The Rule of Twelve

You can figure this out easily. About the time that people started going to sea and had a respectable notion of time, they discovered the rule of twelve. (This rule works for most bodies of water in most times, with Cook Inlet in Alaska and the Bay of Fundy being the notable exceptions. The onset of a rising tide is at times the front of a wave surging landwards over the sand. We call this a "tidal bore," and it's caused as a flood tide is funneled into a long, narrow, and shallow inlet. The walls of water that mark a tide there aren't under our general rule.)

The rule goes like this: The tide will raise one-twelfth of its total rise in the first hour of the flood. It will rise two-twelfths in the second hour, three-twelfths in the third hour, three-twelfths in the fourth hour, two-twelfths in the fifth hour, and the remaining one-twelfth in the sixth hour. Turn that around, and you'll see how much water will ebb away during a falling tide.

Let's apply the rule to a hypothetical easy-to-figure tide. There will be a tidal difference of 6 feet between high and low tide. That makes

Tides dramatically affect our paddling environment. This kayaker is paddling his way through a maze of rockbound channels. If the tide drops just a little bit more, he will be stranded, perhaps a long impassable way from water. Six hours from now, the tide will have risen to cover these rocks and to flood the tiny beaches, allowing the surf to churn itself into an impassable foam. By learning how to predict the tide hour by hour throughout the cycle, you can safely navigate such obstructions.

each twelfth equal to 6 inches. In the first hour after low tide, the water will rise just 6 inches, or ½ foot. In the second hour, the water will rise 1 foot, and in the third hour, it will rise 1½ feet. During the fourth hour, it will rise another 1½ feet. In the fifth hour, the water will rise 1 foot, and in the final, sixth, hour, it will rise ½ foot.

It doesn't take a lot of figuring to realize that not much water will move during those first and sixth hours, and that currents will be at their weakest at that time. More water moves during the second and fifth hours, so expect more currents then. Currents should be at their most brisk during the high water rise of the third and fourth hours.

And that brings us to currents.

Currents: Water in Horizontal Motion

Water isn't spontaneously created. Okay, during some of the Pacific Northwest rainfalls, that point is debatable, but as far as tides and currents go, the water comes from somewhere and goes somewhere else. All this rushing about as the tide rises and falls creates currents. Because of the relatively slow speed at which you and I paddle, we are going to be affected by currents. The more we know of them, the more we can take advantage of them and the less we will do ineffectual battle with their muscle. Current tables tell us more about dashing hither and yon. Current tables are lists that predict current speed at specific times, for specific locations—just like tide tables.

Don't assume which way a current will flow. Direction and velocity depend on the profiles of the shoreline and the bottom, and the water pouring between two islands can be kicked into a totally unexpected direction by a reef. Start by comparing the little current arrows marked on your chart with the maximum ebb and flood noted next to each arrow, and expand that with the numbers from your current tables. Remember that much of this work was done for commercial vessels that must stick to the center of the channels; in our kayaks we can dance along the edge of the shore, poke into bays, sneak up on islands, and paddle in waters where the main current is broken up into eddies and swirls.

Using the Moon's Muscles

Even if the tidal range is just a few feet, the resulting currents will affect your passage. If you're going with the current, you'll catch a free ride. If you're working up against the current, you'll expend your energy and make only a little headway. If you cross a current, you may be swept far away from your intended landing.

Excuse me while I grab your kayak when you attempt to turn back to shore. What I said sounded like a bucketful of work and difficulties, and what you should have been hearing was that the movement of the waters is the best thing since free public transit. Which it is. A hundred or so years back, Native American paddlers could drift the channels all through the inland sea of the Pacific Northwest to get wherever they wanted to go, riding a current for a few hours, lying in the lee of an island, and then catching a connecting current across the sound. The people of the rainy Northwest coast came close to perfecting the art of using the currents to help their travels, and I assume seagoing folks everywhere learned this same art of riding the currents to their destination.

Let's say that we want to paddle 5 miles down a particular channel. We already know that our over-the-water cruising speed is 3 knots, but, at the peak of the ebb tide or the peak of the flood tide, there is a 2-knot current flowing in the channel. If we time our launch so that we're going in the same direction as the current, we can make the trip in just one hour.

If we didn't pay attention to the current and launched when the maximum current was flowing *against* us, it would take us five hours to make good that same distance. We would paddle against the current at our cruising speed of 3 knots, but we would be swept backward by the current at a rate of 2 knots—which means that we would make good speed of just 1 knot over the bottom. With a "real" speed of 1 knot, we would work for five hours to make good that same distance. Whew!

I think I'll use the currents.

What if we have to force our way against a current? We can sneak around much of its force. The current will be strongest in the deepest and straightest part of a channel—a matter of friction. The drag of the bottom and the drag of the shore will slow a current, so don't paddle down the middle of the marine street. Sneak over next to the shore and glide along in the eddies formed by projecting points. An eddy is sort of like a shadow in the bright light of a current; it's a back current flowing into the low-pressure zone left behind an obstacle in the main current flow. Hop from the eddy behind one island to the eddy behind another. If the channel curves and you have an easy crossing, consider paddling the inside of the curve rather than the outside. If the current persists against you, no matter what you try, don't fight it. Beach at the first nice cove and brew up a pot of tea. Read a book, take a photo, or play your flute. Learn to enjoy the moments you snatch out of time.

If you must paddle from one large body of water to another through a narrow and constricted passage, expect turbulent water in that passage as the currents race through. Wait for slack water if you can. What I've done, on waters I know well, is to start into the channel just before slack water, with the last vestiges of the current on my bow, and sprint as far as I can as the waters shift direction. I catch the first few minutes of the beginning tidal flow on my stern. Do not do this without a lot of forethought, study, and plenty of local knowledge.

The force of the sea in a constricted channel can be frightening—and if you're not frightened, you have little grasp of what's happening all around you.

Predicting Current Flows

Current flow is a lot like tidal movement—its strength builds gradually. The current isn't zero at slack time and 3 knots five seconds later, and it doesn't hold at 3 knots for the whole six hours of flow. Just like the tides' rule of twelve, we have a handy little theorem—the rule of three—that can help us determine the strength of a current throughout the tidal cycle. Don't bet your dinner on this, since local conditions can affect flows, but you will be able to deduce a good approximation of the current. (An aside: *Deduce* is a good word. You'll hear old salts talking about "dead reckoning" as they chart their position, and this has nothing to do with their life expectancy. *Dead* is a misspelling of *ded,* as in *deduced.*)

To make the rule of three work for you, first look at your tide tables and the times for the high and low tides for the day you're planning your trip. The high and low tides will be about six hours apart, but for this illustration we'll assume the tidal cycle takes exactly six hours. The maximum predicted current speed is 3 knots. At the start of the tidal cycle—right at high tide or low tide—the water won't be moving and the current speed will be zero. One hour into the tidal cycle, the current flow will be moving at one-third of its predicted maximum speed, or 1 knot. At the second hour of the tidal cycle, the flow will have accelerated to two-thirds of its maximum velocity, or 2 knots. At the end of the third hour of the tidal cycle, the current will have reached three-thirds, or all of its maximum speed—in this case, 3 knots. During the fourth hour of the cycle the current will begin to slow, until at the end of the fourth hour it will be at two-thirds of its maximum speed, which in our case would be 2 knots. It will continue to slow through the fifth hour, until at the end of the hour it will be at one-third of its maximum speed, or 1 knot. During the sixth hour of the cycle it will continue to slow, until at the end of the sixth hour—which is the end of the tidal cycle in our illustration—the current speed will be at zero.

You just divide the maximum current speed by three. At the end of the first and fifth hours of the tidal cycle, the current flow is one-third of the maximum. At the end of the second and fourth hours, it is two-thirds of the maximum flow. At the end of the third hour, it is at its maximum speed.

If you have to paddle against this current, it makes sense to paddle in the early or late part of the tide, when the current is at its slowest. When you have to paddle across this current, you can judge how far down-current you will be carried by the flowing water.

Spring and Neap Tides

When reading of the sea, you're going to run across the terms *spring tide* and *neap tide*. Don't confuse these Old Saxon words with the seasons. "Spring" comes from *springan*, which translates as "to swell." *Spring tides* give you the highest high tides and the lowest lows during any month or lunar cycle. You'll find them when the moon is full or when it is new—in other words, when the moon, Earth, and sun are all in a line and the pull of gravity is along that axis. Because the moon, although smaller, is much closer to the Earth than is the sun, its relative gravitational force is greater—roughly twice that of the sun.

Neap tides also occur twice a month, during the first and third quarters of the moon. When the moon is between the Earth and the sun, the face of the moon aimed at the Earth is in shadow, and the moon appears dark (a new moon). When the moon passes through one-quarter of its orbit around the Earth, half the moon will be illuminated by the sun and half will be in shadow. In the second quarter the moon moves around until it is directly opposite the sun from our viewpoint on the Earth, and it appears as a fully illuminated disk (full moon). In its third quarter it moves three-quarters of the way around its orbit, and again, is half lit and half shadowed. By the fourth quarter it has moved back between the Earth and the sun, and the face we see is in shadow.

During the first and third quarters, the sun and the moon don't work together, and the gravitational pull of the moon can't quite tug up as much ocean water as at other times in the cycle. The high tides aren't quite as high, and the low tides aren't quite as low. The Saxons, who had a fairly good knowledge of the sea, called the tides during this time of the month *neafte*, which translates as "scarcity."

Disappearing Landmarks

Forgetting about the tide is usually just embarrassing and not critical. We temporarily lost a campsite because when we launched, we used a wildly sculpted boulder on the beach as a perfect landmark with which to locate the camp, just back off the beach. Four hours later the currents marked its position with a boil.

Fernando Jose Vasconcelos Soares; licensed by Shutterstock.com

CHAPTER 17

Resources and the Rule of Thirds

We're not the first to have paddled this way. We're gliding in the wake of many generations of paddlers, and the hard-won knowledge of those who have crossed the waters before us is ours for the taking. It is far better to take advantage of their knowledge than to re-create the mistakes from which they've learned.

As they have shown us, there's not a store on every corner. Time didn't stop when we took off our wristwatches; drinking water doesn't always come from a convenient tap. As we venture out on the water in our kayaks we must learn to treasure our reserves of vital resources. These might be time, water, equipment, or food—whatever we need for the successful completion of our task.

A darned good rule of thumb is to divide our paddling task into two equal parts, and divide the resources we bring to the task into three equal parts. Tasks? Parts? Doesn't that sound all too complicated and regimented? Before you give up and wander off, let's make an imaginary trip and see how it works.

We'll pretend that we're launching from the shores of Johnstone Strait, high up on Canada's western coast, and that over the next seven days we plan to paddle around a group of islands and return to our launch site. The high point of our trip will be a stop at a First Peoples village with standing totem poles. We've already contacted the band that owns this village, and they've granted us permission to land. The totem poles are located exactly halfway around the chain of islands, so reaching them is the midpoint of our task.

Now, let's divide our critical components into thirds. Critical components? Well, certain factors are critical to the success and safety of our trip. Food is one. Drinking water is another. Fuel for our stove is yet another. Time, especially for the paddler, is a fourth. We'll start, arbitrarily, with time.

We want to spend a full day at the now-empty village, looking at the totem poles and traditional houses. That leaves us with six paddling days, which we divide into three blocks of two days each.

You and I can chart out a paddling schedule that will bring us to the midpoint of our trip at the end of our second day—the first third of our paddling time. Heck, we know that we paddle at a speed of about 3 knots, and four to five hours is plenty of time to spend swinging a paddle. So we can cover 12 to 15 miles in a day, with plenty of time for sightseeing, photographing, fishing (you already have a Canadian license), and lounging in camp. At the end of the second day we should be landing at the village. A day with a night at each end is what we've budgeted for the village—probably less than we want, but it's what we have.

Under ideal conditions, then, the second third of our time will carry us back to the put-in over two days, and with a night camping. That's well within our abilities.

This allows us to bank two full days against the unexpected. With this great luxury of time in reserve, I'm not going to see you pacing the beach early in the morning, wondering if that rising wind will make the next channel crossing too arduous for us. We won't have to drive ourselves late into darkness on the last day, fearing that any delay will plunge those waiting for us into worry and anxiety. If we have time in the bank, we don't have to paddle out on the edges of the good-sense envelope.

We can also squander some of the precious time by poking into an inlet in search of rumored petroglyphs, or photographing the rich colors of paintbrush or fireweed against the bleached patterns of driftwood, or drifting over the shallows with row upon row of purple sand dollars canted up on their side. With time in our pockets, we can discover a new standard of richness.

The same goes for our food. Keep a reserve. Hoard a few meals deep in the ends of our boat for a wind-bound afternoon. We're planning a seven-day trip, and that means twenty-eight meals. Kayakers can eat a lot, though, so we've actually packed thirty-two meals for this trip. That's twenty meals for the four days of paddling and one at the village, plus eight meals for the two days we might fritter away coming back home. And food for an extra day, just because we might have an unexpected delay.

Some years back, my wife and I had only book knowledge of the Northwest Territories and the Mackenzie River when we paddled out of Great Slave Lake heading north, and the winds that pummeled us every afternoon shocked us. A wind that rolled in with rabbit-tail clouds at 2:30 p.m. each afternoon? A little physics makes it all clear: The sun bakes Canada's wheat-growing plains, and the heated air over those plains rises. Denser, cooler air flows into the plains, and the easiest channels for it to flow along are the river valleys. The solar heating kicks in throughout the morning, and the air movements become noticeable right about the same time each day. That's why upstream winds in the early afternoon are common on rivers—like the Mackenzie—that extend from the ocean into a hot interior. (The opposite phenomenon can be observed while paddling in Chile, where you can feel a mass of cold, dense air pooled over the glaciated interior cascading down the mountain valleys toward the warmer sea. The fierce winds can overturn well-equipped yachts and send kayaks caroming over ripped-apart waves.)

The first afternoon, as we paddled across the wide and shallow Mill Lake, the winds were a surprise. We scurried to shelter on a sandbar that was just attempting to grow into an island. This was mosquito heaven, and we had the tent up in record time as we watched the recently placid surface of the lake churn into some fairly respectable waves. By evening it was calm again, and we put in a few more hours of paddling. We had plenty of time in the bank, so we didn't have to force our way into the wind and the chop. We had a well-planned food reserve, including desserts and special treats, so that we could pamper ourselves without dipping into daily menus. And, most importantly, the knowledge that we had these reserves allowed us to enjoy the trip rather than forcing us to maintain an uncomfortable schedule.

Time, food, and water are the obvious critical factors. Carry more food than your minimum schedule says you'll need. Keep a store of potable water in reserve lest you cannot find the next spring. Keep a little time on the clock because you can get caught on the beach when the wind howls.

Like many aspects of kayaking, the technique is easier than the implementation, but do try to follow it. Divide your tasks in two, and your resources in thirds. The last third is your insurance.

CHAPTER 18
Taking Your Kids Kayaking

Do you remember seeing that little cartoon I have taped up over my desk? You laughed when you saw the dejected horse harnessed backward to a cart, with the driver (facing over the back of the cart) saying: "I think I've found our problem."

That's what kayaking with kids is all about. Putting the horse before the cart. Since we as grown-ups are bigger, stronger, and, we like to think, wiser than kids, we assume that what we want to do is best. Sorry if I'm shaking my head. The happiest kayaking trips we've ever taken were those in which we were able to become the kind of people our kids would like to take kayaking with them.

Let's imagine (it's a real stretch, but this is imagination) that I've been kayaking for a whole bunch of years, a lot of them in the lightly explored regions you'd love to see. It's probably not true that my charts are illustrated with fanciful creatures, and blank areas labeled HERE BE DRAGONS. What you do know (in our imaginary world) is that I've been a professional guide and paddling instructor, and that mutual friends keep telling you how much fun they've had on our trips. Then, out of the blue, I ask: "Wanna go paddling for a couple of weeks up the coast?" Of course, you're going to be treated just like a lot of kids have been as families paddle off on vacation.

Excited?

Well, first of all, we'll leave in the middle of rush-hour traffic on a Friday afternoon. You're probably more tired than grouchy, even though we were up most of last night, rummaging through boxes in the garage for the camping gear we hadn't put away properly the last time we tried this. There's no room in the front seat for you, so you'll be wedged in the back

Olga Lyubkina; licensed by Shutterstock.com

with the pile of bags we didn't get packed right. We put food in some of them, so don't squash anything. Sorry that we didn't leave you enough room to stretch out, even though we'll be driving all night, and no matter what you say, we're going to tell you to be quiet and we'll get there as soon as we can. Oh, yeah—we also haven't explained to you where we're going, but we have made it clear that you can't take any of your favorite things. And we're going to complain bitterly if you say you have to go to the bathroom. "Hold it," I think, will be the operative words.

Larger people—grown-ups—can paddle all day with pleasure. Smaller people—kids—need a place to play, a place to rest, snacks, and frequent breaks to shake their sillies out. Which only goes to prove that smaller is smarter.

We jounce down the rough road to the launch site just after dawn on Saturday, but you can't see the water. A bag fell over on you. We quickly carry our kayak to the beach and begin to shuttle a mountain of gear from the car to the boat. That's right, singular: *boat.* It's a big touring kayak with two cockpits and a large center hatch. That's not necessarily good, because we're dropping bags into the center as we hurry to make the tide. You're left with a dwarfish pocket, far too small to stretch out your legs and with no room whatsoever to play. As we push off we advise you: "Don't move—this kayak is tippy!"

We missed the tide, so the two paddlers are tired and irritated. They're tired, you're bored. We land just after the light has gone so we can't find firewood right away, and, once we do, we manage to burn the dinner since we're more involved with putting up the tent than cooking. Do we ignore you? Nope. Almost constantly we're saying, "Sit down and stay put—you could get lost out here!" Or, our second favorite: "Don't get dirty, and for God's sake, don't go down to the water and get wet!"

Just think; you've got another twelve days of this to look forward to.

Are we having fun yet? No? Well, now that you've begun a kayaking trip from a child's perspective, maybe you've learned a lesson: Kids are willing to have fun and ready to go adventuring, as long as we adults don't work too hard to mess it up.

No wonder some kids give up on camping and want to go to the arcade and play video games instead.

How to Make Your Trip Fun for All Ages

Do you really want to have a fun trip? Start with (a drum roll here, please) the basics. Where do you want to go, when do you want to go, with whom do you want to go, and why do you want to go? A lot of adults don't really ask themselves and the group these kinds of questions before they take a trip, and they wonder why they're not having wonderful experiences. If part of your family wants to voyage through high-latitude wilderness—say, into iceberg-dotted LeConte Bay on Alaska's Panhandle, or along the rocky Maine coast—and others want to loll on tropical beaches, languidly drifting from spa to resort, you may have some problems. Unless you can come to an agreement, you're going to have disappointment. The kids have to take part in this decision-making process. You can make them go, but you can't force them to enjoy themselves, or to let you enjoy yourself. That's a group effort.

If your family has never taken a kayaking vacation, don't grab your seven-year-old and tell him camping is more fun than a week in Disney World. You will lose credibility the first time it rains. Sell your children on the fun. Sell them on the adventure.

It's hard to sell them on history. Don't tell 'em about the Gold Rush. Go pan gold. Don't stress the economic necessity of the westward fishing industry. Grab a hook and a line. Don't read a book about voyageurs eating their moccasins before pressing on to a spring wilderness. Instead, help them cook up a batch of spaghetti and wonder if this tastes like moccasins.

Make it live.

Children do not live in the abstract. Tell them you're retracing one of the fur trade routes, and you'll be answered with a yawn.

Preteens, with experience and a bit of training, are perfectly capable of paddling their own kayaks. It's up to you to make sure the water is within their capabilities.

Make it live for them, make them live in the story, and you'll have an excited crew.

We planned to paddle down Canada's Dease River, across little blobs of lakes and along thin trickles of rivers that were well suited to the long sleekness of a cruising kayak. During the wet evenings of the previous winter, we had pored over books and journals, seeking the stories of the explorers and fur traders who had mapped this river. We were looking for, and found, the site of a Hudson's Bay Company trading post at the farthest stretch of the company's reach. It lay on a remote point of Dease Lake where the company had dug in its fingers for only one winter and then had let it slip back into obscurity.

Could we sell that knowledge to a nine-year-old? Not likely. What we did was beach our fiberglass boats on the shore where the traders' birch-bark canoes would have beached

Photos courtesy of Eric Stuhaug

Give your preteen a turn at the cookstove. Here, at a water trails campground, a kid is building mac-n-cheese.

If cocoa is the drink of choice, let one of the kids boil up the water to make it—even if you have to fire up the stove so they may cook.

and hunted through the scrub for depressions where their cabin would have stood. We found it! We camped where the post had been, made moccasins as traders long ago had done before abandoning their post (okay, ours were from a Tandy kit), sang old voyageur songs, and cooked our version of the last meal the traders had cooked here. The traders had boiled the lacings from their snowshoes for their last meal before setting off downriver. We sat around the fire in our homemade moccasins and made faces, pretending the long strands of pasta were boiled rawhide.

Childish? Sure. But that's the point. Bring your trip into the environment and experience of the children. Find a real person from history and follow that person's steps. Make appropriate costumes, reinvent meals, learn the songs. Make it a game.

Learn a coyote call, and see if you can have a coyote answer you. Look for fossils. We made a game of finding old log cabins and seeing who could find the most ways in which the pioneers joined the logs at the corners (we've found more than twenty). Is it important to do this in order to learn to paddle? No. But if you can invent games that include children in the party, you'll find your days in the kayak are much more pleasurable.

Paddling along the Alaskan coast on another trip, we didn't discover gold. We did mine garnets out of a clay bank. Gems? Whose eyes are you looking through? We discovered gems. Someone else may not have valued them as highly as we did.

How old should a child be before you start off on a kayak voyage? Hey, you might as well ask how long is a ball of string? You have to narrow down your question before you can expect an answer.

Some of our friends resumed boat camping when their son was less than a year old. He loves it. They've camped with an infant, a toddler, and now with a child. They would be

How old should a child be before a kayak voyage? Old enough to have fun! And old enough to have parents that set a trip within the abilities of a child. You might be limited to a half-hour paddle across a pond, but that can be thrilling to a child.

the first to warn that while it has been fun, it's also been a challenging journey. Both of the adults are incredibly good boaters. If they were any less, they would have exposed both themselves and their child to danger. They are both meticulous (and probably obsessive) planners. I've sat down with them as they dissected a problem and developed a series of alternative appropriate responses. Fancy talk, that, but what it means is that they figure out the problems they might face and plan—heck, they practice—ways of dealing with each of these problems.

It can be done, with grace and elegance. What do you do with a diaper bucket? What works to keep an infant cool—or warm? How do you keep appropriate food from spoiling? Solve the problems you think you might face before you paddle.

For me—or, more appropriately, for all of us, because these have to be communal decisions—kayak camping hinges on the daytime diaper bucket. Logistically, the bucket is a pain. A child who still requires diapers in the daytime is a demanding passenger. Once they don't need daytime diapers anymore (usually around the age of two or three), that's when you cease to be the totality of that child's world, and you can join him or her in discovering the universe. Children at that age are still small enough so that a kayak can be both a playpen and a high chair. They're old enough to join you on easy "hikes" above the beach in search of petroglyphs, old cabins, and camera viewpoints. You can cover vast amounts of beach within a few steps.

Even without diapers, toddlers may create problems. It is difficult to find comfortable PFDs for them. Kids will fuss and fidget, and you'll be tempted to strip those bulky PFDs off them so they can play. Don't.

Kids and PFDs

Do you want to teach a child to wear a PFD? No problem. Wear one anytime you're in a boat—hot or not—and use this as an unspoken illustration of what to do. Kids will emulate you. If you wear a PFD every time you're in a boat, your children will assume that this is the way of the world, and they will don theirs. If you live in a "Do as I say, not as I do" world, in which you demand standards of your children that you don't in yourself—well, you're going to be worn down by a long trail of bickering. There are some great safety products available for kids, including equipment made by Stohlquist, Kokatat, MTI, Extrasport, NRS, and Stearns.

Photo courtesy Bending Branches

Put a gaggle of kids on a sit-on-top in suitable water, equip them with a little knowledge and good PFDs, and watch over them without being seen; that's a recipe for a major expedition to the ends of the Earth (or at least the other side of the pond).

Don't think you can get by with a PFD that your kid will grow into. A couple of years ago, in Connecticut, we ran a very simple demonstration. We coached three little girls with long blonde hair and put them all in adult PFDs. All three had been carefully (and secretly) coached to grasp the bottom edge of their PFDs, and all three bobbed around in the pool. All the parents and grandparents in the audience patted themselves on the back for having the right number of life jackets on their boats. Then, at a secret signal, the three girls released the bottom edges of the PFDs—and all three of them dropped until their arms caught on the lower edge of the armholes, and all you could see of them was their blonde hair floating on the surface. You wouldn't believe the rush on kids' PFDs that followed.

Here's the parental rule: Help your child into a PFD. When they are comfortable, lift up on the shoulder straps. If it slips so that their nose whacks the zipper during this test, it will do the same in the water.

Second rule? A PFD that doesn't fit can't be altered with scissors or a needle and thread. If it can't be adjusted with its own straps to fit properly, part company with it.

PFDs have to be beyond the essential. You don't have to nudge a paddling partner and ask: "Did you remember to bring your heart?" Your PFD falls in the same category.

Clothing and Gear

Loud noises are great. Loud noises with a purpose are even better. Every child and adult in your party should carry a whistle—the louder the better. Put one on a lanyard around your neck and one around each child's neck as well. The human voice can fade away in the bush or on the water, but a full-lung blast on a good whistle can be heard for a mile or more. Listen to the awe-inspiring blast from a Storm or a Fox 40, both of which are loud even when wet, and use them as the criteria for the whistles you'll carry.

Make coaching into a game and convert noise into communication. Kids shriek when they're having fun, and that's cool. Teach everyone that when they see a bear, to yell "Bear!," and the same holds true for any other animal. There are cougars in the woods, and wolves. We might think deer and raccoon are cute, but they can be dangerous. So can elk and moose. Kids can call for help without being terrified.

Kids are not small adults. Parents sometimes forget that. Kayaking can be hot, can be cold, can be spray in your face or the sun beating down on you. Children have neither the body mass nor the acquired stoicism to cope with weather that's not too far outside of their comfort range. Yes, you'll see a child demanding to frolic in an October surf, or wearing a down vest in July, but you'll also see a child who is almost instantly transformed from comfortable to miserable.

Let your kids enjoy the dressing up of kayaking. We can start from the top. Like you, a child needs a hat. A hat will protect their face, their ears, and their necks from sunburn and from rain. Most kids, if you give them a voice in the selection, will wear a favorite hat until it's a ragged ruin. Think a floppy fisherman's felt cruiser, a boonie hat, a Seattle Sombrero, or a Tilley hat. Don't think somber. Let the kids find the wildest colors in the shop. For them, it is stylin'. For you, it's visibility. Lime green and international orange with strips of reflective tape is way cool. Remember a chin strap.

Trousers and tops—one word only. Layer. You may be in shorts country, or floating among icebergs, but conditions can change quickly. If it is hot enough for shorts, remember that sooner than you expect, it will be chilly enough for long pants. What is true one way is equally true the other. Most children will be in a constant flurry of changing clothes, and that's perfectly all right. Set a few basic rules, such as that every item has to be repacked once doffed, and keep a weather eye cocked. You'll find that most children have no idea of when they will be too cold or too hot, and your counsel will be appreciated, even if they don't admit to it.

Foul-weather gear should be readily at hand. And I use the term *foul weather* rather than *rain* deliberately. Foul weather includes rain, but also means wind and spray. Look for a stout jacket that works as an outer layer of personal armor. It has to allow for freedom of movement (even over layers of clothing), it has to ward off the bite of the wind, and it has to protect vital core heat from the robbing fingers of spray and rain. Don't settle for a thin, plastic garment, because your child will soon outgrow it, and because you'll never paddle under conditions where your child will need the extra comfort. Kokatat, NRS, and Patagonia (among others) make excellent paddling clothing for children and adults. Even if the price is outside your recreation budget, you should be paddling with others, and odds are that at least one of your companions knows where to buy used gear at an affordable price.

Don't forget young eyes. Shield them with sunglasses, and shield the sunglasses with retainers. Might not hurt to pack a spare pair away.

I believe in bright, fluorescent colors and am not overly concerned with color-coordinating. Why? No matter how firm the rule, some article of clothing will be dropped and forgotten. Camouflage patterns or drab colors blend into the background and may be overlooked. Although we might rather not think about it, bright clothing is also easier to spot if someone wanders off from camp and gets a bit dislocated.

Footwear for kids? Go poke a stick in a wasp nest and you'll stir up less controversy. Generally, what works for adults also works for children, but children sometimes have an absolute sense of style. If you can, go along with their desires—they go along with yours. Inexpensive sneakers work, but they will get wet and they will stay wet. Some folks prefer Alaska oxfords—stout rubber boots with laces to snug them tight. Still others swear by river sandals—Teva, Merrell, Keen, Timberland, and Chaco are all well known, and there are many others—worn with or without socks. I like the sandals-and-no-socks approach for play near the water, with a pair of warm and dry socks all set to put on when the child is off the water for the day. If you'll be hiking up off the water, rely on lace-up boots with ankle and foot support and a sole that blocks the sharp-y things you'll find on the ground. Since I've equally supported sneakers, boots, and even wet-suit booties in the past, I suspect that I may well switch my footwear preference at some time in the future.

The BOX

There are two other absolute essentials in kayaking with kids. These are just as important for adults, but we sometimes forget to offer children the same considerations we expect for ourselves. The first is their box. That's BOX, and it is personal, private, and absolute. They can bring anything on the trip with them, as long as it fits in the box. An action figure, a battered toy car, a set of tiny dishes—whatever eases the transition from a secure and well-ordered home into the confusing, stimulating, and surprising world of the kayak is perfectly fine. You might have ideas on what's proper, and in that case you can put what you need in your box. If your child wants to take a tattered stuffed bear along to keep away the night creatures, that's his or her right.

Electronic toys, including games, won't survive well in a kayaking environment. Plus, they'll eat batteries. If you start well ahead of time, your child can be led to understand this. If you spring it upon them at the last minute you'll have words.

Heck, you don't even need special toys. The bilge pump you should carry along anyway makes a perfectly great blunderbuss to fight off pirates. In a year or so he might even learn that this same pump can trigger a water fight between boats.

THE Box

The second absolute is THE box. THE box is slated for opening at predetermined times. Those times are not based on how people behave, or on the emotional state of the boxee. When it is time, THE box is opened. Make it the responsibility of the children to know when THE box is to be opened, to bring them into the drama and excitement of the opening.

THE box was born during a quiet-water trip in northern Canada, when our paddling companions placed a large wrapped and taped cardboard box in their boat with the smug announcement that it would be opened on Tuesday evening—two full days away. Despite cajoling, threats, and some outright begging, not a hint was given for two days. Come Tuesday evening, the box was presented with all proper ceremony and carefully unwrapped, and there, packed in dry ice and insulated with wads of newsprint, was a selection of Popsicles.

Why this effort? Because we all deserve treats. Never, ever say that we can't open the box because someone hasn't been good, or someone hasn't helped gather firewood, or even that someone hasn't cleaned a plate. So what? The box and its supply of treats come from a universe beyond our failings or successes, and we simply take pleasure in what is offered.

The Popsicles started THE box, and in subsequent voyages we've found fudge, glow-in-the-dark Frisbees, and even the fabric dome and instructions for a do-it-yourself sauna.

Sharing the Fun

Think back to that imaginary trip when we crammed you in the center hole of our big cruising kayak and made you sit by the hour. What was the worst part of it? I'll wager the most frustrating aspect was the knowledge that you were merely luggage, a spectator while everyone else was a participant. Would your children feel any differently?

A young child, just out of the toddler stage, is not going to be a significant motor on your voyages. That said, they'll only learn by doing.

They need a paddle. What they don't need is an adult paddle. As an adult, you're comfortable with an oval paddle shaft somewhere in the range of 1 by 1⅛ inches to 1⅛ by 1¼ inches thick, and with a length of around 220 centimeters. How would you like a paddle shaft 2½ inches in diameter, on a paddle 300 centimeters long? Your hands would be exhausted just trying to wrap around that big cylinder, and your shoulders would ache from attempting to twirl that log. Not to mention the fact that the blades would be so huge, you couldn't manipulate them in the water.

And you're going to hand that giant piece of equipment to a child and urge him or her to have fun?

A child doesn't need a "good" paddle, but a youngster does need a practical-size paddle. We made our first kid's paddle with the blades

Find a paddle the right length and with a shaft fitting his hands, top it off with a properly fitting **PFD** (and because this was on white water, a helmet), stir in some supportive training, and a ten-year-old can fall in love with paddling. A whitewater slalom course is way more fun than a video game, and he doesn't even have to know that this kind of paddling is a classroom for kayaking skills.

from an inexpensive raft's oars and a shaft from a piece of carefully sanded and varnished doweling. Efficient? Not in the slightest. But the kid could comfortably grasp it and could mimic the paddling actions of the adults. As his paddling skills increased, he acquired better paddles.

We found two ways to encourage his participation. One, when he was of an age to be in a cockpit safely by himself, was to team him with the strongest paddler and let him paddle in the bow of a double. He'd paddle when he felt like it, and he played with his toy trucks curled up in the bottom of the hull when he didn't.

The second method developed in our three-holer cruising boat, as an absolute rule. Two of us paddled and one rested in the center hatch. Whoever was paddling could ask for a switch at any time, or whoever was resting could ask for a switch, and we would make it— at the first available beach. Not at a preset time, not with a "We'll paddle for an hour and make up some time and then you can paddle," and not with a "We just switched—be patient!" Instead, "I want to paddle" or "I want to rest" meant an immediate detour to the beach.

The first couple of trips were a closely linked series of launches and landings. I suspect that the adults were being tested as to the commitment of their promises, but that's not the kind of question I could gracefully ask. Besides, now when I want to rest, the rule is still in effect, and, now in his forties, my son is willing to beach the boat and let me loll amidships.

Children realize there don't have to be "chores" in setting up camp. Chores are work, and most of us will avoid work, or at least be slackers. Make it a cooperative game, or at least a team play, and be willing to switch tasks.

When our son was seven and a week out on a long voyage, he announced that he was tired of collecting firewood while the two adults put up the tent, built the fire, and put on the coffee. He wanted the tent and fire duty.

Make a child the official photographer for your trip. There are a bunch of water-resistant (that's legalese for being able to be in the water but not down 100 meters or so), simple-to-operate digital cameras that won't break your wallet. You can find used ones for what you and three friends would spend for lattes.

Putting up the tent is complicated and far more suitable for the knowledge and experience of an adult mentality than the mindless scurrying about in search of firewood. I don't know if that was his opinion, but it was certainly mine. But we agreed to switch jobs, nevertheless.

The first few times he put up the tent, he certainly took a long time. Not only that, he pointed out to me what kinds of fallen twigs and branches were needed to build and maintain a good cooking fire, and how I had taken the lazy way rather than collecting what was necessary.

Switching tasks can be humbling.

Washing up comes at the end of the meal, and the person who is washing the dishes feels left out of the camaraderie as everyone else lolls back with a full belly and comfortably tired muscles. Everyone gets to take a turn at cleaning up. Don't delegate it to just one person, nor to the kids. Rotate the roles, and let everyone learn to enjoy them.

If you're willing to share the best, be willing to share the rest. We created a rotating roster, with one person (two, in a larger party) responsible for planning, preparing, serving, and cleaning up all the meals in one day. You may have difficulty imagining having to eat a meal concocted by an eight-year-old. But it's an eye-opener to find out they think the same about you. And in my case, the eight-year-old planned some pretty good meals. Here's the dinner menu he prepared and presented, with the only adult help being the buying of the materials (we were within a day of a store).

> Red wine, Tang, or coffee before dinner
>
> Tossed green salad
>
> Macaroni mixed with canned chili
>
> Peas
>
> Rolls and butter
>
> Dessert: Canned chocolate fudge topping heated in a double boiler, served with fondue forks and a selection of marshmallows, orange slices, apple slices, and banana sections
>
> Coffee

Breakfast had been cold cereal with tea, while lunch was pilot crackers with peanut butter washed down with Tang and sweetened with candy bars.

After our son washed up the dinner dishes, he had no kitchen duties until the rest of us in the party had taken our turn behind the stove. The combination of several days off and the (well-deserved) praise for his meals made his tour as chef a fun and positive experience, rather than a tail-dragging chore that it would be better to avoid.

Is it easier for an adult to share these duties? The four most popular words in the English language might be "Let me show you" or perhaps "Let me do that." The most supportive phrase in the English language (and the most difficult for me) consists of the words not spoken as I sit with my mouth shut. We must help when help is requested, and offer support that is absolute and invisible as our children try new things, but we must also painfully and honestly sit back and let them do what they are trying to do.

Kids and Books

We were huddled up under a rain fly, bundled to avoid the bite of an ice-chilled wind, the evening the dragon attacked and the kids had to flee for their lives.

Well, actually, we were cruising in the Alaska Panhandle, with the end of each day marked by reading aloud a chapter from the book we had brought along. It takes no great skill to read aloud, and while many of us look back with fond memories at being read to, that seems to have been something our parents did for us—we think of ourselves as the readees rather than the readers. We were several families on that trip, with a handful of kids who had never read *The Hobbit* nor had it read to them. The first night, when we ventured into Tolkien's world, the kids thought themselves too sophisticated to listen, so they sat out on the fringes and pretended not to pay attention. During the reading of the second chapter, the kids circled right around the fire and the adults lurked on the fringes—too old in their own minds to listen to a fable, but unwilling to miss a word.

On the one rainy evening of the two-week trip, the kids put up a rain fly and built a fire so we had a place to read. As drizzle finger-tapped at the lean-to fly and waves groaned against glacier ice, we read of Bilbo finding the dragon's hoard and of the dragon soaring unexpectedly around the cliff and lunging at the Hobbit and the dwarves. Just then, a nervous girl nudged a fire log and overturned the coffeepot into the glowing ashes. As the eruption and steam settled away, there wasn't a kid to be seen!

You don't have to be a skilled and evocative reader. You just have to be open enough to enjoy the book and to draw comfort from a small body pressed up against your side as the dragon stalks your heroes. While reading is fun, don't forget to share the entertainment. Pass the book to a child after a while.

Don't take the advice here as gospel. What worked for us may not work for you. These memories are not an assembly kit for joyous expeditions, but they may get you started building your own.

A Final Word

There's a terrible disease running rampant among adults, and one of its side effects is the ability to ruin just about any paddling vacation. I think people catch it at work, or from watching exercise infomercials. It's called "Neffie." Spelled NFE, which is the acronym for Not Far Enough. Most of the adults I know, myself included, want to jump into a kayak and paddle and paddle. And paddle. A kid—and kids are smarter than adults because their brains haven't been worn down by a lifetime of demands to work harder and faster—knows that somewhere between three and five hours is long enough to be in a kayak. Big people want to paddle for ten hours or more, to make some more distance. And even then, it's Not Far Enough.

The kids are right. If you want to make speed, take an airplane. Writer Bob Pirsig said once, "We were making good time. We just weren't going very fast." Every kid knows that a kayak opens up the world because it gives you plenty of time to see that world. It doesn't pass by as a blur outside your window.

If you see a beach, stop. If you see a big rock in the middle of a slow stream, swing into the eddy behind the rock and enjoy the swirls of water and the turbulence along the eddy lines. You'll share more of the world with your child, and that's one of the reasons you went paddling. Your blood pressure will go down and you'll live longer. And maybe you'll get a chance to see how neat little whirlpools are curling out from a rock.

Three to five hours in a kayak? That means maybe 9 to 15 miles. It's enough.

CHAPTER 19

First Aid and the Paddler

Witthyap; licensed by Shutterstock.com

several books, and you're not going to become proficient from a chapter in this one.

Being proficient, as you should be, and having a heads-up about some common kayaking problems aren't the same thing, but can put you on the right track.

Remember how the ball of your hand and the web between your thumb and index finger were tender after you paddled for a bit? The most common minor injury from kayaking is a blistered hand—which, since that's your engine, isn't all that minor. Try paddling after the fact and you'll understand. You'll have pressure on your hand, you'll experience some friction, and a wet paddling environment can soften your skin. What can you do? Prevention is always good advice. If you haven't been paddling much, start by wearing paddling gloves. They look like fingerless cycling or golf gloves and do a good job of protection while providing a nice grip on your paddle. It's also a good idea to apply a chemical such as Tuf-Skin ahead of time to build up an artificial callus. A severe blister may mean you'll have to be towed, and then the blister is both painful and embarrassing.

The sun burns. You'll be out in the full force of it on the water all day. You'll also be doubly exposed by reflected rays from that glowing orb. You can blister, bleed, and inflict serious, long-term, and possibly fatal damage to your skin from overexposure. That includes cancer. Prevention, again, is the best way to go. Wear a floppy-brimmed hat, clothing to block burning rays, sunglasses, and a good waterproof sunblock. You're more likely to find what you need in a dive or surf shop if your kayak shop doesn't carry that item. Remember to coat your hands and ears. Don't believe that once you tan you won't burn. One of the nastiest

You're going to need a special tool for the next few minutes. Fortunately, you most likely have it in your home. Dig out your faithful old phone book (that's the tool) and look up three numbers: your local Red Cross chapter, your county's Office of Emergency Management (or something similar), or the business number for your local fire department. At least one of these will offer a series of first-aid courses in your area. Sign up for the basic class, and follow that up with CPR and every advanced class they offer. Heck, if your fire department accepts volunteers, combine your education with a little public service. First aid is worthy of burns I remember was on an African-American girl who thought she was immune from the hammer of the sun. She won a trip to a doctor but fortunately didn't scar.

You could also develop sore wrists. If you do, don't paddle, and see a doctor if pain persists. You could have a case of inflamed tendons or the start of a repetitive-motion injury. It's my belief that this often happens to worried paddlers who grip the shaft too hard or those who paddle with feathered paddles of more than 80 degrees. Some paddlers will suffer shoulder pain, as often as not caused by paddle blades that are too large.

It's hot, you're working hard, and water is in short supply. That's an invitation to disaster. Drink plenty of liquids. Then drink some more. You should drink before you're thirsty and eat before you're hungry, and this advice applies to paddlers, too. If you're dehydrated or have low blood sugar, you won't make good decisions and may become faint. On a day trip or longer, take note of your urine. If it's dark and pungent, you aren't drinking enough water. Sweets will not provide you with energy. You need complex carbohydrates, and plenty of them. Think about keeping spaghetti or noodles on the menu.

If you find yourself with a severe headache, a likely cause is that you forgot your sunglasses. Wear them when the sun is strong, along with a hat or cap with a deep bill. Eye drops can go a long way toward soothing burning eyes.

If you find yourself with back pain (I mean, deep, I-hate-to-move pain), probably you don't have proper lumbar support. You're also likely slouching as though you're in a chaise lounge. Depending on your stomach, take along an over-the-counter pain reliever to ease the discomfort of overused muscles.

Paddle wisely. Don't go out for a three-week trip at the beginning of the season. You probably can't paddle 50 miles a day. For that matter, you can't drive for ten hours and paddle for ten hours the same day. Lightly stretch

Photo courtesy Ocean Kayak

The most common problems you might run into on the water are sunburn, blisters (on your hands from paddling), and dehydration. Carry and use lots of sunblock, cover up with sun-blocking clothing, wear a hat and sunglasses, either slowly build up the amount of paddling you do or else wear paddling gloves, and drink way, way more water and sports drinks than you think possible.

your muscles before you put them under pressure. The whole idea of kayak cruising is to have fun. Don't punish any part of your body in the process.

Make it a point to know the medical needs of your paddling friends. It could be that your group should carry something like the EpiPen (epinephrine auto injectors) prescribed by medical professionals. Epinephrine injection is used to treat life-threatening allergic reactions caused by insect bites, foods, medications, latex, and other causes. Symptoms of allergic reaction include wheezing, shortness of breath, low blood pressure, hives, itching, swelling, stomach cramps, diarrhea, and loss of bladder control.

Diarrhea is more than an inconvenience if you're out on the water. There's just no real good spot to find relief when you're in a kayak.

Last thought: Remember those phone numbers you looked up? Start calling, and set yourself up with a good first-aid course.

CHAPTER 20

Water, Water Everywhere and Not a Drop to Drink

Traveler; licensed by Shutterstock.com

We float on water. We're surrounded by water. Water splashes on our faces and falls from the sky on us. "With all that water," you reasonably ask, "why is it so hard to get something to drink?" The answer to that is simple, and if you don't know the answer, it can be way uncomfortable.

Most water is salt water, and while salt water has a lot of things going for it, we're not biologically able to drink it. The rest of it is called "fresh," and that's a misnomer if there ever was one. A lot of freshwater is so gooped up with natural chemicals or minerals, it's undrinkable. Some of it is polluted by our

own agricultural or human wastes, road run-offs, or chemical pollution. I suspect we pour a heck of a lot more crap in the water from our lawns and washing our cars than we face from industries, but that's just an opinion. To make it worse, all freshwater is filled with bugs and other nasties.

You don't have to look at water like that. We do have some tools at our disposal to do righteous battle with the creatures lurking in those clear depths.

There are, in an extremely simplified sense, three kinds of bad guys we're liable to run across: protozoan cysts, such as *Cryptosporidium parvum* or *Giardia lamblia;* bacteria such as E. coli or salmonella (and many others); or viruses such as hepatitis A, enterovirus, rotavirus, or norovirus, among a host of others.

Protozoans and bacteria can be filtered out of the water quite effectively. Viruses, which are reportedly kind of rare in North American waters, can scoot right through a filter but can be whacked by a water purifier.

You're looking kind of vague. A water filter pushes raw water through a microfilter, which acts as a very effective sieve and doesn't let protozoa or bacteria through. A water purifier also uses a microfilter, but adds a chemical treatment or sometimes a UV light to eliminate all three of the gangs.

You can get by if you boil your water for at least a minute, but think about how much time and fuel it's going to take to boil the gallon or two of water that each paddler in your group will need every day.

You can irradiate your water with a task-specific UV light. Remember to bring plenty of spare batteries.

You can treat your water with chlorine dioxide tablets, or, less effectively, iodine.

How much water can you drink in a day? Double that for a day in a kayak. The sun and wind will dehydrate you, and your body will perspire to keep you cool. As you dry out you'll lose concentration, you'll be grouchy, and you'll be weaker. Constipation looms, as will cracked lips. If you're drinking enough you'll feel the need to pee every couple of hours or so, and your urine will be light in color and not pungent.

It takes from a quarter to half an hour for chemicals to work their magic, but with cold or murky water, that can stretch out to four hours. Iodine is not effective against *Cryptosporidium,* and is not suitable for pregnant women or people with a thyroid condition.

All the filters and purifiers I've used (a nonscientific survey) required pumping the water. Some were easy to pump, some hard. Some were fast, others were slow. Some have permanent filter cartridges, and force clean water back through the filter to clean it. Others have replaceable filter cartridges, which, although quicker to replace, leave you with more garbage.

If you have the luxury of a base camp, because it takes a little time and space to set up, a gravity-fed system has advantages for a group. Basically, you hang up a big bag of water and let it drain through a microfilter into a clean, sterile container.

Whatever system works for you, consider souping up the unit. You're gonna be pumping water up from some source and feeding that raw water into your system. If you use a pre-filter, even a coarse one, on the thirsty end of your intake tube, you'll vastly extend your filter life. What about those times when you don't have an intake tube strainer, or you dropped it over the side? Or, heaven forbid, accidently squashed it? Try wrapping a clean bandanna around the open end of the intake tube. It won't take away the little nasties, but it will filter out the big globs that will clog your important filter.

If you're treating water with a combination of methods, make sure you do it in the right order. Use your chemicals first, and let it sit for hours. Then filter the water either with a pump or with a gravity feed. If taste is a concern, as the last step, run the water through a carbon filter. A carbon filter might reduce the effectiveness of your chemicals if used before the halogens have worked their magic.

If you think about it, you will have a water source, potentially polluted, and a system for getting rid of the bad guys. You might start with a designated dirty water carrier. That's the folding bucket you use to scoop raw water up out of the source, carefully pouring it into your treatment system. It can help keep the bad guys where they belong and away from your precious treated water (and your stomach).

I've never used a small manual desalinator. You might be headed for an area where there simply isn't a freshwater source. The ones I've heard about produce a little over a gallon of potable water per hour. On the other hand, they cost about the same as your tricked-out kayak.

In an emergency—and just being a little thirsty doesn't constitute an emergency—you might dig a small pit on the beach right where the moist sand and the dry sand meet. Freshwater is lighter than salt, and a layer of freshwater may often be found at the top of the water table. This is not pure water, and you may well pay a miserable price for drinking it.

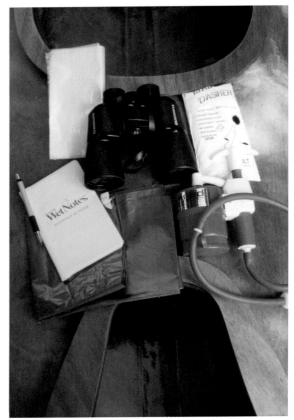

There's a water-filtration unit in my bag of beach tools, this one from **General Ecology**. We pack a notebook and pencil, plastic bags for treasure (and to scoop out raw water for the filter), binoculars, and a rain poncho, but the filter is the first thing in the boat.

CHAPTER 21

Nattily Attired

"I say," cautioned old Henry Thoreau, "beware of all enterprises that require new clothes, and not rather a new wearer of clothes. If you have any enterprise before you, try it in your old clothes."

That was good advice back on the shores of Walden Pond, and it is still good advice when it comes to kayak cruising today. You don't need new clothes to clamber into your kayak and go paddling. Slip into an old pair of pants, a T-shirt, and a pair of flip-flops and you're ready for the water. Oh, you'll probably want a long-billed hat to keep the sun out of your eyes. You'll wear a PFD, but that goes without saying.

That's not going to outfit you for all kinds of paddling, in all kinds of weather. It will get you out on calm water for a balmy afternoon.

Fortunately, on most day trips in mild weather, you won't have to be concerned about all the possibilities. After a few seasons of paddling, you'll have so many opinions on what to wear and bring that you'll be a source of advice to others.

What should you wear in a kayak? Let's get out of the kayak for a minute and go for a long trip. You'll need to select the best single set of clothes you could wear for a one-day cross-country airplane flight, a brisk scramble through one of the city's parks, and then a long afternoon of very high-pressure business meetings. Staring at your closet with baffled eyes?

You've just discovered the principal challenge facing your kayak wardrobe. You have to plan for a variety of paddling environments.

So it's drizzling a little bit, and the sky isn't as blue as you might wish. With a good paddling jacket covering your top and the rest of you warmly sheltered inside your kayak, you can't ask for a better day on the water.

Your lower body is sheltered from the wind and waves. Your upper body is in the full grip of the elements. Paddling is going to keep you warm—sometimes too warm. The sea is fractions of an inch away and can precipitously chill you. Since you're in a damp environment, the air constantly erodes your body temperature.

Live with a simple rule: Enjoy the sunshine, but dress for the water temperature.

The Challenges of Kayak Clothing

I suspect that if you get two kayakers together you'll have three separate opinions of the best kayaking attire. Part of this makes perfect sense. What you might wear on a sunny afternoon in July will be different than your choice while paddling through a thin skin of ice in December. Likewise, your choice of clothing

for a four-week voyage of exploration is going to be different than what you'll choose for a short ride over to a laid-back picnic.

What's a poor paddler to do?

I'm no fashion maven, but being unnecessarily wet or cold more times than I can count, I've learned some of the virtues of being comfy. So here's my totally biased fashion closet.

I wear shorts from the middle of spring through late fall—knee-length to reduce chafing, a light synthetic for quick drying, a mesh liner for the same reason, and with mesh drains in the pockets to let water (but not possessions) out. We used to call them guide shorts; some marketers now call 'em board shorts. You'll find nice ones at NRS, ExOfficio, Patagonia, and Kokatat, among others. If it's a cool day I might switch to long pants made the same way. Zip-off legs that convert pants into shorts work pretty well.

If it's a bit cooler in the mornings or evenings, I might slip a pair of synthetic fleece warm-ups over my shorts. Mid-weight fleece dries quickly and will keep off some wind.

While paddling a sit-on-top, I prefer neoprene shorts. Some are all neoprene, some have a Lycra front; what I choose to wear depends on water temps and the level of exertion.

On cooler days in a touring kayak I might dig through the ski bag for polypro or COOL-MAX bottoms. They are lightweight, quick-drying, and nonbinding.

Above deck I start with a similar synthetic, short-sleeved T-shirt. For a little more protection I'll add either a short-sleeved or a long-sleeved shirt with sun-blocking material. The long sleeves are more for sun protection. The next layer would be a fleece pullover, sometimes over the shirt and sometimes in place of it. Wool feels good but fleece dries better. Top layer if needed is a lightweight paddling jacket. For milder weather I'd pick one with hook-and-loop closures on neoprene cuffs, and a similar closure at the neck. Mine has an adjustable waist step. Paddling generates heat, so I'm as concerned about ventilation as I am about shelter.

I'm a big believer in hats—not only to keep off the rain, but also to shelter tender skin from the sun. Baseball caps leave your ears and neck exposed. Foreign Legion caps with long bills and a skirt hanging down over your ears and neck work well, if that's your style. Be warned: Without a comfortable chin strap, your hat can

Photo courtesy Brian Henry / Ocean River

Wind will pick up spray and chop, and throw the wet back at you. Your spray deck will keep your boat dry, and your paddling jacket will keep you warm and dry.

The Seattle Sombrero (yeah, that's really its name) was designed by Outdoor Research for the paddling environment. It has a broad brim to keep the sun or the rain off your face, ears, and neck, a chin strap to keep it from blowing away, and it's made of Gore-Tex, so that it is at once waterproof and breathable.

be kidnapped by even a mild breeze, and at the worst possible moment.

You might have noticed a few common threads there. Watch for synthetic, quick-drying materials. Layer up with clothes that can trap air close to the skin topped with protection from the wind. Protect yourself from the sun.

When it comes to protection, don't forget your eyes. Good polarized sunglasses will improve your vision. They will also protect delicate eye tissue from damage. A good pair will also help to prevent headaches and painful shoulders. Most of us squint in bright, glaring light. We tense when we tighten, and that turns our shoulders and upper back into a band of pain. Tight muscles in your neck kick off a headache.

It's all too easy to drop your sunglasses, and that splashing noise as they slip overboard is horrid. I use Chums retainers because they fit my glasses, and me. Whatever brand you like is cool, as long as they grip your glasses.

Last, but not least: When the temperature dips into the forties and there's a wind nibbling at me, I like pogies. A pogie is a combination

of bag and palmless mitten that wraps around your paddle shaft. Your hand fits into the wrist opening, and you can grasp the paddle shaft inside the bag—while the nylon or neoprene fabric keeps the cold wind and spray off your bare hands. If I haven't been boating for a while, I might wear a pair of paddling gloves. Think of bicycling or golf gloves, with a spandex back and synthetic leather palms that reduce the possibility of blistering but still allow you a good grip on the paddle. About half of each of your fingers is exposed. Check out NRS, Stohlquist, Sea to Summit, or Kokatat to find ones that will best fit your hands.

When it comes to paddling comfort, I put my foot down . . . into an evolving chain of footwear. Some ideas were better than others.

If you're doing any amount of boating, you're going to want a pair of water shoes. Mine lace up, and give my foot plenty of support. Water will quickly drain out, and the drain holes are small enough so that I don't wedge pieces of gravel between my foot and the insole. I just hate that. Soles offer protection from sharp or pointy things, insulate my foot from hot or cold ground, and stick pretty good so that I don't slip around. With full uppers, not just straps like my sandals, water shoes help keep sunburn off the tops of my feet. Sunburned feet hurt! I'll caution you: This is specialized footwear, and you won't find them in a discount store. Check out kayaking or rafting shops and some of the dedicated outdoor stores with lots of kayaking gear. While other cobblers make equally good shoes, check out Teva's Gnarkosi shoes. I'd use them as a measure against whatever shoe fits you.

And then there are those bad days. If the weather looks to be horrible, if the trek to the put-in is crappy, if we're faced with portages of questionable worth—heck, if the ground is sloppy and slick, I just feel like I want more comfort on my feet. Make that more comfort and more support. I'll strap on a pair of

I must be getting soft as I age, because I prefer the comfort, support, and protection of a good boating shoe such as these **Teva Gnarkosi** to damp sneakers. Kayak water shoes will drain quickly, dry rapidly, and don't have room for those dratted little pebbles that creep between my sandal soles and my feet.

Teva Avator SR neoprene boots when I need an ankle-high (or thereabouts) boot, one with plenty of arch and foot support, adequate drain holes that won't suck debris into the boot, and an opening that can be cinched down to prevent crap from washing into it.

Here's a big thing to remember. Different manufacturers shape their boots and shoes on different lasts. A size 10 shoe from Manufacturer A might be the most comfortable and best fit you've ever had. A similarly purposed size 10 shoe from Manufacturer B may send you to the ground, writhing in pain. They both could be excellent shoes, but they fit your unique foot differently. It's up to you to find a shoe that meets your needs, and, even more importantly, fits your foot.

I started boatin' wearing watersports sandals when a white X tan line over your toes and a similar loop of white around your ankles were the equivalent of a secret lodge handshake. I still like sandals, but now will sometimes wear them with Gore-Tex waterproof (yet breathable) socks. When it's chilly I'll pull on thin fleece socks first.

An old pair of cheap sneakers is okay in a warm season, offering some support and plenty of protection to your soles when scrambling around a beach. Beware not only of sharp things but also of searing your feet on a sunhot stretch of sand. On the downside, soggy sneakers are less than comfortable, and can act like sandpaper on soft, damp skin.

For a while I tried mid-calf rubber gardening boots. (Marine supply stores sell much more expensive and elegant deck boots.) In theory these kept my feet warm and dry—but the theory had a flaw. I would continually step

Need more foot support and protection from a lousy put-in, stony beach, or canyon? I switch over to a bootie like the Teva Avator. They don't come with that green stripe across the toe; I was walking around in the bay, and that's kelp.

into water just a bit deeper than my boots were tall. I'd slosh into my kayak and the full boots would drain back upon me. Sponge time. Rubber boots aren't breathable, and I'd sweat as I warmed while paddling. Odiferous. And last, I don't have small feet. In a high-volume touring kayak this wasn't a challenge, but in a low-decked, low-volume kayak, space is at a premium.

Wetsuit neoprene booties with a semi-rigid sole, a holdover from river-paddling days, are pretty neat, but after a few days my feet wrinkle up, and the booties—well, they need a good deodorant.

Flip-flops are cheap, uncomfortable, offer little support or protection, and come off when you swim. If you walk on the beach they'll collect gravel under your arches and toes.

Last but not least is going barefoot. It can feel good, but it can also lead to scuffed,

scratched, or abraded feet, which do not feel good.

Wetsuits and Dry Suits

I'd like to make a really simplistic generalization: Wetsuits, normally made from something like neoprene, keep you warm but not dry. In fact, they work better while wet. Dry suits, made of a thin, coated fabric, keep you dry but not necessarily warm. Both offer good protection when you're in the water.

There are lots of magic numbers in kayaking, and 100 is one for clothing and thermal protection. If the combined air and water temperature is under 100 degrees, you'll need some level of thermal protection.

Wetsuits, especially in the thinner weights, are a practical safety item with a few drawbacks. One, you have to don your suit ahead of time; I've never met a person who could put

Different shoes for different folks. This kid loading his kayak really preferred rubber gardening boots to any other footwear. He wanted something good for jumping in puddles, chasing crabs, tromping through brush, and, occasionally, boarding his kayak.

one on in the water. Two, they trap your body heat very well, and you'll toast under most conditions. Three, they also can become rank (at least mine can).

Most of the paddlers I hang with, if they feel the need for thermal protection, lean toward thinner-weight "shorty" wetsuits. Think of a form-fitting pair of coveralls with the arms bobbed like a T-shirt and the legs cropped above the knee. They protect your body core. Most will wear a paddling jacket with mostly watertight neoprene cuffs and a closable neck to keep off wind and spray.

Remember that your kayak keeps you in two separate environments. From the waist up you're exposed to the elements; from the waist down you're enclosed in a windproof and waterproof hull. Your body wants to be kept warm above the deck, and kept cool belowdecks.

My personal choice would be for neoprene shorts topped with a short-sleeved jacket or perhaps even a vest. These are easier to put on and take off than a single-piece shorty. I suspect most women would choose shorts and a top, just for convenience.

A full-on dry suit is a marvelous thing. Imagine coveralls made of waterproof materials, with latex gaskets at your wrists and neck, and with latex socks. Add a built-in storm hood. It will have a honking-big zipper with closures to allow you entry, and will have a substantial front "relief" zipper for, well, relief. It will also cost you a grand. If you are going to paddle where you need this level of protection, that's money well spent. I don't think you're going to paddle there in the near future, and it brings up paddling conditions that I'd just as soon avoid.

Something to think about: Some dry suits and some wetsuits are made with drop seats. Women paddlers may appreciate this. There's another gadget that is used by women helicopter pilots as well as women mountaineers. The Freshette feminine urinary director is a palm-sized flexible funnel-like device with a flexible

I hate lifting my arm and having a trickle of water dribble down the ticklish spots onto my torso, so I have a paddling jacket with latex wrist gaskets that are close to watertight. They are a little more difficult to don and have to be treated with 303 UV protectant a few times a year, but I'm willing to pay that price. The gaskets are protected by an overcuff while paddling.

drain tube. It requires minimal undressing for discreet use, and may help you avoid nasty plants, miserable weather, and steep ground. Most male paddlers I know rely on a pee bottle when out on the water. The Freshette gives women the same possibilities.

I want a paddling jacket waist that can be snugged in, to create a dam against water deflected up from my spray deck. It doesn't happen often, and my PFD will usually deflect it, but a dollop of cold water landing on your belly is a brisk reminder that something wasn't fastened properly.

If you're working pretty hard you'll get warm, and when you're in a fleece top and a paddling jacket, that can be very warm. That's why I like a neck that can be opened to vent out the heat.

You want to get rid of excess heat, but you equally don't want spray and rain to flood down your front. That's why having a neck that will securely close can be a comfort.

For nasty conditions (my definition of nasty, not world-class nasty), I choose the semi-dry-suit little brother to that ultimate suit. I have waterproof pants with ankle straps that can be compressed to near-waterproofness. Mine are high-waisted, with an adjustable waistband. I top it off with a Kokatat Gore-Tex TecTour anorak. Mine has gasketed sleeves for waterproofness (I hate having water drip up my sleeves into the ticklish parts), an adjustable splash collar mated with an adjustable storm hood, and a cinchable waistband over a double-tunnel skirt that mates with my spray

deck. The hood and sleeves are striped with reflective tape.

Since you asked, I have a Kokatat TecTour anorak. Other manufacturers make equally good jackets, but like having a choice of shoes, this jacket fits me. When you start looking for technical clothing, browse through such companies as Kokatat, NRS, Stohlquist Water-Ware, or OS Systems for ideas.

I sometimes wear a lighter paddling jacket with neoprene cuffs that fasten with hook-and-loop closures and a neck with the same closures.

Out of merely personal choice I don't use jackets with neck gaskets. Although they are comfortable and waterproof, I can't open them for ventilation. That's my quirk; you might like them. Nor do I have a short-sleeved paddling jacket. Lots of people like them.

If the water is really nasty, I stay on the beach. I'm not in enough of a hurry to go anywhere to have to attire myself in ultimate survival gear.

A hook-and-loop closure over a neoprene cuff makes a pretty darned good barrier against wayward water. They are easier to don and adjust than gaskets. You can also find them on the cuffs of waterproof pants, for the same reason.

CHAPTER 22

Rack 'Em Up

I picked you up this morning on the way to the beach, you and your kayak. I've been to your house a few times, now. You live pretty close to the middle of town. I can find my way there without directions. This isn't about my route-finding skills (heck, I used a cheat sheet with your address), but it is about your ability to choose where you want to paddle.

You look a bit baffled right now, but in a minute it will make sense. If you were fortunate enough to live on a protected cove right on the beach, on a body of water so wonderful and diverse that you could (and would) spend the rest of your life exploring it, and the kayak shop from which you bought your boat would deliver it right to your dock, and your kayak were so well equipped that you'd never have to bring it to town for another gadget or doodad,

then read no further. 'Fess up; you don't live there yet.

The challenge is finding out how to get from where you are to where you want to be.

You want to paddle from this beach straight out to that island just a couple of miles out. It looks like a perfect spot for a quiet picnic. Maybe you want to see the orca pods cavorting in British Columbia's Johnstone Strait. Perhaps you want to seek buried treasure (or at least sunshine) along the sand-rimmed cays of Florida's 10,000 Islands. What about paddling from inn to picturesque inn along the rocky coastline of the Maine Island Trail, believed to be the first designated water trail in the United States?

How are you going to get yourself, your paddle, and your kayak from your garage,

197

Some sets of wheels, such as this Kayak Kaddy, are small enough to fit through a hatch when you arrive at the water. Others you can simply disassemble, a two-minute job, and easily stow away.

where you store everything, to the put-in for the voyage of your dreams?

Car Racks for Carrying Kayaks

You could, if you were so inclined, toss your kayak atop your car, open the windows, and thread a rope through the windows and over the top of the car and the kayak. Loop it around a bunch of times, tie the rope ends together with a granny knot, and off you go. You'd beat up the top of your car, you might get rained upon (and certainly couldn't listen to your CDs), and you'd probably hang a significant bend right about the middle of your boat. Fortunately, there's a better way of transporting your kayak.

One of the first things you should do during the whole process of buying and equipping your kayak is to tear yourself away from the enticing accessory shelves and amble over to the rack department. Brace yourself, because unless you're already into outdoor sports, you're going to be thumped with a severe case of sticker shock. "That much? Just for some little vertical posts, a couple of crosspieces, and a pair of little slings to hold a kayak?"

In a word, yes. It's easy to start by putting a couple of hundred-dollar bills on the counter and then piling on more when you begin adding all the bells and whistles to the rack. Remember, though, that what you're doing is not just buying a conglomeration of aluminum struts; you're also acquiring a carefully engineered system that will support the thousand-dollar (at a minimum, and probably a lot more) kayak that you want to transport, and in so doing, will keep it firmly attached to your vehicle. In any paddling group there will be someone who is all too familiar with the wry and bitter joke of the driver looking out the car window at a kayak in free fall and saying: "Boy, that boat looks a lot like mine."

It happens.

If you aren't fairly knowledgeable about racks already, you're best off sticking to one of the two major brands: Yakima or Thule. After all, they became the dominant players in the cartop transport game for the good reason that they both work well. Let's look more closely at your kayak rack. The towers are those posts that extend more or less vertically from your vehicle. They come in pairs, one for each side of your car. They also come in various heights, depending on the profile of your roof. You mean you didn't notice that all vehicle roofs aren't flat? Some cars (regrettably few these days) have rain gutters that extend

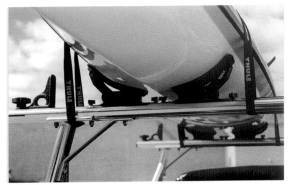

Saddles hold and cushion your kayak, and straps secure it to the rack and to your vehicle.

along both sides of the top above the windows. One style of tower clamps right to these gutters. Another tower style has a broad foot and rests atop the car roof with clamps that extend around and grip the top of the door frame. Still another style clamps to the factory-mounted "luggage racks" atop some vehicles. Beware of these factory rail systems. Many aren't designed for the weight of one or two kayaks, or for the wind load when you're buzzing down the freeway at the speed limit.

The crosspiece, no great surprise, is the horizontal bar that extends from the tower on one side to the tower on the other. The crosspiece actually fits right through the top of the tower and is clamped into place.

The cradle is a metal bracket that supports a fabric or rubber "sling" upon which your kayak rests. The cradle is mounted on the crosspiece. If you want to carry a pair of boats, most crosspieces will hold two side-by-side cradles, and the longest crosspieces—which, as often as not, may protrude well out beyond the sides of your vehicle—could even hold three.

Some of these cradle systems will support your kayak on its side, others flat. There are rollers, rubber pads, paddled skeletal aluminum tubing . . . you get the idea. There are a bunch of different configurations, all designed to hold your particular kayak firmly and safely. With some designs you lift your kayak into place. With others, you can slide your kayak on (often with the aid of extendable bars to keep your kayak and vehicle apart). You'll need two sets of cradles, one for the front end and one for the back end of your cartop rack.

If you wheel around in a pickup, you'll mount one set of towers and crossbar on your roof, but you'll use two elevated "towers" at

Why bother with a cartop carrier and the hassle of finding parking when you live close to the water? Just take your kayak for a stroll with a boat cart.

the rear of your pickup bed, towers as high as the one you mounted on the roof, with the second crossbar and cradles.

I've seen some sports cars, all coupes, with one crossbar over the roof and a pickup-like mount over the rear bumper. I don't think that's an off-the-shelf system, but a good kayak or rack shop might be able to fit one on your vehicle.

Fortunately, you (and I) won't have to figure out the proper tower foot, the proper tower height, and the proper crosspiece length. Both Yakima and Thule have installation guides, and all you have to do is look for your vehicle make and model and you'll find the dimensions you need listed in the book.

As much as I would rather not think about this, go ahead and spring for a set of locks. One set of locks will hold the towers to your car, and another (usually a cable lock) will hold your boat to the rack. I deeply resent having to recommend to you that you need locks, but that's the way of the world.

Generally speaking, and with the help of adapters, you can mix carriers and cradles from either manufacturer atop the roof racks from either. If you already have a roof-rack system—say, for skis or bikes—it makes some sense to stick with the same manufacturer for your kayak supports.

Let the shop set up your rack, fitting it to your vehicle and showing you how to adjust and fasten the towers. Beforehand, you might want to mount eyebolts on your front and rear bumpers, to tie your kayak's bow and stern lines. Some paddlers will loop the bow lines around tow hooks found at the front part (on many makes) of your vehicle's frame. You can also use a towing system's trailer hitch for lashing down your stern line.

Most of us will lash our kayaks in place on the roof rack, with lines around the two crossbars. Those two lines should hold your kayak in its cradles. The bow and stern lines provide security in case of a frayed line around the crossbar, or an inexpertly tied knot. Despite all the claims of absolute boat security and safety, you saw me tie down bow and stern lines on your kayak before you left your driveway.

Would you like to learn a way to dramatically shorten your kayak? All you have to do is leave the stern line flapping free and back your vehicle up. Invariably, you'll back over that free line and crack your kayak right at the rear cradle.

You can get by with a set of gutter clamps bolted to a 2x4, with maybe a little rug for padding. That's the classic homemade canoe rack. And for most canoes, resting upside down on their gunwales, it works pretty well. But kayaks don't have a broad, flat surface on which to rest. If you cinch down the lines holding your kayak to a flat bar—such as a 2x4—you can stress-crack the hull of a fiberglass boat or deform the hull of a plastic boat.

Ropes work perfectly well to lash a boat onto your rack. I'd suggest a soft synthetic, such as Dacron or nylon, just to protect the finish of your boat. Better, though, is the synthetic and low-stretch fabric webbing offered by both Thule and Yakima. Loop the webbing through the slots on both sides of the cradle, and cinch it down snugly through a cam fastener. I suspect that if the rack would hold to the gutters, you could lift your vehicle with those straps, but I'm not about to check.

Loading Your Kayak

Loading a kayak, if you're substantially shorter than your vehicle, can be a struggle. Malone Auto Racks builds a loading system that lowers its cradles to about waist-high beside your vehicle. You place and secure your kayak on the cradles, and then ratchet your kayak to its travel position atop your car. I've never used one.

Another method for loading a kayak was demonstrated to me by an old codger with a pop-top VW camper and a heavy boat that I would have been challenged to load. He did it without even breathing hard. His technique was simplicity itself. He had a 3-inch pipe, about 3 feet longer than his car was tall, with a 3-foot horizontal extension at the top. Think of a tower crane at a construction site, and you'll get the idea. He had a ring with a short rod, which he inserted into the jack opening on the side of his VW. The long pipe fit into the ring and would swivel within it. A second ring clamped to the crosspiece of his rack. He suspended a block and tackle from the end of the extension atop the pipe, and would hook this into a sling within the boat cockpit. He could easily lift the boat with the mechanical advantage of the blocks, and could then swivel the pipe to place his kayak right over the cradle. The parts could be quickly disassembled and fit within the camper (the long pipe on the rack), and off he would go.

If a high lift is a high barrier to moving your kayak, you can pack your kayaks on a specially designed trailer. Your best source of advice, once again, is your kayak shop or a good sports-rack shop.

These methods will get your boat from your home to the launch site. You and a friend can lift your kayak with the T-grips at the bow and stern and easily pack an empty boat down to the water's edge. Kayaks aren't shaped for a balanced load, however. You'll kind of shuffle, and tilt to one side, and if the trek is more than a few dozen meters, you may well want to stop and switch hands.

Boat Carts

Humping a kayak from your vehicle to where you want to launch can be a strain on your back, your legs, and your patience. Unfortunately, there's just no easy way to carry a kayak—empty or loaded—for more than a few steps. Fortunately, you can just let the good times roll by resting your kayak on wheels.

For long carries you might want to investigate one of a half-dozen or so small folding boat carts. Basically, these consist of a pair of wheels, a small frame incorporating a simple cradle, and webbing to lash the kayak to the cradle. Fasten the boat cart just behind the cockpit, pick up the bow T-grip, and take your boat for an easy walk. Narrow, high-pressure tires roll easily, on paved or hard paths, even on or off ferries. Wide, low-pressure tires work great on soft beaches, boggy ground, or in the muck.

Boat carts take terrible abuse, even though you wouldn't think so. Take them apart after each immersion, clean them, wax them, and check their bolts and their webbing. If the cart is not strong, it will fail at the worst possible moment. But then again, that's the reality of many machines.

A boat cart is a tremendous aid in moving your kayak to the water. Wide tires let you roll your boat down muddy trails, across soft beaches, and over rocks and cobbles.

Photo courtesy Ocean Kayak

CHAPTER 23

Let's Go Voyaging

That's an ear-to-ear grin plastered across your face. And rightly so. The last few times we've met here on the beach, you've gotten a pretty good grip on the basic kayak paddle strokes, mastered the essentials of how to get yourself out of trouble, learned how to find your way from place to place, and even given some thought on how to paddle with kids. All that, and you've launched from this beach and paddled in our protected little bay. You (and I) think it's time for a more adventurous trip.

Let's put it all together and take a trip out to the islands. If you want, we'll take it easy. No driving a great distance, no attempt to see who can carry the most, and no sprinting for the buoys. Just an outing on a pleasant day.

What the heck—you can paddle a kayak; I'm going to follow you. You're the leader on this trip. You're not only going to paddle this trip, you're going to be in charge.

This trip, like any other, begins well before we get to the water's edge. We have to have a destination, with the courses and directions from here to there. We should have a couple of alternate landings, just in case of . . . whatever. If we're going to be paddling for more than about three hours, we might want a lunch and relief stop, or we need a heads-up so that we can plan for a lunch we can eat in our kayaks. The route, the destination, the people involved, and the approximate time we're expected home should be listed on a float plan, which is left in the hands of a family member or friend. If we run into trouble (okay, it rarely happens, but . . .), that person can summon help. (Be sure and alert that person when we return home!)

First thing when we arrive at the beach, all of us will assess weather conditions and how we feel. Are we up to the planned trip, or will it be pushing the skills of some of us? Our destination is a plan, not a goal, because all too often we feel obligated to push harder to reach a goal. If we feel tired, sore, or even a little concerned about the environment, we might just peel off to an alternate and closer destination.

We're probably going to want to get off the water early if we're camping in these popular waters, because many campsites fill up quickly.

Great! You thought to provide each kayak with a copy of your route, including all of the alternate campsites and courses, as well as a rendezvous point in the unlikely event of separation.

We usually don't do this as a military formation, but it's a good idea to check the safety gear we should be carrying: a PFD for each paddler (should be worn), an extra paddle for each kayak, a bilge pump (and possibly a scoop bailer), signaling devices (whistle, mirror), a first-aid kit, compass, lots of water, snacks, and the right clothing, plus an extra layer suitable for the conditions. I like to carry a big contractor-grade plastic trash bag in my PFD. It can be a tent, a minimal sleeping bag, or a poncho as needed, and at the end of the trip can be used to collect some of the trash that others have scattered about. I also have sunblock and lip balm in the mesh pocket of my spray deck.

Because I am a cautious sort, I carry along a VHS marine radio. I can contact other boats or the Coast Guard, and I have several different weather radio channels available at the flip of a switch. On some trips we've been known to carry small walkie-talkies for boat-to-boat communication.

Gear for each kayak should include an extra paddle, chemical light sticks, a throw bag (holding about 20 meters of floating rope and a convenient way of throwing one end to another person), a sponge, a flashlight, a pump, a tow line, and a bailing scoop.

Most of us will also eyeball everyone's kayaks as we board. A last check that storage bags are closed and secured, gear is secured to the kayak, spray decks are secured, and hatch covers are in place.

Last, we won't straggle haphazardly off the beach in your wake. We'll push off as a group, or, if so prearranged, in a couple of smaller groups. There is safety (and company) in numbers.

Launching

Starting as we did in a sheltered bay, launching was simple. Paddling isn't always get-in-and-go, however. We could have been on an exposed beach, with waves crashing down on the packed sand. Sure, there are paddlers who feel that you should be able to leap off tall rocks into the foam, and others who demand that you should be able to smash through 6-foot surf on your way to the open water, but I'd just as soon sit in the sun and enjoy the day. Time may come, though, when we don't have an option.

First of all, let's put a few parameters on what constitutes paddling surf. If the surf is less than a couple of feet high and just slides up on sloping sand, your launch is going to be more on the simple side of the equation. Simple is a relative term, however. We're talking about a huge coil of cyclical force rolling across the ocean with more energy than a schoolroom full of second-graders. The smallest wave can chew you up and spit you out. On a rising tide, launching is even simpler. Set your boat down just higher than the dark mark of the incoming water and wiggle into your boat. As the tide climbs, the water will start to work under your boat and soon you'll be afloat. Sand appears to be the neatest surface, but take a little care. Each grain grabs hold of your hull, and it's hard to break loose. The easiest beach has sand the size of pea gravel, with each little pebble acting like a ball bearing.

For that matter, the flatter the beach, the easier it is to break off and go floating. On a steep beach, where the angle between the beach and the water cranks over to the higher-digit side, you'll end up with your bow in the water and your stern high and dry. So you'll be balancing on the sharp ends of your boat with 71 percent of the world's surface tugging at you, and you'll be rocking back and forth—stable you won't be. The steeper the beach, the more of an angle you're going to have to put into the alignment of your boat. You'll be playing a delicate balancing game, though. You want to move straight off the beach, directly into the waves, and you want to be at the best angle to get your bow and stern off the beach at the same time. As with many aspects of the water world, you're going to end up compromising among the three different demands.

Surf

If the surf is from 2 feet to about 5 feet high, you can get off the beach with care and planning. With smaller waves the odds are you'll rise up and over each crest. In that mid-range you're likely to have a wave slosh over you, and if you're not lucky, that could be two or three waves.

If the surf is 6 feet high or more—well, kick back and enjoy the show. Launching your boat isn't worth risking your hide and hair.

How can you determine the height of the surf? Go stand by the waterline. If you can just see over the tops of the waves, the surf would be about 5½ feet high if you are a 6-footer, or 5 feet high if you stand 5-foot-6. If you can easily see over the waves, kneel down. That puts your eyes at about 3½ to 4 feet up. If you can still see over the waves, plant your rear on the beach and look out; your eyes are now around 2½ feet above the water.

Take a look at the surf. Some waves will march up to the shore and seem to let the top of the wave spill down the front face in a long, controlled slide. These are the easiest to work through. Other waves seem to curl over and let the top of the wave break or collapse in the front of the wave. These are harder to manage. What you'll face in these short, steep waves is water falling directly upon you, and as you struggle up through the foam, you'll wade right into the circular energy form of the wave body.

Surf is not uniform. You might have bad dumping (breaking) surf at one end of a crescent of beach, and small, spilling surf at the other end. If that's the case, I know where I'm going to launch. For that matter, doesn't it look like the surf is only ripples up there beyond the point, where the kelp seems to form a breakwater and the little offshore rocks break up the oncoming energy patterns of the waves? Take your kayak in that direction. A carry on the beach is preferable to a thrash in the surf. Also, look beyond the immediate surf line. Is there a clear passage you might follow once you're through the first waves?

We'll start our passage through the surf by getting in the slosh just at the beach line, with paddle in hand and our spray skirt already around our midsection. Watch for a pattern to develop in the size of the waves coming in, and ready yourself. Some people count the seconds

Breaking wave

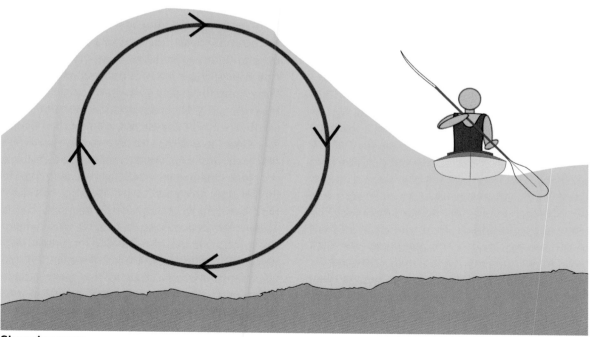

Slumping wave

between each swoosh of water rumbling up the beach, while others look for the visual pattern of towering waves versus waves that are smaller and friendlier. Your goal is to be in your boat, your spray skirt snapped into place, and your paddle driving just after the largest waves in a set have slid up the beach. Keep your hands out in the low-gear end of your blade, and drive ahead with plenty of power. The first time you try this, you'll want to keep the slop out of your boat, and you may try to get in too far up the beach . . . which means you'll sit there and try to scoot along while the beach holds you firmly. Until the big wave comes and grabs you. Commit yourself with vigor and élan.

If you are high and dry, try scooting yourself forward with each wavelet that piddles away under you. Use a hand on one side and the knuckles of your other hand wrapped around your paddle on the opposite side. Yes, you can lean back and really pry on your paddle, but if you do so, think about how much you paid for your lightweight cruising stick. Now, if you'd only asked for more heft on the blade . . . ? Use your hands instead.

With luck, you'll slosh through the foam and maybe have to climb a swell or two. The idea is to charge at right angles (or perpendicular) into the oncoming waves. This approach may or may not put you at right angles to the beach. Push your weight aft to bring up your bow as you start into a swell, and then shove forward as you pass over the top of the wave.

Well, you made it unscathed, but I didn't. I'm going to get popped by a small wave—one of those 2- to 3-footers that were lurking. I'll plant my paddle blade in the most solid part of the wave I can find and pull myself forward (with my chin down). One school of thought is to shut your eyes and hold your paddle over your head. This method depends on the same kind of aid that parted the Red Sea, and most of us do not have that kind of communication system, or influence. With one of the big graybacks, your best bet is to hunch forward (to prevent the wave energy from grabbing your chest) and power ahead with everything you have. A 5-footer will thump you hard, and in all honesty, you can get a bit disoriented under the froth of a breaking wave. The absolutely worst thing you can do is cower down and hope nothing will happen if the wave doesn't notice you. It doesn't even know you exist to begin with. A wave is merely programmed to whoosh up the beach. If it grabs you and flings you over on your back and drags you upside down up the beach, it isn't even aware of it.

Many novice paddlers fall victim to one of two basic mistakes when first attempting to launch into surf. Fortunately, there are remedies for each one.

Mistake number one is to paddle through a small set of waves and then sit up to relax. There's a bigger set all primed to grab you. Keep hammering forward until you're well clear of the surf zone.

What if you don't have time to get your spray deck snapped down before the wash from a wave grabs you, and you're willy-nilly in the soup? Go for it! If you don't do anything, you're in major trouble. That's the ultimate rule in paddling. If you're doing something, even the wrong thing, you can always correct yourself. Your strokes will help stabilize your boat. If you do nothing, you will wallow in disaster. You have no stability, no power, no maneuverability . . . and no chance.

You might have heard that you should deliberately roll your boat and let the bottom take the full force of a dumping surf. Right. That means your head is hanging down from the other side of your boat. The reason the surf is dumping is that the wave has tripped on the shallows—so guess what part of you is closest to the bottom? In my opinion, if you find yourself upside down with anything less than a bombproof roll (and if you had one, I'd be at your knee, learning from you), try a fast

Let's Talk about It

The combination of waves, wind, and seabirds can be noisy, and it's hard to understand someone shouting from a kayak, even when they're not very far away. We
usually use simple hand signals for basic communication, plus a whistle. Five short
blasts on a whistle means "danger." One long blast means "I'm looking for you," and
is answered by two blasts, meaning "I'm here." If you point your extended paddle
at me and pat your head, you're asking "Are you all right?" I can signal "I'm okay" by
patting my head in reply. These aren't carved in stone, but they work for us. As long
as the signals are simple and agreed to by everyone in your party, they work great.

Come this way

A vertical paddle means that it's safe
or proper to come directly toward
the upraised paddle. If the paddle is
being waved in a tight circle, it's a
request for the entire party to come
to the paddle.

Go that way

A paddle extended and slightly angled upward
indicates the direction a paddler should head.
It does not—and everyone in your group should
understand this—point at a danger or hazard that
should be avoided.

Stop go back

A paddle held horizontally over your head in both
hands says "Stop! Go back!" and is a warning that
the paddler being signaled is heading into danger.
Feel free to give five blasts on your whistle to
emphasize this command.

roll followed by a wet exit. If you can hold onto the offshore end of your boat, great—it will be easier to work it inshore. But don't get your hand tangled in the grab loop, and for your own sake, don't get between your boat and the shore. You're going to feel like a lost sock in a clothes dryer, turning around and around, and you definitely don't want a ton or more of sodden kayak smashing down on you.

Now for mistake number two, which may be even bigger than mistake number one: It's a lot easier to get off a beach than it is to get back on. Where will you land? Waves are a creature of wind, and if our destination is downwind, you might as well figure that we will be landing with the wind at our backs. I hope that you looked at your chart and found us a place to land out of the prevailing wind and waves.

Leeward and Windward

I'll pop in another couple of nautical terms you should know; they both refer to the position of an object in relationship to you. Anything windward is upwind of your boat, or in the direction from which the wind and the weather are coming. Anything downwind of your kayak is leeward.

Remember—these are only directions relative to you, and are not locations.

When you're going to land, it's usually better to do so on a shore that is windward of you. The wind is blowing from the land, over the shore, and out across the water. As you paddle into the wind and get closer to the shore, wave action will usually decrease. If you paddle downwind toward a shore that is leeward of you, the wind will impart more energy to the wave system, and the wave action at the beach will be more intense.

It gets confusing if you forget that windward and leeward are only as significant as their relationship to you. If you are on the island of Hawaii, the "windward shore" is upwind from where you are standing. Keep the wind in your

face and walk across the island until you come to the shore, and you'll find a shore battered by high surf and wind. If you are in your kayak just a quarter-mile farther upwind, the relative direction of that shore is dramatically altered. From your kayak, that shore is now described as a "lee" shore, and lies leeward of you. It hasn't changed—you've moved. Now its position, relative to the wind you're experiencing, is different.

As a rule of thumb, it's easier to land on a shore *from which* the wind blows rather than on a shore *toward which* the wind blows.

Is there a protected beach from which to launch, and is there a protected beach upon which to land? Finding those are part of the planning process. I know you spent some time locating likely protected landing zones along our route today.

Colliding Currents

You lead me down the bay and through the narrow entrance that dumps into more open water. It's a couple of hours after high tide, and the ebb is in steady flow, so we make good time. However, you warn me that the water looks all swirly right in the entrance. Good call—it is. You're paddling right into the confluence of two tidal flows, and you'll find swirling and disturbed currents where they meet. You could find some good chop and sharply defined eddy lines. Be ready to brace. You'll also see some waves reflecting off the northern point, setting up sharp, peaked waves that seem to rise and fall in jagged mountains. You might see these off any point, caused by the reflected waves moving in and out of sync with the wind-driven waves. The reflected waves pass through the pattern of the wind-driven waves, and where they coincide, special waves called *clapotis* can seem to explode from the water's surface. Some folks might choose to sneak along the beach to miss the major collision of the two tidal streams. Beware, though, because that might put you in the surf zone below the confluence. You'll have to call this on a situation-by-situation basis.

Where would you look for wildlife? At the break between two kinds of habitat. That's true for birds, elk, whales, and fish. All of these creatures live in one habitat and hunt in the other. The confluence of tidal currents is a pretty good spot to fish, although you'll need to consider bottom structure and water temperature, too. Most bottom-dwelling fish—including the whole family of rockfish that are the best eating of any marine creature—don't like to battle swift currents, but they do like new crops of food to come drifting in like clouds of manna.

Riding the Currents

We're still in a narrow channel, and the current here can build to a brisk 4 or 5 knots. But that's in the middle, and we could probably sneak back against it by working along the shore. However, I hope you looked at the chart before leading me this way. Right in the narrowest part of the channel ahead, a big ridge sticks up out of the seafloor. While it's too far below the surface to pose any rocky danger to us, or even to a big ship, it does block the current stream—which in turn can create a series of breaking waves called an *overfall*. I'd just as soon skirt by them.

The Nearest Shelter

I have my hand-bearing compass out, taking sights, and you drop back to ask what I'm doing. Simple enough. If anything goes wrong, I want to know the direction in which to paddle to the most available safe landing. Not necessarily the nearest—if I had to paddle 2 miles to a protected beach right into the teeth of the current, it could take me a couple of hours. With the current, wind, and waves at my back, however, I could cover 6 or 7 miles easily in just an hour.

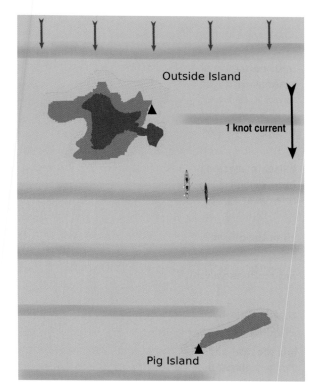

Closest, in our paddling world, is more often measured in time than in distance. We left our camp at the triangle on Outside Island, heading for Pig Island, with the wind, waves, and current on our sterns. Fifteen minutes after we left Outside, about a mile from our launch, we decided to head for shelter. Pig is still 2 miles away. Pig is closer, because we have the boost from the current and the wind, and we won't face the obstacles of the waves.

Yeah, you charted out hidey-holes for us, and I appreciate that. Just knowing where the safety spot is may be comforting, but it doesn't answer all our needs. We have to know where we are in order to find the safe landing.

Assuming fog closed in, which is possible any month of the year, I know which way to head to get to the nearest landing. It's a habit I fell into long ago. You're not worried, because you know I'm taking care of this. But on the other hand, what if we get separated in the fog? Keeping track of where you are all along the voyage is a good habit to form, for safety and convenience. We all should know in which direction and for how long we should paddle in order to re-form a scattered group at a safe landing spot.

Waves

Sliding down the front of a big roller is an intimidating experience, and one that will test your bracing and other boat-handling skills. No matter how you cut it, a cruising kayak is not an ideal surfing machine. You're also offering the wind even more distance in which to build up the waves and surf. While crashing through the surf on a lee shore ranges between embarrassing and dangerous, it may be preferable to dumping far at sea. Scooting right next to an islet, cranking around into a sharp turn across the eddy line behind it, and then making a soft landing is . . . well, it sounds easier than it is. Ocean rollers are not necessarily a hazard. The period of the wave is so long that you'll have a hard time really looking at it. You'll be in a trough and the horizon will be close in, and as the grayback passes underneath you, the horizon will magically spread

out. You may not even feel the slow climb and dip as it passes, and you'll barely register the fact that sometimes you'll be able to see your fellow paddlers nearby, and sometimes you won't.

Think of a big hair curler just rolling around in the open water. The energy pattern in a wave looks something like that, with the energy coil moving along and the water staying horizontally in place. Water at the leading edge of the wave will be forced down, and water on the back of the wave will be lifted up, but you won't see a lot of horizontal displacement. Problems arise when the water is shallow enough so that the bottom of the energy coil trips on the seafloor. The wave runs out of water needed for the front end to dip and the back to lift, and instead of a smooth pattern moving along, we suddenly have a breaking wave, with the front face eroding away.

Our plan is to turn west at the bottom of this channel and head up to a secluded little anchorage for lunch. Good plan, but as we make the turn from this channel into the other one, we'll have the current right on our

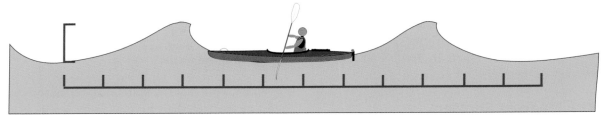

In open water, if the height of the waves (from trough to crest) is greater than six times the distance from crest to crest, the waves will start to break and spume will fly.

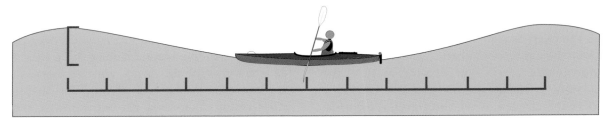

If the height of the wave is less than six times the period (that's the crest-to-crest distance), you'll just bob up and down over smooth and safe waves.

bow. We could charge straight into it for three hours, or until the tide changes, but neither of us wants to work that hard. You cling tightly to one shore. Again, a good call. The current will be the strongest in the middle and in the deepest channel—so let's avoid those places. Instead, we'll sneak up behind the points jutting out into the channel and take advantage of the eddies behind each. We'll have to be on our toes, because we'll have to cross those lines where the main current is flowing one way and the back current of the eddy, the other. With plenty of speed and caution, we'll slide right through. Plus, since we're ready to stabilize our kayaks with a bracing stroke, we'll be alert enough to avoid the situations in which one is required. We'll look more closely at eddies in a couple of paragraphs.

We can sneak up in the lee of an island or a rock the same way. We'll stay out of the main current and skip from eddy to eddy. River paddlers since the day of the birch-bark canoe knew of, and used, these same eddies as they rested behind rocks, points, or even big logs— all of which sheltered them from the full force of the river's current.

Ferries

This channel arcs in a graceful curve through most of its length, and right now you have us on the outside of the turn. To the outside is where the current will be directed. If we stay on this shore, we'll have the current pushing us right into the beach . . . not to mention we'll have to overpower the current even to move ahead. Why work that hard? We'll have to ferry across to the other shore. We could wait until we pass by this little cloud of islands, but maybe we should share the work of crossing the channel with the natural assistance of the eddies. If we cross behind the islands, we'll manage either to be in an eddy, or at least to be sheltered from the full thrust of the current, as long as we are in the islands. We won't have

to work as hard, and we won't be shoved back down-channel.

Our plan is to ferry over behind one island, paddle up its eddy as far as we need to, and then ferry across the narrow cut between that island and the next. So now we're tucked in behind a big rock at one end of an islet, and it's time to really understand eddies.

Look right off the edge of the rock. There's a swirly line in the water peeling off from the rock. If we had the wings of a seagull, we could look down on this channel and see the water pouring out the lower end. The islet we're sheltered behind breaks up the smooth flow of the water and directs some of the current to each side. The current doesn't immediately close around the islet. In fact, it takes quite a distance for the two pieces of current to join again after being split. You don't end up with a true hole in the water behind the islet, but you do end up with water flowing back into this area from downstream, where the current streams join together. The water molecules might see the hole, but it takes them a little time to peel off from the main current and work back into the hole. As a result, you literally have a reverse current flowing into the hole behind an obstruction.

At the same time, since water likes to cling to itself, you have two currents in opposing directions rubbing up against each other. I've seen the wall created between strong currents rise to an abrupt 6 or 8 inches, which is nearly cockpit-high on a cruising kayak. From a cockpit that wall looks huge!

What happens when you attempt to cross this line? One current will grab your bow and send it one way while the other current will send your stern in the opposite direction. If you're not prepared, the sudden jerk of the water can spill you right over!

How do you get across safely?

Your first weapon is *speed*. Hit the line with vigor, and keep moving!

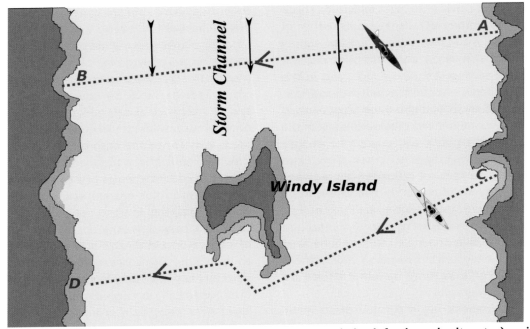

To cross a current without being swept downstream (holds true in both fresh- and salt water), point the bow of your kayak somewhere between right into the current and your destination on the far shore. The angle depends on the force of the current. You want to be at an angle so that you can balance the distance you cover upstream with the amount you'll be carried downstream as you crab sideways over the current. The paddler in the red boat decided to muscle his way across in one jump. The paddler in the yellow boat is making the shorter jump to Windy Island, and will rest for a moment in the lee of the island before making a second jump to the far shore. Not only will he be less exposed during the crossing, but he'll also have an intermediate landing spot if needed.

Your second weapon is *angle*. Depending on the relative velocity of the two current streams, you want to pierce the line at an angle of 45 to 70 degrees to the outside current. If you try too steep an angle—just easing across the line—you'll get tossed back. If you try too broad an angle—say, straight across the eddy line—your bow will be twisted about and you'll head down-current. If you mean to do that, that's all right, of course. This is called a *peel-out*, whether you do it on a river or on the ocean. But if your goal is to ferry across the current to the next islet and eddy, you have to be able to hold your angle.

Your third weapon is your *lean and bracing stroke*. At the very least, cross the eddy line flat and paddle on your down-current side as you cross the line. Even better, tilt your boat a bit so that you're showing a bit of bottom to the outside current. You'll skid over the grasping fingers of the current rather than dipping your up-current gunwale and letting the sea get ahold of your edge. If it does and you can't rock back in a great down-current brace, you're about to become a swimmer. (I learned that in more than one river.)

That was some hard work. I'm going to rest for a second by sliding up on this kelp. Kelp is neat. It works just like the old fishing-boat trick of putting a bag soaked in thick oil upwind of a vessel. Oil leaking from the bag would coat the water surface and quash turbulent waves.

Kelp, a more environmentally safe substance, has the same effect with its thick fronds.

Ferrying is not easy work. And I'm tired of trying to keep my boat on the right heading. What I'll do is lean the boat over a bit on the down-current side to change its underbody shape. Each stroke I use to drive the boat forward will then slightly turn the kayak's bow into the current. As I glide ahead, with the wind off my bow, the combination of the wind and waves will attempt to push my bow down-current. As a result, I'll go along in a straight line without paddling a lot of corrective strokes and putting a lot of strain on one arm. What I've done by leaning my boat is to create an underbody in which one side becomes straighter—or nearer the keel line—while the other side becomes more curved as the gunwale is lowered into the waterline. Think of a capital letter D; your kayak will turn toward the straight side of the D and away from the curved side.

Wind

As we come clear of the islands, the wind is right on our bows. Wind is no friend to the paddler on the water. Few of us can paddle for any distance into the teeth of a 15-knot wind, and once the wind starts knocking the tops off the waves, we face some difficulty. Sure, master mariners know how to cope with this, but

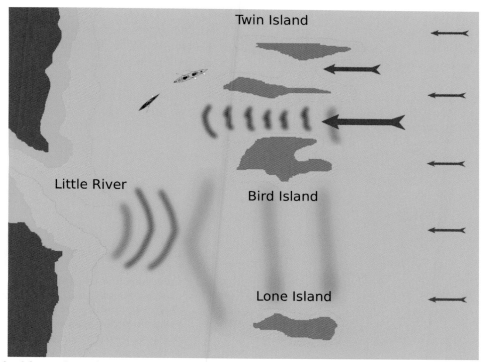

Twin Island

Little River

Bird Island

Lone Island

We launched from the point on the north side of Little River and we want to camp on Twin Island. If we paddle straight out, between Bird and Lone, we'll be working hard right into the wind, as shown by the red arrows. Instead, we angle north and east, hiding in the wind shadow (and the waves) behind Bird Island. The narrow channel between Bird and Twin will concentrate the wind and let the waves build up, so we'll stay behind Bird as long as possible before darting over to Twin. Twin looks almost like two islands connected by a narrow and low neck. The wind might be whistling through there, so we'll tuck in behind the southern hill and creep around the point. We can land anywhere in the bay and look for our campsite.

the rule of prudent seamanship is to avoid as many challenges as possible. Experienced kayakers are humble when they venture out onto the water, and for good reason. We're small, we have limited stamina, and we're fragile. Not only that, but the never-ending slog of pushing right into the teeth of an unrelenting wind ruins my good mood. After a bit, that is.

If we have to climb up the face of each wave only to be stopped by a blast of wind at the top, we're going to tire pretty quickly. Let's head to the shore that will give us the most protection. Heading right for shore, however, would put us in the trough of the waves, so we'd not only be rocked about, but also carried down-channel by the current (after all, the tide hasn't changed yet). Instead, we'll turn so that we're at an angle of around 45 degrees to the wind and waves. I haven't been saying that all our maneuvers tie together for no reason.

We're ferrying across the wind and waves. At some point we'll find wind and waves that aren't rolling out of the same point, and then we'll have to angle across the waves and accept the wind. What we've done, in effect, is to take a long switchback across the face of the waves instead of a short and steep climb. Quartering doesn't work, though, if it merely leads you farther out to sea and away from shelter.

A Sheltered Landing

As much as possible, you keep us in the shelter of small islands and points as we work up-current, and you've found us a tiny bay on the lee side of an island in which to land. I'm proud of you. We're coming into a steep little beach, but one that trails off from a relatively steep sand and gravel surface into a very gradually sloped mud surface. At dead low tide we would have faced a long trudge through the goo.

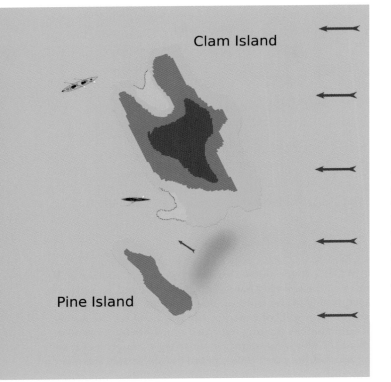

Clam Island

Pine Island

Landing on an exposed beach is perfectly possible for a kayak, but I'd rather scurry around the point and glide across calm water as I land. You found us two sheltered landings on Clam Island, away from the wind and waves coming toward us from the right (or east) side of the chart. The bay on the north side of Clam drains at a really low tide (see the grungy green?), but since we'll come ashore at near high tide, we'll float over the shallows. We could also land behind the little intertidal strip on the south— perhaps a bit more exposed to wind and waves between Clam and Pine, but still a great spot. Good job!

How did you know about the slope? Simple enough. You just looked at the depth numbers on the chart. The numbers changed quickly near shore, but then stayed the same for a long and tapering distance. On the chart, the drying portions of the beach were marked in green, and you could easily pick out the potential problem. The chart also indicated the *sndy* areas of sand and the *mdy* areas of mud. You picked that up from *US Chart No. 1,* the key to all our navigation charts.

Landing on an Exposed Beach

I'm glad you planned ahead, because I hate landing on an exposed beach. First of all, you can't see much from the outside of the surf line. You can't see if you'll be landing on a smooth beach, rocks, or logs. That's right, logs. Which could be churning around at the surf line! I told you I don't like this. We could be faced with spilling waves or a harsh, dumping surf. Your first (and best) option—okay, I'm biased—is to go somewhere else.

I don't think just stooging around outside the surf line waiting for conditions to improve is a viable option for cruising kayakers. If you're waiting for the current to slow coming out of a bay at the turn of a tide, or overfalls to subside in a tidal race, then yes, you have a point. But wind-driven waves on a beach probably have more endurance than you do.

Heave to (that has nothing to do with seasickness—it means to turn your bow into the wind and rest while you more or less hold your position) and let's consider our options.

We might not be able to see over the backs of the waves as they advance toward the shore, but we do have the tools to give us a reasonably accurate picture of what's happening at, or beyond, the wave break: our charts and our tide tables.

As you remember, a wave is a circular pattern of energy rolling through the water. When it runs into the bottom, it trips—with

Driftwood logs look like a nice place to tie up a kayak or sit and enjoy the view. Remember, those logs floated in, either on a high tide or the waves of a storm. You really, really don't want to be grabbing your gear when waves are tossing those multiton logs around like matchsticks.

the release of all the energy imparted to it by the wind. If the bottom slopes very gently, the energy of the wave is going to stumble along and dissipate slowly. Water will spill off the top and front of the wave in a rather gentle break. If the bottom shelves rapidly, if it is steep, the energy of the wave is going to trip as it abruptly hits the seafloor, and the wave is going to come apart with sound and fury.

How are we going to know the bottom profile? Look at the chart. If we have a long, shallow gradient working into the beach, we're probably going to have a spilling-type wave. If we have a bottom identified as mud or sand, we're probably going to have a spilling-type wave. If we have a bay with outlying rocks or reefs that can trip a wave, we're likely to find protected waters inside. That's also an alert: Rocks, like toadstools, rarely appear alone; an outlying reef or rocky islet may indicate more rocks within the bay. Check the tide tables. Most sandy or muddy bays will have a gently sloping bottom, with steeper inclines at the beach line. If we land during the lower part of the tidal cycle, we'll be on the flatter bottom rather than the steeper beach. For that matter, if we land lower on the beach profile, we'll have less chance of coming ashore on, or in, the driftwood—which can include logs.

On the other side of the coin, if we have an abrupt transition from deep water to a very narrow, shallow zone (the blue area on most charts), we can be suspicious of the potential of breaking waves. If the cove bottom near the shore is identified as rocky, or we see the symbol for rocks along the intertidal zone (the green area on most charts), we can suppose the beach profile is steeper. Yes, you can land on a steeper, rocky beach, but you face the risk of sliding back down the beach into the next incoming wave. Lee Moyers, an outstanding paddler as well as kayak designer, put the best face on approaching such a beach. He calls them not so much a challenge for the paddler as a great photo opportunity for friends safely on the beach.

The chart and a little common sense offer other safe landing hints. If the beach is an absolutely straight line, the bottom profile is absolutely uniform, and the waves are coming in perfectly perpendicular to the beach, there's little to choose from. That's highly unlikely in the real world. We'll probably want to land in a cove or bay, which from overhead will look much like a crescent. The further the crescent shape of the bay is carved into the shoreline, the more likely we'll find smaller (or gentler) surf near the outside edges, or horns. The waves will come straight into the center of the crescent, unabated. However, the waves will curve from their straight-in approach to slide up the side beaches, and this will dissipate some of the energy.

We're more likely to see the waves approach the overall beach at an angle, however slight. All other things being equal, the end of the crescent that makes the waves turn the most will have the least surf.

These are all hints and indications rather than absolute rules. You have to use a lot of common sense, a good deal of forethought, the ability to plan for alternative landing sites, and the self-confidence to look at a particular beach and say, "Nah . . . that's not for me today."

After all that, I have to confess that with a proper boat and the right beach, surfing is simply a kick. Kayak touring is the water equivalent of cross-country skiing; surfing is running the slalom gates.

When I said that waiting around wasn't much of an option, I meant just splashing around with no plan, and hoping. You should be patient. Come in reasonably close to the surf line (go ahead, back in if you are nervous, and have your getaway ready), and focus on the pattern of waves surging to the beach. Your plan is to come in with the smaller waves that seem to follow in the shadow of the big guys. Surfers like to fly down the front of the waves, their bodies arched in the curl and their smiles primed for any passing camera. I, however, have no desire to send 17 feet or more of cruising kayak down the front of a wave! Earlier in this book we found that some boats are made to turn and some are made to go straight—well, kayaks go straight and surfboards turn. The front of a wave is possibly not the best kayaking environment.

Really put your muscles to the paddle and try to climb high on the back of one of the smaller waves as you approach the shore.

For a more-controlled ride to the beach, or just for a boost from where you are to where you want to be, slip just over the top of the wave onto its front face, but turn so that you're descending the front face at an angle. That's what the lead kayaker is doing, as his partner sets up to catch the next wave. The lead paddler is leaning slightly into the wave for balance and is reaching over the top of the wave with a low brace for stability and control.

Too far forward and you run the risk of being part of the falling water on the front. Too far back and the backwash will pull you into the following wave. Those two dragons should be enough to keep you on the wave's back—but the fact remains that even with a wave nipping at your heels, you won't go much faster than 5 or 6 knots, while a wave can double that velocity. Ride one wave as long as you can, and as it surges ahead of you, pick up the next. You could very well ride through the surf on these waves and then slog through the slop to shore.

You want to come in at right angles to the motion of the waves. At the same time, you want to hit the beach at an angle. Remember, the beach slants up at an angle to the water surface (even though the water doesn't appear very level in the surf zone). By coming in at an angle, you decrease the apparent steepness of the beach, and you'll be less likely to hang

All this time we've chatted about landing on a beach. Sometimes there isn't a beach. Sometimes we end up being hauled onto a ledge above the water.

up, suspended by your bow and stern. For that matter, you'll be less likely to bury your bow in the beach and have the next wave slew you about and send you tumbling.

A very experienced paddler—or one who has no choice but to attempt a landing on a hostile shore—can angle across the waves to a fast ride ashore. Work your way into the trough and turn until you're just about parallel to the movement of the waves. Paddle forward to hold plenty of speed (and, if possible, away from the first break of the waves), and as the wave starts to pick you up, use a stern rudder to angle your bow down and across the wave toward shore. Don't come straight in! If you bury your bow, you face at best an uncontrolled

broach, and possibly even a tip stand that will lead to a flip. This can be anything from very uncomfortable to very dangerous.

Now convert that stern rudder to a low brace (remember how these moves work together). If the wave face is steep, lean into the wave and grab a high brace with your paddle high into the foam. The wave will eventually break, but a good brace should keep you surging toward shore.

If your angle allows it, drive right up on the beach. The backwash from each wave will attempt to suck you back out, so ready yourself for a quick exit and a full-muscled tug of your boat up the beach. The waves will chase you, demanding another chance at you and your boat.

Here's another landing technique you can try (I've never done it, but I've seen it done). Gingerly back toward the beach. This is one of those times you should have your rudder or skeg out of the water! Work your way in toward shore slowly and carefully, looking back over your shoulder. What's the advantage of sneaking up to shore this way? If things look bad, you're in position for a quick getaway. I wouldn't do it in any degree of surf, say over 4 feet, and I'm not certain I would even do it then, but some paddlers like this technique.

In the Water

What follows is information you don't need, about an event that will never happen to you under circumstances that will never come together. It's a kind of Halloween tale, and though you may find it scary, it shouldn't frighten you off the water. Paddling a touring kayak is 90 percent or more preparation, and a small bit of reaction to changing circumstances. With forethought, caution, and a healthy respect for the environment in which we play, you may never find yourself in a situation more uncomfortable than wet feet and a damp behind. But in the worst of all worlds . . .

Okay, so something went wrong and you've had an upsetting experience. After this is all over, you should sit down with a cup of something warm and attempt to reconstruct the series of events that put you in the water. In doing so, you'll discover alternative courses of action that might have avoided the flip. But for now, you're in the water—in the surf zone, or in water churned by big waves hurrying to join the surf—and you've misplaced your kayak.

Be very clear on this: What we're talking about is a very narrow set of circumstances. You should be paddling with someone else, and that other person should be able to pick you up. Even if you get churned up in Nature's version of a washing machine, you should keep in contact with your kayak. You've already

practiced Eskimo-rolling, paddle-float self-rescues, and assisted rescues. You should be able to return to your boat, get back in, pump it out, and resume your journey.

But this time, you can't. You've lost your kayak, and you have to swim.

Most of us don't think about our breathing. It happens, almost automatically. When you're swimming in rough seas, however, that's a luxury you no longer have. When you're pummeled by a breaking wave, when you're twirled about in the energy core of a wave until you're disoriented, you have to hold your breath. When you bob to the surface in a trough, you have to breathe. Controlling your breathing, and knowing that you're able to control your breathing, are the first steps in regaining the serenity to extricate yourself from the water's grasp.

Once you've gotten over the confusion of being tossed about in the energy patterns of the waves and you have a fair idea of where shore and safety lie, it's time to swim. In swimming, you could run into one of two currents—both frightening, both frustrating. You can't outfight them, but you can outthink them.

Let's start by looking at what happens on a beach exposed to wave action. Following the uprush of water onto the beach after the breaking of a wave, the seaward backrush occurs. The returning water is called a *backwash*. Waves approaching the beach at an angle produce a current parallel to the beach within the surf zone. The speed of this current rarely exceeds 1 knot, but can reach up to 3 knots.

Concentrated energy from the wave front can form barriers to the backwash, which is deflected along the beach to areas of less resistance. The backwash will accumulate at weak points and will pour seaward as it forms rip currents through the surf. The large volume of returning water retards the incoming waves. The waves on one (or both) sides of the rip, not being retarded by the backwash, advance faster and farther up the beach. From there they move along the beach as feeder currents, increasing the volume of water flowing out at the rip. The rip may form at an indentation on an otherwise-straight beach, along underwater obstructions such as a shoal or bar, or where the energy of the wave fronts is refracted and diverged. Mind you, that's a simple explanation of a complex phenomenon, but fortunately when you're swimming, you really don't have to remember all the root causes.

If there are higher waves to both sides of you, and they're advancing to the beach while you're being swept away from the shore, odds are you're in a rip current. If you attempt to swim to shore against the current, you'll tire long before the water does, and you'll go inexorably through the neck of the rip, where it punches through the surf, and wind up outside the breaker line where the current dissipates.

What to do? Swim parallel to the beach, more or less across the current. Once clear of the outrushing current, use the energy of the shore-bound waves to paddle your way in.

What happens if, as you attempt to swim toward shore, you get the feeling that the world is whizzing by you? Basically, you're going for a ride in a long-shore current that parallels the shore. You might even find that you're being carried at an angle away from the shore.

Don't fight this current. Ride with it, swimming with the current but at an angle toward the shore. You're going to find yourself fixating on a particular shoreside feature, and you're going to want to reach that feature, be it a point, a rock, or even a beachside tree. What can happen is that you'll be swept past the object of your desire and you'll fruitlessly battle the current to reach that one ideal spot. But remember that your goal is to get to shore, not to a particular point on the shore. Even if you could swim just as fast as the force of the current, the net result is that you'd stay in just one place until you were exhausted. Me, I can't swim that fast. Olympians may hit 5 miles per hour in a short sprint; the average swimmer is pressed to top 2 miles per hour. Tired, clothed, bashed about in the waves, I doubt I could manage 1 mile per hour. I'd just as soon save what strength and body heat I have and ferry out of the current to shore.

Let's say you are caught in the seaward current at the mouth of a river. While it may sweep you a ways off the beach, it will dissipate rapidly. React just as if you were in a rip current and ferry your way out of the current.

Tides sweeping in or out of bays can generate very strong currents; I've seen 11-knot currents in restricted passages such as British Columbia's Surge Narrows. That's hauling. You can't fight a current like that, but you can beat it by ferrying with the current and stroking toward a reachable shore.

You're shaking your head. You, of all people, would never venture near smoking mountains of water crashing onto rugged shores. First of all, who's talking about 20-foot-tall cliffs of foam poised above the beach? Surf can also be a couple of feet high, on lakes as well as the sea. Secondly, currents will push and tug at your kayak just as they do on a swimmer. You can take advantage of currents at the beach, or you can waste your time and energy fighting them. The choice is up to you, but only if you've invested the time to understand the how and why of currents in the beach zone.

On the Shore
As we look around the sheltered bay you've guided us to, you judge that the beach is safe and suitable. That's an important step, one that many people overlook. Too many people commit to a plan and forget to check reality. While kayaking, a plan is the general framework from which you hang your actions as suitable for the moment. I'm fairly sure that the wind isn't going to change while we're ashore and create

a flock of monster waves crashing right on this arc of welcoming crescent beach—but I don't think I'm willing to bet the farm on my hunch. So I'm paddling over to the west end of this little bay, where a ridge of rock hooks out and offers a curling arm of shelter. It's the old belt-and-suspenders theory again—I want a double safety net. If there is a turn in the weather, I think I'll be able to launch in the shelter of the rocks and make a comfortable swing into the water beyond the bay rather than have to fight my way off the beach.

Let's enjoy a well-deserved lunch and plenty of exploration and recuperation time. We'll drink plenty of water, because we both used up lots of fluids on the way here. We've also dug into our energy reserves, so we need to refuel for the rest of the trip.

Be polite to the island. When nature calls, dig a small hole—maybe 6 inches or so in diameter, and just a few inches down through the topsoil and humus. That's where nature's treatment plant lives and operates. If you go deeper, you're building an insulated, sterile box for your wastes. If you leave them unburied . . . well, I doubt if you'd be that rude. From a biologist's viewpoint, liquid wastes belong on a beach. In today's regulatory world (and crowded campsites), this may not be an option. Know, as they say, before you go.

Heating your food presents a dilemma. If you build a fire, you scar the soil and leave an unsightly carbon ring. If you use a butane or liquid-fuel stove, you're burning petrochemicals. I'm inclined to go with a small liquid-fuel stove for cooking, but in an area with lots of driftwood, a fire may be more appropriate. Whatever you do, remember the advice of the old frontiersman. A big fire will make you sweat, not because of its heat but because of lugging all that wood. A small fire will keep you just as warm because you may approach it more closely, and because it's far easier to cook upon.

Plotting the Course Home

I fell asleep when you were off exploring, and now it's late afternoon. Our take-out is on an almost-featureless beach off to the west, and, as near as we can tell, the beach looks the same for miles and miles. Should we lay out a compass course right to the beach and paddle that line? Well, there's a wind coming from the north, so we'll be set to the south. We will also be crossing shallows and meandering channels, so the tidal currents are hard to predict. Over on the other side of our island, in the deep channel, you can forecast the current, but it's going to be devilish on those flats. Do you trust your course?

Just use the neat trick that we learned in chapter 15: Going Wrong Makes It Right. If we land just south of the take-out but get confused and trudge south in search of the car, we could walk for miles. If we overcorrect and land on the north side of the car and hike north, same story. Only if we land to one side of the car and hike in the opposite direction will we find our way home. That means our odds of reaching the car are two out of four, or 50 percent. But by going the wrong way, we can improve those odds to 100 percent. A lot of navigators habitually set their course to land on one side of their goal and then run down the beach line. Chart a course well to the north of the car. We can then hike south, and there's the car. As we get better at this, we can cut the error factor down.

As we work our way south along the beach line after our landfall, you spot the notch in the sand dunes that marks the trail, and the end of our trip. Though you don't mention it, I've seen a change in you. When we started paddling together, you would have doubted your ability to plan out and paddle a trip like this. Tides, currents, wind, and waves. And a route. It would have been too confusing. Funny how you can start with a few simple skills, and by using them one step at a time, you reach your goal.

A Personal Scale of Paddling Conditions

I try to remember that good time, as in "making good time," refers to the pleasures of what we see and do rather than the distance and speed we go.

Water is a constant variable, and difficult to pin down when describing the challenges of paddling across it. A particular route may be sheltered from wind and wave, which would indicate it was easy, but strong currents might make it too difficult for the less-experienced. A rocky or cliff-bound shore will impose a higher degree of challenge than a route following sandy beaches. Stronger winds demand stronger skills, while calms welcome the less-experienced.

Distances to be covered also impact the choice of a route. Ten miles between launch and take-out will take three to four hours in calm water. That's a good (and tiring) trip for a less-skilled and -conditioned paddler. Twenty-five miles, less than a half-hour in a car, will take a competent paddler eight to nine hours to cover. That's figuring in time to take a photo, eat, drink several bottles of water, and stretch tired muscles.

What follows are quick sketches of three levels of paddling conditions. Changes in wind, weather, waves, the shoreline, and temperatures can radically change the degree of difficulty. With miles in your wake and a realistic appraisal of your own skills and condition, you'll use these reference points to assess your planned route. This does not represent some universal law or proclamation; it's merely my assessment of my own comfort levels. I've sat on a beach and sipped a mug of tea while I watched other kayaks on the water. I've also paddled while others chose to stay ashore. Use this as the beginning of a guide for yourself.

1. **Easy.** Suitable for beginner-level skills. Surface ranges from mirror-smooth to small waves of less than 1 foot. Tops of the waves are smooth and glassy, and are not breaking. Wind speeds are between calm and 6 knots, enough to feel on your face or to rustle leaves. There is no significant surf action along the shore. Waters are quite sheltered by the mainland and offshore islands. The shore is immediately at hand, and poses no great difficulty while landing. Rescues would be relatively easy and could include beaching.

2. **Challenging.** Suitable for paddlers with some training and experience. Winds range from 7 to 16 knots, Force 3 and 4, or from a gentle breeze to a moderate breeze. A moderate breeze will move small tree limbs and raise up loose paper or leaves. Waves can be 2 to 3 feet high. You'll see some whitecaps or cresting waves in a gentle breeze, and a fair number as wind strength increases to a moderate breeze. Waves may wash over a kayak deck, with the risk of swamping or capsizing. Sheltering islands and the shore will decrease wave action. Paddlers are still close to the safety of shore. Surf, if any, is relatively easy to cross.

3. **Difficult.** Paddlers need experience, confidence, and good boat-handling skills. Rescues, self- or of others, are difficult. Winds are Force 5 to 6, fresh breeze to strong breeze, or between 17 and 27 knots. Small trees may be set swaying, and you can hear wind whistling in wires. Waves are longer and run up to 5 feet from trough to crest. Whitecaps are everywhere, and spray is spitting off their tops. Wind is building up waves for a greater distance, with greater power. Currents will be up to about 4 knots, faster than you can paddle. You are farther from shore, and the channels between islands are broader, allowing more wind and wave action. Crossing the shore surf is significantly harder and requires greater skill and power. Shores may be rocky or irregular and present challenges when landing. It is becoming noisy and chaotic, and communication between boats (and even paddlers in tandems) is more difficult.

The American Canoe Association's Scale of Difficulty for Coastal Waters extends through three more steps, mirroring the sport's six stages of difficulty for whitewater boating. Class 4, for coastal paddling, is Very Difficult, up to Class 6, Life-Threatening. Other classifications simply label everything from Beaufort Force 7 (a moderate gale, or 33 knots) and up as Extreme. For most of us, the outer reaches of Difficult paddling is just what the name implies: difficult. That means it's time to get off the water, check that everyone is okay, and get on the phone or radio to inform your loved ones at home that you're lolling on the beach for a time. If you can't reach home, tell the Coast Guard where you are, and that you're safe and happy on the hard until the weather abates. Don't send those brave folks out into the crappy weather looking for you.

Remember: Sea kayaking is a sport to be enjoyed—not merely endured, and certainly not something merely to be survived. When things start getting a bit sketchy, head for shelter. Brew up some tea, sing a song, and plan on a better crossing later.

CHAPTER 24
Kayak Camping

iphoto: licensed by Shutterstock.com

We've been paddling together for a bit, and as we've glided along, I've come to realize that you want to expand your paddling horizons. Better put, you want to paddle *over* the horizon and discover for yourself just what a great little craft you're on the way to mastering.

Good for you!

How do you want to go? With forethought and good planning, you can map out a route that lets you paddle between inns. Snoozing in a featherbed and waking up to a gourmet breakfast makes exploration mighty appealing.

What would you think of a guided multi-day paddle along Hawaii's Little Na Pali Coast?

Your guides would move all the camping gear from one park to the next, prepare all your meals, supplying your kayaks and leading you over warm waters filled with tropical fish and giant turtles. As you paddle just outside the waves, you'll look to the north at paradise or to the south at Antarctica. You can find the same care in the Bahamas if you prefer the Atlantic to the Pacific.

Heck, I know you. You want to do this more on your own. You've done a lot of camping, out of cars or with a backpack, and you're ready to go.

One great solution is sprouting all over the country, flowing from the Maine Island Trail. Water trails are lineal parks for human-powered vessels, with campsites spaced about a day's easy paddle apart. Sometimes these developed campgrounds are on public property, and sometimes they're a public-private partnership. You'll pay a price for using these parks, but you have the advantage of developed campgrounds and a reservation system. Check with your state parks department for local information.

If you are paddling through National Forest lands in Alaska, you can hop from comfortable cabin to cabin. You can reserve them, and the cost is on the low side of moderate.

You're quick to point out that we're paddling touring kayaks, and you want to go touring. And you want the experience to be self-contained touring. Sounds good to me.

Earth, air, fire, and water: The old Greeks thought they had figured out the basic building blocks of the universe, but if nothing else, they defined the four factors that are critical to camping out of your kayak. You need earth as a place to pitch your tent, fire to cook your meals, water to drink, and air to blow the

224

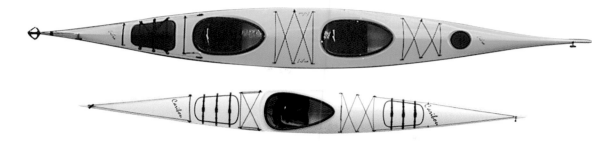

Photos courtesy Brian Henry / Ocean River

If you look at the double and single kayaks above, you'll see that the single boat has about the same amount of room from its front hatch to the tip of the bow as does the double. On the other end, the single has about the same (or perhaps just a bit more) amount of room from its rear hatch to the tip of its stern than does the double. The double does pick up some room in the middle between the cockpits, but part of that is taken up by the stern paddler's feet. The double does offer a bit more room around the paddlers, just because it has two cockpits. All in all, a double may carry about a quarter to a third more than a single kayak. Both these Current Design kayaks—the double is a Libra, the single, a Caribou—are rigged with elastic cords ahead of the cockpits for charts or other quickly accessible gear, and with cleats just aft of the cockpit (or rear cockpit) for a paddle-float self-rescue system.

bugs somewhere else. As we're paddling along together, let's chat about what makes these four factors work together.

If you crawl inside your touring kayak with a tape measure, you'll figure out that you have about three times as much storage space as found in an expedition backpack. That's for a single kayak. A tandem has about four times the volume of your backpack. By the way your eyes just lit up, I'm sure you've figured out that a kayak is as close to a perfect people-powered camping vehicle as you're liable to find. You're right.

Before starting to cram all your earthly possessions into your kayak, slow up. First of all, everything you pack must slide aboard

You can cram a lot into a kayak, but you'd be wise to pare away that which you don't really need from that which you do. You'll spend a lot of time packing, unpacking, and just lugging all that stuff around.

through narrow hatches and small cockpits. You'll either pack your gear into a lot of small bags, or figure out how to pack in sausage-shaped bags.

We both know that stuff expands to fill the space available, but we also know that the more we pack into our kayaks, the more we're going to have to push through the water, and the more we're going to have to carry up the beach. Comfortable camping is an exercise in simplicity, and it's almost true that the less you take along, the more comfortable you are. The opposite side of that is the fact you have the ability to carry along those things that are truly valuable.

Certain items we'll accept as givens: a tent with rain fly and ground cloth, sleeping bag and pad, cooking utensils, a tarp to protect your kitchen. If you have a small tent, fine. If you're still shopping, consider a slightly larger model giving you room to sit up, sprawl out, or play cards with your companions. Sometimes it rains on trips. I cherish a chair to rest in of an evening. I pack along a Crazy Creek Lounger, which consists of a fabric cover with side straps that form a back. Inside it is a self-inflating mattress, which at night goes under my sleeping bag.

A Choice of Fire

I paddle with two distinct types of folks: Some think of food as fuel and want it to be as simple and quick as possible; others think of food as a social event to be relished and treasured. I don't really understand the first group, and they probably don't understand me. You have to understand your own needs when assembling your kitchen.

Unless you want to eat only raw food, you're going to be faced with cooking, and cooking presupposes fire. Both campfire and stove have environmental impacts, and if you're going to travel gently on the land, you should consider the benefits and drawbacks of each.

I admit that I'm atavistic enough to really enjoy the flickering light, the smell, and the crackle of a campfire—to lean back in a chair with a mug of tea and a dulcimer, and to play the stars out of the deepening hues of the evening sky. But a fire is not suitable at all times and in all places. To use an open fire, for enjoyment or for cooking, mandates certain requirements. There must be a plentiful supply of down and dead wood. You have to be in an area of limited human use, both to ensure that supply of wood, and to give the area a chance to heal the scars from the fire. You also have to be willing to eradicate the marks of the fire before moving on. You might use a fire pan, or confine your fire to an existing fire ring.

If your camp can't meet those absolute requirements, you have no choice but to use a stove. With a stove you won't have ashes or a fire ring, nor will you burn the silvering chunks of driftwood or fallen limbs. But you will be using a machine that took substantial amounts of energy to fabricate, and you will be burning nonrenewable fossil fuels. On the other hand, you'll have an almost-instant source of easily regulated heat despite rain, wind, or dark of night. With a stove you can concentrate your skills on cooking rather than on the art of fire tending.

I sublimate my need for a flickering fire with a collapsible candle lantern. Mostly. The little lantern gives a bit of firelight in a wind-proof glass and is an evening focal piece.

After that as a warning, what's your real choice? Accept the best of both worlds, and tailor your kitchen to the resources available.

A hint, if you will: In an environment rich in downed wood, search for branches no bigger than your wrist or forearm, and carry them back to your camp whole. Buck the limbs to fire-length only as you use them, and don't set up a woodpile. Why? Full-length branches can be scattered out to be invisible while cut wood is an enduring eyesore.

We usually use a multi-fuel **MSR** stove, for the ease of finding its fuel. Our **MSR Flex 3** cook set gives us a couple of pots, dishes, and three cups. Others make equally good cook sets, but the founder of **MSR** was a climbing and paddling acquaintance. I suspect that a fair bit of unhappy tummies on camping trips come from inadequate camp hygiene, so we carry along a 10-liter collapsible sink from Sea to Summit. When folded up, it's about the size of a personal CD player.

When it comes to stoves, you have a lot of choices. We use a multi-fuel stove (which can burn white gas / stove fuel, diesel or kerosene), and as likely as not will bring two stoves along. Part of that is "belt-and-suspenders" backup, in case of failure, and part of it is because sometimes two burners just come in handy. They are light, compact, easily regulated, and convenient—all big pluses for a lazy camper such as myself. I'm willing to trade off their noise (and they do roar) for their clean heat.

Portable Kitchen

My kitchen is fairly simple. I pack 2- and 3-liter pots with nonstick lining and add a 10-inch sauté pan with nonstick lining, oven, teakettle, pot gripper, and hot pad (odds are you'll use both), plastic cutting board, wooden or plastic spatula, good knife, measuring cup, and a couple of 2½-liter water bags. Don't underestimate the value of a sharp knife. I've found that

a Blackie Collins–designed Gerber knife holds its edge well and locks into a sheath.

You can assemble the pots, pans, plates, and cups you need any way you like, but for ease of compact stowing and how well they work, take a good look at the MSR Flex 3 or the GSI Pinnacle Camper series. Both of them have insulated metal cups with lids. I've burned my lips on the old single-wall metal Sierra cups and won't do that anymore.

The Outback Oven revolutionized camp cuisine. It is essentially a small convection oven that you perch atop a single-burner camp stove. With one, you can bake up biscuits, pizza, or a plate of brownies. For breakfast or dessert, slice up an apple or two, top with brown sugar and cinnamon, dot with a couple of teaspoons of butter, and bake for twenty minutes. Take one of these ovens along in its compact package, and you'll expand your meal horizons and save fuel at the same time.

I admit it, I like my coffee. I could make do with one of the instants, but I figure that a small Italian espresso maker—I carry a small Bialetti Moka—is worth it. We all should have room for our little luxuries.

Those few campers who come down with tummy problems often blame them on bad water. I suspect as often as not it's from bad hygiene. Yeah, like you, I think washing up is a pain, especially when you're trying to wash utensils, plates, and pots in one small cooking pot. So take along the kitchen sink for cleanup. To make that easier, I use a midsize (10-liter capacity) fabric-and-flexible-frame Sea to Summit portable camp sink that folds down into a case not much bigger than a portable CD player. We could probably make do with the 5-liter sink, but there's washing to do beyond pots on a longish trip.

If you want, you can choose to eat the type of meals where someone has to ask whether they're eating chicken or broccoli—but you don't have to. Spice up your food, and camp

We all deserve a few treats. One of mine is a stovetop espresso maker. It makes the day start brighter, and soothes out the evening as we sit and chat.

meals will turn from drudgery into delight. A basic collection of spices includes basil, bay leaves, cayenne, chili powder, cinnamon, cumin, curry, dill, nutmeg, oregano, rosemary, pepper, salt, and thyme.

Tempt your taste buds with a few more condiments: brown sugar, garlic cloves, mustard, mushrooms, oil (corn oil, olive oil, peanut oil—match your palate and enjoy), salsa, soy sauce, dried tomatoes, and wine (decant into a Platypus water bag and use in a pasta sauce or in a dip for mussels). Hot sauce is a near-must.

If you're like me, you're going to find it easier to keep all the spices, condiments, and can openers in one place. A pouch made by Outdoor Research, called the Outdoor Kitchen, comes with a dozen or so bottles for condiments, a few bottles for oils, pouches for your kitchen tools, and mesh pockets for scrubbers, towels, and soap. Unzip it, hang it near your stove, and half your kitchen is in place.

I know of three ways to pack your food; two of them make you obsessive, and the third is an exercise in frustration.

The frustrating one (call it character-building) has you cramming all your food into

With the proper licenses and in the right season, the sea can yield up delicious meals. This youth learned to catch rockfish, and subsequently learned that the person who catches the fish also fillets them. Because he caught several extra fish, he paddled out to a yacht on the bay and offered the excess fillets to the sailors. In return they gave him a couple of pounds of homemade fudge. Karma does work.

"I know the lunch stuff is in here . . . somewhere." Preplanning makes a lunch stop a little less hectic.

the largest bag you can find. When it's time to cook, you paw through the entire bag and end up dumping it on the ground. You'll cherry-pick (if you're weak like me) your favorite foods at first, and then by the end of the trip, end up with mismatched foods you'll wonder why you packed in the first place. It's also interesting when you attempt to push this big bag through a small hatch into your kayak.

Another way is to collect a series of smaller, color-coded bags. Well before you launch, prepackage all the ingredients for each meal into separate bags. One group of paddlers insists that you should put all your breakfasts in a red bag, second breakfasts in a yellow bag, late lunches in a blue bag, dinners in a green bag, and treats in a clear bag. You equally could build a meals bag for each day, with one breakfast, one second breakfast, one lunch, one dinner, and one treat in each bag. Both work. Yes, that's four meals a day, plus a treat, but paddling can be hard work.

Those aren't individual servings, unless you are paddling alone. That's one meal each, for however many people you are cooking for.

One thing to remember: Any day may have a long crossing over midday, and you should plan lunches that can be eaten while afloat. You can mark those days when you're plotting out your trip. When possible, we prefer to break from paddling with lunches (and relief) ashore.

Whatever method you adopt, remember that you're going to be exercising fairly vigorously, and you're going to be eating more than you expect. Increase portion sizes; don't skimp on foods with a higher fat content; and remember to bring along desserts and evening snacks. Our rule of thumb is that we'll eat one more meal per day than we do at home. We've tried simply increasing the size of each of the three meals, but we do better with a good breakfast, early lunch, dinner, and supper.

Oh, yeah: Remember to label each meal. I've found it handy to include *all* cooking

Don't store fresh food in your tent or in your kayak. We're not alone out here, and a hungry bruin regards all food as belonging to him.

of the biological contaminants sounds great, but it still lets you sip 3 percent of the bugs. The closer you get to 100 percent filtration, the more comfortable you'll be. Water filters come in three flavors: a filtering system, a filtering system with carbon treatment, and UV treatment. Filtering takes care of the larger guys while chemical or light treatment works on viruses.

Also, most of the little nasties are dense creatures. You might find an attractive little waterfall tumbling into a small pool, but the creatures bouncing down that waterfall are going to hit the slower water in the pool and sink to the bottom. Eventually they're going to wash on through; the pool won't turn into a biological soup, but think where the greatest concentrations of contaminants will congregate in a stream. Few filters will weed out chemical or heavy-metal concentrations, so you're potentially better off avoiding still pools at the bottom of quick stretches of moving water.

With your water containers filled, move on away from the favored habitat of all those biting and stinging creatures and look for a more-habitable campsite. If you have a choice, you're going to find a gentle gravel beach tucked in behind a point. A large log tossed above the high-tide line during a severe winter storm serves as a table and kitchen. Gravel? Sure. Our culture seems to put a high value on sand beaches, but sand gets into everything. On the ridge of the point itself, exposed to any breeze, you'll find a flat place for your tent. Cherish that breeze, because it will keep your camp free of those flying, biting creatures. A small bowl is not as comfortable a campsite: It will shelter the mosquitoes and flies, it will pool up with cooler air, and, in most cases, it will be damper than a more-exposed spot on the ridge.

directions inside each meal bag, and to identify each component. When I'm first packing, everything is distinguishable, but a few days out, I can't tell one from the other.

A Real-World Campsite

There is, somewhere in our collective subconscious, an archetypal campsite on the banks of a trickling brook where we can dip pristine water from the stream and loll on the sandy beach.

In the world through which we actually paddle, there is no pristine water; virtually all the streams are filled with little nasties. And when we stop to fill our water bottles, we find that they are surrounded by a horde of slightly larger nasties: mosquitoes, biting flies, no-see-ums, and other flying appetites.

Appreciate streams for their beauty, but pump your water supplies through your water filters. Read the specs for your filter carefully. The filter that will remove 97 percent

I have a nightmare that I'll rise in the morning to discover a bare beach where my kayak had been the night before. When searching out a campsite, consider where you'll secure

If possible, your camp should be 70 or so adult steps from the beach. That's the recommended 200 feet. Your "sanitary wastes" area should be another 70 steps from your tent, and also 70 steps from the beach.

your kayak. A steep beach will be harder to land on, and you'll have to carry your kayak up the slope above the reach of the tide. A flat beach means a long carry across the flats if you land at less than high tide, or a long carry to the water if you want to launch before the tide comes back in. I've camped on slopes that were easy to land on but were impossible to launch from at most stages of the tide. Whatever beach you discover, I'd suggest carrying your boat well above the reach of the tide and then tying it securely with the bow, and perhaps even the stern, painter. And after all that, check it during different stages of the tide.

Generally speaking, hoisting your kayak atop that line of drift logs is the second dumbest place you can stow it. Those logs floated there, perhaps with a storm surge and pushed by waves. You really don't want to attempt to rescue your kayak from a maelstrom of surging, crushing waves.

What's dumber? Coming in at dead low tide and firmly tying your kayak to a stout rock. Think what happens as the tide rises.

As a pretty good rule, your campsite should be about 70 adult steps from the water, or 200 feet. You should be the same distance from your drinking water source. Solid wastes? About 70 or more steps in the opposite direction from your drinking-water source. Your kitchen area, because of the traffic there, should be on mineralized soil or rock to minimize compaction.

Do you remember how to dig a latrine? Forget it. Today's low-impact camping utilizes "cat holes," which is a minor hole maybe 6 inches deep and upwards of 6 inches across.

If you dig a deep pit, you've excavated down into a sterile soil environment, and the contents will be preserved for a long, long time. The active biological agents are in the top few inches of the soil.

When you and I are out here on the water, we're going to be guided by the moon and sun. The tides will determine our days, and the winds will establish our courses and distances. Those are truths we just have to live with, and in the real world are no more confining than gravity. What we can do, within those boundaries, is set our own schedules so that we're off the water relatively early on a paddling day. It's going to take an hour to two hours to land, unpack the kayaks, and set up camp. It will take at least that long to repack and launch when we're ready to push on.

When we can, it's often easier to make a long passage on a traveling day and set up a base camp as a home for several days. We can then set out on daylong mini-expeditions from this camp in boats that are lighter and more responsive, without the budgeted time for establishing a camp each day.

I've mentioned a few brand-name products. These are ones that have worked very satisfactorily for me. Don't rush out to equip yourself the same way, but you might use these as standards against which to measure the items you choose for yourself.

We've put in enough work setting up this camp. I'm going to take a break, get out my chair, and see if I can entice the evening stars out with my dulcimer.

Paddling is fun. Camping is fun. Kicking back and playing a dulcimer and pennywhistle is fun. Unpacking everything in the evening, setting up camp, repacking in the morning, and pushing on is less fun. Try finding a base camp where you can perch for several days, heading out on voyages of exploration and discovery while having a comfortable camp waiting for you at the end of the day.

Reward yourself by setting up an early camp, do a little exploring, and then find the perfect point from which to watch the sunset. That's why we came out here, anyway.

Dabjola; licensed by Shutterstock.com

CHAPTER 25

River Paddling

There is a difference in paddling on the ocean and on big rivers: One of them has saltier water. That's flippant, and I know your question was serious. In truth, though, the two environments are remarkably similar. Rivers don't represent some ideal of untrammeled freedom. In some areas you must register and license your kayak. Some areas may impose a fee for use. Local or state governments may place requirements on safety equipment or access. Some rivers may be paddled only under a permit system, and you might have to wait years to obtain a paddling permit. Know before you go!

Let's start with a clear distinction. We're not talking about white water, big rapids, or steep creeks. Those are way fun to paddle, and with the right boats and training, you can spend days and miles bouncing in the froth. That's a

A pod of kids in kayaks slows for a chat with a canoe on the **Stikine River in Canada.**

whole 'nother world. Right now you're talking about the bigger, quieter rivers that are more highways than playgrounds.

Class I and II rivers are placid, smooth-flowing streams. This isn't to say that you don't need a sizable helping of boating skills and common sense, but it does divide smoothly flowing streams from the fun and spray of white water.

In paddling-speak, these are considered Class I or Class II rivers. Class I is considered Easy, and involves moving water with riffles and small waves. We'll run into few obstructions, and all of those will be obvious and easy to skirt. These rivers, temperatures permitting, invite swimmers and pose little risk to them. You can rescue yourself quite handily without assistance. Class II is suitable for the Novice and may have some bumpy stretches, rapids that are pierced with wide, clear channels that are easily identified as you approach. You can't simply drift through obstacles, and you may have to do some maneuvering, but rocks and waves are easily missed. In the event of a mishap you might appreciate someone standing by, but you can take care of yourself easily.

River classifications extend onward to Class VI, or Extreme, and at the top end describe the edge of impossibility.

I implied that a river might be classified, and I don't want to mislead you. I'm really talking about segments or lengths of a river. A river

Rivers aren't necessarily whitewater playgrounds; on most you can just kick back and relax as you float along.

might begin as a trickle too small to paddle high in the mountains, grow into a mass of whitewater foam carving a deep canyon, burst out onto the plains with a long series of easy waves, and end at the sea as a placid near-pond.

Can we cruise and camp along these rivers in our kayaks? Mostly, yes. We'd probably want a more-maneuverable cruising kayak than is best for the sea. Consider the recreational kayak, around 15 feet long, with a 25- or 26-inch beam, and a large cockpit if you want to paddle a solo boat. For a double, look at a Klepper, a Feathercraft Klondike, or a Nautiraid Grand Raid. While these are all folding kayaks, it is their dimensions you should look at: They are all about 17 feet long, 32 to 36 inches across the beam, and all have a single open cockpit for both paddlers. Double spray decks are available. Look around and you can find similar plastic or composite kayaks.

Why this configuration? Shorter kayaks are easier to turn; beamier kayaks can be tilted to the side, bringing their bows and sterns to the surface and making turns still easier; and the big cockpits make it a whole heck of a lot easier to load and unload.

If you were crossing Montana's Fort Peck Reservoir or were down on Lake Powell, you may be subject to wind and waves that match the ocean, and in those locations you might prefer the integrity of a small cockpit.

In most places we won't have charts for these rivers. We'll use topographic maps and, when available, guidebooks. When you look at the topo map of your river you'll see that the contour lines crossing the river all form vee shapes, with the apex of the vee pointing upstream. The closer these lines appear together, the steeper the average gradient of the river, and possibly the stronger the current flow.

You'll use a topo map to find your way on most rivers, although some of the huge rivers with scads of commercial traffic are charted. Just remember that the vee where a contour line crosses a river always points upstream, and the closer the contour lines are together, the steeper the slope.

Heck, I've been with groups that forgot the contour vees point upstream, and planned a trip from downstream to a campsite upstream. Most of us won't do well paddling against even a 2- to 3-knot current.

Are you up for a day on the river?

Most flatwater or ocean trips are out and back, which means we can leave our vehicles at the launch beach and return to that same beach. Most river trips are point to point, meaning we start upstream and paddle to a take-out at a predesignated point downstream. You got it. We need to have at least one vehicle at the take-out to shuttle drivers back to the put-in to retrieve their vehicles. It's easy to get a car or driver to the wrong end, and it's equally easy to get lost on the route between the take-out and put-in. It's also easy to separate the car keys from the cars. Every paddler I know has a ridiculous story to tell about that.

With the car shuttle behind us, let's set to paddling.

When we launched our kayaks from an ocean beach we always tried to keep our bows into the waves. Wind and waves are the dominant factors in marine paddling. Here on the river we'll launch with our bows upstream. Current is the dominant factor on a river.

If we launch with our bows angled downstream, the current will force us back against the bank. If we launch straight out into the current, the force of the river will shove our bow downstream, and we'll pinwheel about for a bit. We'll launch at an angle of around 30 to

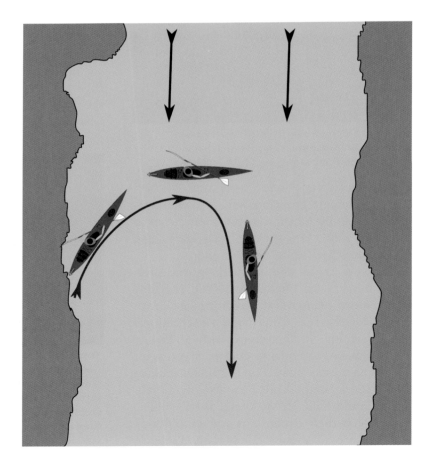

Launch with your bow angled into the river current, and as you clear the bank, turn across the current and continue the turn until you point downstream. A high brace off your downstream bow will help pull you around, while a low brace off your downstream stern will swing you around with a loss of forward speed.

45 degrees into the current. Our first paddle stroke will probably be on the downstream side of our kayak, which will give us the power to hold our angle to the current. Starting on the upstream side will turn us across or down the current.

Hold that angle to the current for your first couple of strokes, until you clear the bank, and then ease around to point downstream. You might want to do a low brace a bit behind you on the downstream side, and this will bring your kayak around nicely. Equally, you could do a high brace on the downstream side up ahead of your knees. On salt water our braces were balanced by the speed of our kayak; here on the river, we brace against the currents in the river.

"This is sweet," you crow, as the current carries us downstream. It is.

We are approaching our first bend in the river. When the river is going straight, and there are no underwater obstructions, the strongest current will be in the deepest middle part of the stream. That makes sense.

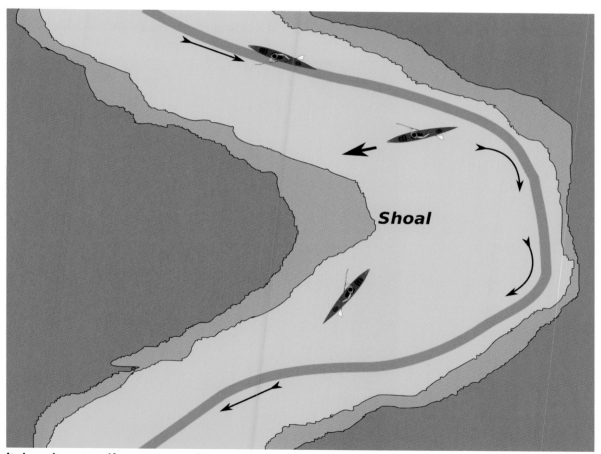

It doesn't matter if you are on a river or the sea—the current flowing down a channel will move to the outside of a bend. The water will carve the channel deeper on the outside, and the outside bank will be much steeper. The water will drop its load of silt and sand on the inside of a bend, creating a shoal or bar. Cautious boaters will back-set or ferry across the current to reach the slower water on the inside of the bend, staying aware of the shallower water.

This changes with a bend. The river carves the outside of the bend deeper and builds shoals on the inside of the bend. The fastest current will be along the outside edge of the bend. For us paddlers, this is a mixed blessing.

In a very few cases the river can force us up against the bank as its course changes. This is called a *headwall*. It can be upsetting in every sense of the word.

The river is also eroding the bank on the outside of the bend. The current just rubs against the land like sandpaper and chews it away. This is also where it's most likely to erode the soil out from underneath a tree's roots and send it toppling into the river—not a good thing. Not because it might topple on us, but because once it is down in the water, the current can still flow through its limbs. The current, carrying us to the outside of the bend, may move us right into those limbs and entangle us. It is significantly difficult to extricate ourselves from one of these strainers.

What should we do? Avoid it! Turning our bow toward the inside of the bend and paddling ahead is marginally effective, but the current will continue to sweep us to the outside. A better approach is to "ferry" our way to the inside of the bend. In a lot of cases we can turn our kayaks so that our sterns are angled toward the inside shore and then we can back-paddle.

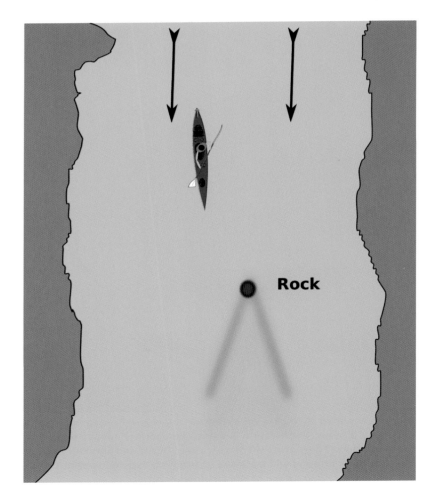

A "vee" shape pointing upstream is a strong hint that there is a rock lurking just upstream of the apex of the vee. With skill and practice you can slip into the eddy within the vee and pause, mid-river—great for checking out river conditions or waiting for your friends.

Yeah, just paddle backward. This is a *back ferry*. We will slide across the river to the inside of the bend.

If the current is stronger, we might swing our kayaks around so that our bows are pointed somewhat upriver. We'll turn so that we're heading a bit toward the inside shore, perhaps 30 to 45 degrees away from the current, and paddle ahead. We'll slide sideways to the shore.

Ferrying allows us to slide from one side of the river to the other without being carried downstream. It's a good skill to acquire.

Be careful when skirting the inside of the bend. You can be too aggressive and run yourself right up on the shallows.

Hey, we just zipped right around the bend with nary a problem. You point ahead, uncertain. There's a bump of water sticking right up in the middle of the river. You might not want to sleep on it, but that's called a *pillow*. There's a rock or similar obstruction on the river bottom just upstream of the bump. The current bounces off the rock and humps a mound of water up on the surface. If the upstream and downstream sides of the pillow are smooth, the obstruction is usually deep or the current is slight. If the downstream side of the pillow is rough and roily, the obstruction is near the surface.

I'd go around it unless I was familiar with it.

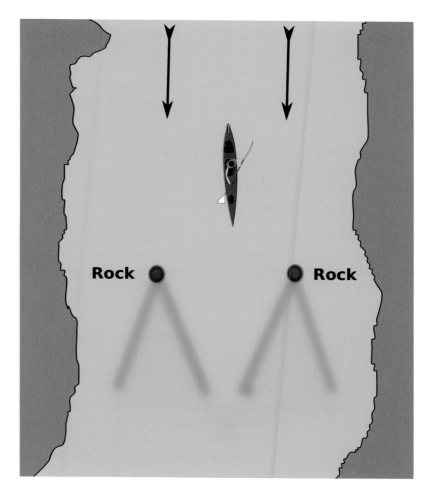

Rock   Rock

A vee shape pointing downstream often indicates a channel between two rocks. The rocks are at the upstream ends of the legs of the vee. The downstream apex of the vee can be marked with a set of waves that seem to stand in one place, caused by the converging eddy lines from the rocks. Take warning: Rocks tend to come in bunches, and you must keep a sharp lookout for them, especially when they're hidden in the disturbed waters of the converging eddy lines.

First you saw a pillow, and now you see a sharply delineated "vee" pointing right at you. Why is the river pointing at you?

A vee of disturbed water pointing upstream tells you that there is a rock or obstruction at the surface of the river, right at the apex of the vee. I'd avoid that point, if I were you. The disturbed water behind the rock is an eddy, and the two lines splaying out from the rock downstream are eddy lines—the place where the downstream flow of the river rubs up against the water flowing upstream to fill in the hole behind the rock.

Who would have thought the river would point at the rocks just for you?

"Hey," you shout delightedly, "there it's pointing at a rock downstream!"

Good call, but not right. The river only points up-current or upstream. You're looking at a vee pointing downstream.

What you are seeing are two rocks, one at the upstream end of each of the legs of the vee. The vee marks what is probably a clear passage between the rocks. The bouncy area at the apex of the vee is likely just the waves created by the currents colliding at the bottom of the vee. Be cautious about that vee, because there could be something solid down in the waves.

We paddle a little farther, enjoying the day, and all of us notice that the river is all of a sudden getting narrower. As we enter the narrower section, the current seems to speed up. Well, it is growing faster. The river is pushing a volume of water downriver. If the river is wide and deep, it can keep that same amount of water moving past a point at a slow speed, like a crowd meandering through a mall. If the river narrows, the water has to speed up to keep the same volume moving past a point in that same amount of time—much like people in the mall speeding up to go through a door or narrow hall.

In a wee bit we're going to be through this narrow neck, and some of the paddlers are grinning. They've been here before, and they all like roller coasters.

You see the river suddenly widen. Wider means slower. As our more rapidly moving water flows into the slower water, it mounds up into a train of waves. Hey, if you push a piece of paper along a flat desk, it remains flat; but if you slow down the front with a finger while continuing to push on the trailing edge, it humps up. You're bouncing over those humps as I speak.

A straight line across the surface of the river is not a good thing. If it extends clear across the river, it indicates an abrupt change in river level. Think of a waterfall, a dam, or, in the best of circumstances, a steep chute; none of these things are desirable.

On many of our big rivers various water management agencies attempt to control the current and the channels with "wing" dams (they have other names, too) that angle out from the bank a ways into the river current. By deflecting the current, these dams keep the river corralled within a channel rather than deciding to carve a new riverbed somewhere else. Rivers do that, you know.

So, if you see a straight line edging out from the bank, don't attempt to hop over it. Even if the water is topping the wing dam, the area downstream of the water is turbulent, recirculating, and deadly. A strong current is probably rocketing off the downstream edge of the dam.

While those dams do provide benefits, I'm always inclined to put an "n" at the end of their name.

Out on the salt water, we always keep a close eye on the tides. Fortunately on rivers we don't have to worry about rise and fall. Right? Wrong! Rain on the upper reaches of a river translates into a rise in the water level. The extreme example is a flash flood and a wall of water rushing down the stream. A hot day can increase snowmelt with a less-dramatic but nonetheless real impact. A dam may release

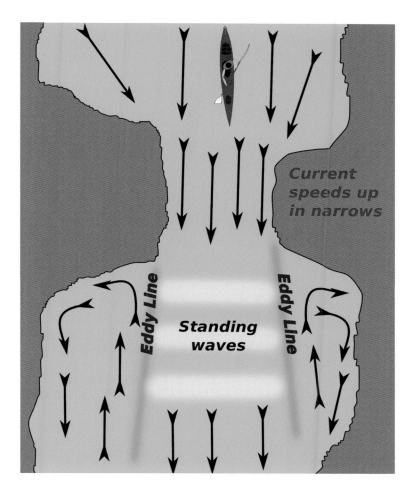

Current
speeds up
in narrows

Eddy Line

Eddy Line

**Standing
waves**

When a river suddenly narrows, the current speeds up in the narrow section. When the river widens, the river current slows. As the faster current from the narrow section slows, the energy is dissipated in a train of waves. The waves remain in one place on the river. If the widening of the river is abrupt, eddies can form on one or both sides of the river. Watch for the eddy lines and the counter-flowing currents if you choose to skirt the waves.

water upstream or on a tributary—triggered by hydroelectric power generation, irrigation needs, water levels mandated for fish preservation, or because a reservoir was overly full.

Most of our weather patterns come from the west. That's a combination of physics and meteorology. River systems—at least, a big number of them—are different. You start off in the morning, paddling in delightfully cool air, the leaves not even quivering on the bankside shrubs. Then about two in the afternoon, a big chuck of wind comes bursting upstream and slaps you alongside the head. It happens at the same time every day. Is that when the river gods wake up?

Nah; it's a combination of physics and meteorology.

The ocean stays at about the same temperature day and night in the short term. (Summer and winter are different, sure, but the temps don't swing wildly from one winter day to the next.) Interior plains are cool at night and heat rapidly when the sun rises. There probably isn't a huge temperature gradient from a river's mouth upstream early in the morning, but then the sun starts to fry the interior plains and the air. Hot air rises. Ocean air comes rushing up the river to fill in behind the rising air; that's our onshore (or upstream) wind. That's why the Columbia Gorge between Washington and

When possible, it's easier to swing your bow into the current and ferry sideways to your planned take-out. Most of us have better control and a stronger stroke moving ahead. You can back-paddle until about motionless in the current and then back-ferry over to the take-out, but this is often more difficult. Notice that I said "current" rather than "upstream" or "upriver." You could be in an eddy with the current flowing in opposition to the main river. As always, paddle in the world that you find, not necessarily the world you expect.

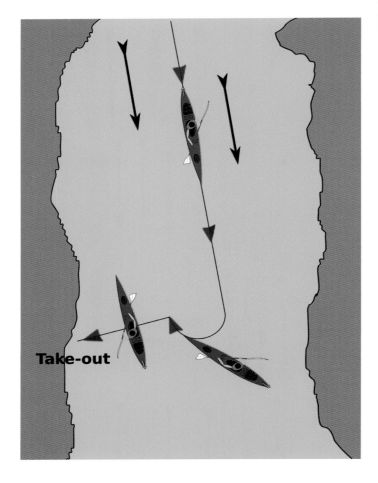

Take-out

Oregon is the world's greatest windsurfing slot, and that's why the wind chased us off the Mackenzie River in Canada every day at two p.m. (we took a two-hour nap each day around that time).

It's getting on to the end of your paddling day, and the take-out is just ahead. Remember how we launched into the current? We're going to land the same way. We'll edge over to the shore as we approach the take-out, and just before we reach it, we'll swing about so that our bows are pointing upstream. Then we'll ferry sideways in a controlled approach to the landing beach.

Let's be realistic. This isn't even an approach to river paddling, but is a brief note about how to consider approaching paddling on moving water. Take a class from a certified instructor. Join a paddling club and learn from your new friends. Join the American Canoe Association (www.americancanoe.org) and advocate for water access and safety. If you catch fire on these vital topics, check out the web pages of the National Water Safety Congress (www.watersafetycongress.org), or on the legal side, the National Association of State Boating Law Administrators (www.nasbla.org).

CHAPTER 26

Sailing

Stories that start "You shoulda been there" always make me cringe, in no small part because in most cases, anyone with even a modicum of good sense would not have wanted to be there—wherever *there* is. In this case, though, you should have, because you would have admired it.

We were camped on a little bump of rock, at the most 50 feet across, sticking up maybe 20 feet out of Canadian salt water. A few ledges along one side were a poor substitute for a beach, but the angled rock steps were the best we could have found that day. A single twisted conifer had forced its way through a split in the rock, and a wider split had filled in with sand and something else until it was level and barely only enough for two tents. At such a place you just

have to sit on one of the ledges and watch the daylight flare into a spectacular sunset. We had made a long day of it, catching the morning tides to work our way through a maze of islands and overfalls, and it felt good to sit on the rocks and sip hot tea liberally laced with honey.

A big tandem kayak came down the far side of the channel, hugging the far shore, riding easily and forcing the three accompanying singles to push hard just to stay with it. The bow paddler in the tandem had opened a big blue-and-white beach umbrella, and it scooped a great bite out of the wind—enough to put a "bone" of white foam curling back from the kayak's bow—and the stern paddler rode the rudder pedals to keep the boat on course for the next bay.

Opportunistic? Sure, but that's what kayak sailing is all about for most of us who like to mess about in small boats. Sails allow us to extend our cruising radius while remaining in the comfort and security of our kayaks. We can grab a little power assist from the wind at one end of the spectrum, or we can trick our boats out with a dazzling array of space-age components to push the very envelope of wind-driven performance. All we need is a scoop of fabric to catch the wind and a rudder to control our direction.

We're not necessarily talking about anything new here. John MacGregor in the 1860s

Today's sailing kayak is a high-efficiency machine. Outriggers provide great stability, airfoil leeboards limit leeward drift, and full-batten sails grab every ounce of energy from the wind. This kayak is set up for three sails, with the mizzen still to be raised.

cruised through Europe in his yawl-rigged cruising kayak, *Rob Roy*. My particular hero is a fantastic man named Dr. Hannes Lindemann, who kayak-sailed the Atlantic twice in the 1950s, once in a dugout and once in an off-the-shelf Klepper folding kayak. He went on to work as a humanitarian physician in Africa. Reading his book inspired me; meeting him across a beached kayak was humbling. Fredrick Voss, in a big-decked canoe, sailed around the world. That kayak is in a museum in Victoria, British Columbia, Canada. Adventurer John Dowd swooshed into a New Zealand port on the breath of a typhoon. The Polynesians spanned the Pacific in their multihull sailing canoes, and the Makah of the Pacific Northwest sailed out in search of whales. So we have a long history of sailing, and a well-earned reputation for quick and comfortable passages.

Sails

Sailing a skinny little kayak? I can see your eyebrows escape up into your hairline as you try your best not to blurt out the question. The simple answer is "Yes."

For starters, let's roughly divide kayak sails into two groups: those designed to go downwind, and those designed to go across, or upwind. That's pretty arbitrary, and you'll find a lot of crossover information, but as a starting point it works.

Downwind sails are set across the wind, and the force of the wind pushes you in the direction the wind is blowing, within an arc of about 45 degrees. Think of all the pirate or Napoleonic sea-battle movies, and you'll get the idea. That big beach umbrella was a perfect example of how downwind sails work.

The other division is the crosswind rigs. On these, the wind blows from sort of on the side, and with proper techniques these can work from downwind to approximately 45 degrees into the wind. If you've watched a "modern" sailboat with a mast and a boom holding the

A sloop-rigged kayak is a perfect family boat for an afternoon's outing.

sail in close to the keel line, you've seen this concept.

Any of these (and there are many variations) require a sailing skill set and constant attention. They can be way fun—in fact, ranging from somewhere between placid to hair-raising fun—and can, when everything goes right, change a long plod to a galloping sprint. They are not every kayaker's cup of tea, so don't let my delight influence you.

If you want to grab some wind on your kayak, you're going to have to juggle three separate balls. Do you want just a little extra muscle to carry you downwind, or do you want a sailing rig that converts your kayak into an all-around sailing vessel? Do you want a simple add-on, or are you willing (or able) to make

some alterations to your kayak? Do you want to keep your sleek kayak design, or are you willing to add (usually detachable) outriggers?

No one can tell you what's best, because you're the only one who understands how you want to kayak.

You say you think you just want a little extra horsepower heading downwind, but you're a kayaker and not a sailor. Since you prefer cruising, you want a simple, easily handled rig that quickly stows away.

Good, because that's available. Think of a sail completely enclosed in a flexible frame, hooked to a bungee cord you already have in front of your cockpit, and trimmed or controlled by two lines leading back to your hands from the shoulders of the circle. You don't have to fuss with a mast or a boom. Sailing is simple. Point your bow downwind with the attached sail flat on the foredeck, and raise the sail by pulling back on the two control lines (*sheets*, in sailor talk). Too much wind? Slack off on the lines, either spilling the wind over the top or completely depowering the sail by dropping it to the deck. Your efficient sailing range is about 30 degrees off each side of the wind, and you probably can tweak that for another 10 degrees. However, one of the big advantages of a downwind sail with a kayak is that you (mostly) don't have to compensate for the sideways force of the wind. Think of all the pictures you've seen of a conventional sailboat heeled over, with the crew poised on the upwind rail. It's more challenging in a kayak, sailing across the wind, or "reaching."

I guess that in a Beaufort Force 3 wind—that's a gentle breeze with wind speeds of 7 to 10 knots, and an occasional whitecap (enough wind to keep a light flag extended, and a tree's leaves in motion)—a downwind sail will push a kayak along a bit faster than most of us would like to paddle.

A rudder is convenient, but by no means necessary. Go ahead; take one control line in each of your hands, and at the same time, hold your paddle. Keep your hands well apart, near the maximum power position, and you'll find that you can steer mostly by subtle motions of the control lines and with an occasional dip or stroke with your paddle. My kayak seems happier with the skeg in the water.

I like to keep my paddle in my hands, ready for a quick brace that so far I've never needed.

WindPaddle makes a sail like this, in several different sizes. The sail is almost dome-shaped within its frame, which means that it's pretty stable when filled by the wind. You can twist the plastic batten of the frame into thirds and stick the collapsed sail rig under your bungee cords for quick stowage.

Advanced Elements (AE), a company that makes a line of inflatable kayaks, offers a semi-circular downwind sail that mounts to deck hardware closer to your bow. Inflatables tend to be a bit beamier than hardshell kayaks, and you might have to futz with mounting points when fitting their sail to a non-AE boat.

With the wind from astern in a downwind rig, there is no force leaning your kayak over to the side. In fact, many downwind sails actually lift up and attempt to raise your bow.

A different take comes from a vee-shaped downwind sail. The booms that support the outside edges of the sail join at a mounting plate on your foredeck. The mounting plate, shaped to fit the profile of your deck, may be adjustable or may be bolted (with a backing plate for strength) permanently in place. The sheets work on the same principle as other downwind sails, and the angle of the sail may be varied for best sailing. The vee shape puts more sail area up higher, getting it out of the surface turbulence and into cleaner air.

Pacific Action Kayak Sails and Spirit Sails are among the manufacturers of this rig.

If you're more into sailing as a tool, look at a spinnaker flying from a rigid mast mounted through your foredeck. These are triangular sails, with the peak of the triangle supported at the top of the mast, and control sheets from the two clews—the outer corners of the sails—coming back to the cockpit. If there is too much wind, simply fold the sail in half so that the two clews are together, and move one sheet from an original clew to a grommet in the center of the lower edge of the sail. Sailors call this *reefing*. Want to sail more or less across the wind? Pull the sail against the mast, bring the two clews together, and you have an airfoil shape that will allow you to sail efficiently across the breeze. A lot of folks make these spinnakers. You can see the rig in action at Easy Rider Canoe & Kayak.

When sailing becomes as big a part of the sport as paddling, look at the TWINS sail rig developed by Balogh Sail Designs. The TWINS rig is basically a pair of triangular sails joined at the mast, with booms that keep the sails fully extended. Sheets come back from the outside ends of the booms to a short rod that allows one-handed control of the entire rig. Slack off on the short control rod and the sails depower by folding together ahead of the mast. The two sails can be folded together for crosswind sailing. The TWINS rig is most

effective to about 45 degrees on each side of downwind.

Sailing downwind is great, but the time will come when you'll want to sail across the wind. Now's the time for what they call fore-and-aft sails, because instead of having the sails spread out to each side of the kayak, the sails will be more or less in a line with the keel. They go from the fore, the front, aft to the rear.

This is going to cause us a couple of problems. When you and I had our bow pointing downwind, with the wind coming over our stern, we were blown right along with the wind. That's cool. Think about what happens when we turn our kayak sideways to the wind. The wind is still going to blow us in the same direction, except now that's sideways. You're right. We have some lateral resistance, but not enough to bother the wind.

We're going to have to add a few more parts to our kayak to use fore-and-aft sails. We have to counter that sideways slip, and

Wind from the side tends to push your sailing kayak over, which is called heeling. Without other tools you have to balance the heeling force by shifting your own weight to the windward side.

fortunately, that's easy enough to do. Let's think about a knife and a cube of soft butter. If you slice through the butter, sharp edge first, the knife moves through the butter easily. If you attempt to push the blade through sideways, it becomes very difficult. If we hang a board off the side of our kayak, parallel to the keel line, it works just like that knife. The board slides easily through the water if you're going ahead, and at the same time helps the kayak resist sliding sideways under the force of the wind. Sailors have been using these for thousands of years, and call them *leeboards*— because they are boards on the lee, or downwind, side of the sailing craft. In most cases the kayak will carry two boards, one on each side. You put the one on the lee side in the water, where it is held at the top and supported by the hull pressing against it. The other board is raised out of the water.

The second problem comes because the leeboards work. Now we have wind pressing on the sail, up high, and the leeboards preventing us from sliding. If we don't watch out we'll topple over on the downwind side. This lean is called *heeling*.

If our sail is relatively low and small, we can shift our weight to the upwind (sailors call it the *weather*) side, and we can counteract the tipping force of the wind. What results is a balancing act, and most of us will be more comfortable with a paddle in our hands, poised for a sudden brace.

If our sail is a little larger, it's doubtful we can shift enough weight to the upwind side to balance ourselves. We can make that work. All we have to do is rig an outrigger.

On paper, an outrigger is simple. It consists of a pole mounted crosswise (more properly, *athwartships*), with one end fastened securely to our kayak and with a float mounted on the other end. Some of these floats can be inflatable, while others are built just like our kayak's hull.

The crossbeam is really called an *aka,* and the float is properly known as an *ama.* Those are Polynesian words, describing the way those island-hopping explorers balanced their seagoing boats for millennia.

Most of the outriggers I've seen (but not all) use two akas, so the ama is held at both its bow and stern.

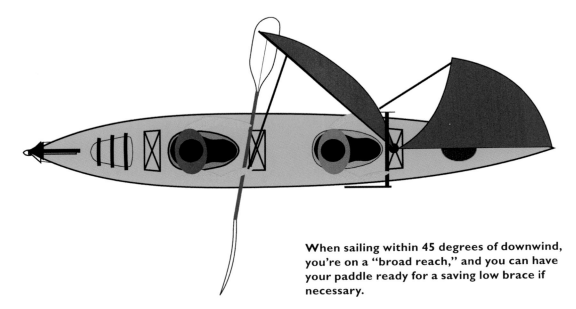

When sailing within 45 degrees of downwind, you're on a "broad reach," and you can have your paddle ready for a saving low brace if necessary.

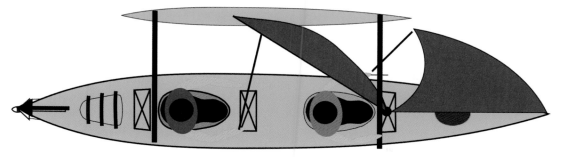

This tandem kayak is being sailed with a single outrigger. If the outrigger is on the downwind side of the kayak, as it is here, its buoyancy supports the force of the wind. If the outrigger was on the windward side it would be less efficient, because only its weight would keep the kayak level. Some kayak sailors will sit on their decks or out on the outrigger supports to add balancing weight.

Right away you caught on to one of the challenges. That ama is only going to support our kayak on one side. That's somewhat true. It is also true that if we're sailing with the aka on the upwind side, the weight of the aka helps to keep us level. Heck, we've even been known to throw a few jugs of water into the aka to help balance us.

There's a more-balanced solution. Let's use long—maybe 10 to 12 feet—amas, with our kayak in the center and an aka on each side. Now we have a very beamy kayak, or really, a trimaran, that will be stable in a lot of wind.

A few seconds of reflection will convince you that your sail will work better when the mast is vertical. You won't be spilling air out

of the sail, and a sail held vertically presents a more-effective area to the wind than one held at an angle. On the other hand, you'll also soon realize that at some point the heeling motion will overcome your balance. Or, splash-and-glub time.

The simplest fore-and-aft rigs are triangular sails that are supported at the top of the mast and at the bow of your kayak, with the control sheet extending back from the clew to the cockpit. They don't have a boom (that long pole sometimes found along the bottom edge of a sail), but are held in shape by the pressure of the wind and the control line or sheet fastened to the lower, aft corner of the sail. With some you can halve the sail area easily,

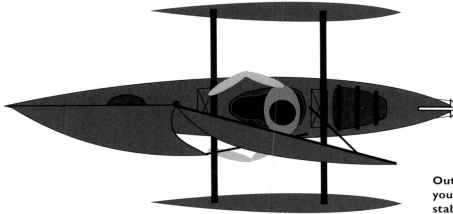

Outriggers on both sides of your kayak create the most stable platform for sailing.

by putting a *cringle* (nautical talk for a grommet or reinforced eye) in the center of the lower edge of the sail. Unhook the tack (that's the place where your sail hooks to the bow of your kayak) and re-hook the tack to the center cringle. Fold the sail in half, and attach the sheet to both grommets at what is now the clew. The folded edge of the sail is now the leading edge, and your effective sail area is halved. Other sails can be rolled up just like a window shade on that line from the top of the mast to the bow. It's called *roller reefing* or *roller furling.*

With sails like these you have a kayak that sails well across the wind, and perhaps as much as 60 degrees into the wind.

The next layer comes with sails that are firmly supported on a line from your bow up to the top of your mast, or are fastened to your mast. This creates a hard leading edge to the sail, and makes the sail a far more efficient airfoil. If you use two sails—a jib ahead of your mast and a mainsail supported from your mast—you increase your sail area for power, and you gain a lot of power from wind blowing through the slot between your sails. You go faster, but you have more sideways pressure on your kayak.

Many of the mainsails you'll see on kayaks as we go cruising, the sails with their leading edge at the mast, have *battens* (thin strips of stiff but flexible material) in pockets in those sails, from the mast to the outside edge. These help give the sail fabric the most efficient shape for sailing across or into the wind.

Sailing

Enough of hardware. Let's go sailing. We'll start in shallow water, where I can hold you as you get ready. First of all, make sure your leeboard and rudder are down in the water. Raise your sail, letting the sheet fly free, and secure your halyard. If you haven't noticed, on this first sail you have a fore-and-aft rig with a single mainsail. Get comfortable, put your feet on the rudder, and pull the sheet in until the boom makes an angle of about 45 degrees with your keel line. I'm holding you (and it's getting more difficult with the pressure from the sail) so that the wind is coming straight in from the side. As I release you, you'll start sailing at right angles to the wind. Hey, it works!

As you start to pick up speed, you'll see that you can easily turn your bow toward the wind with your rudder. But as you do so, the back of the sail begins to shake and you lose speed. Try hauling the sheet in a little tighter, until the angle between the boom and your keel is about 30 degrees. You will now be able to turn your bow further into the wind, until you're sailing a course about 45 degrees from dead into the wind. And that's about as close to sailing straight into the wind as you're going to get.

Now you want to come back to the beach. You have two options in turning: You can turn your bow toward the wind, and with enough speed you'll swing your bow right through the direction from which the wind is blowing, and will be heading back toward the beach with the wind on your other side. Turning by heading into the wind is called *tacking.* You could also turn your bow away from the wind, in a curve downwind, and bring the wind across your stern. Your boom will probably swing from one side to the other with a thump (and with more wind this can be awfully powerful) as you complete your turn. This is called *gybing* or *jibing* (same word, but you'll see it spelled both ways). You will be blown a ways downwind with this kind of turn.

That was fun!

Now you want to go upwind. Pick up a bit of speed and turn until you're headed about 45 degrees into the wind. Sail for a distance—whatever is comfortable, depending on the width of the channel you're in, the force of the wind, the waves, or even your comfort range from shore. Now, with plenty of speed, go ahead and tack—that is, turn into the wind.

A sailing kayak can sail as close to the wind as about 45 degrees, clear around the compass to about 45 degrees into the wind on the other side.

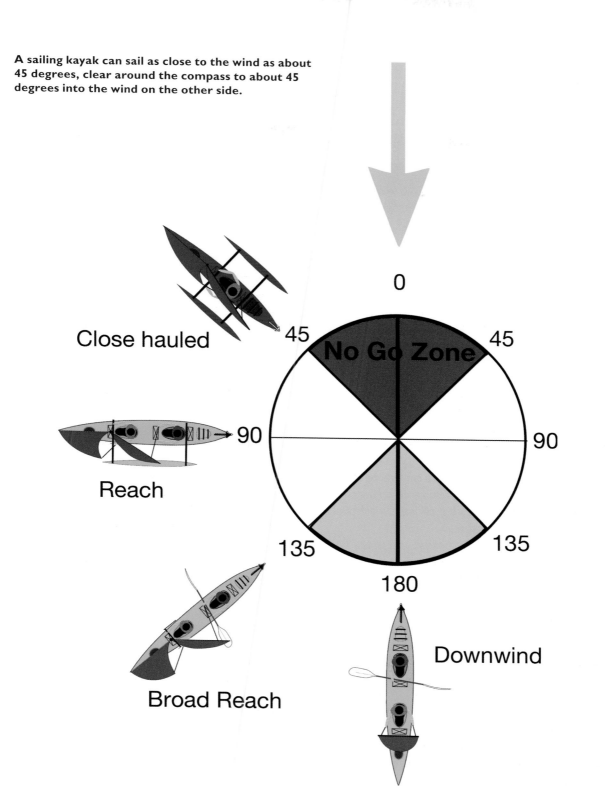

Close hauled

Reach

Broad Reach

No Go Zone

Downwind

0

45

45

90

90

135

135

180

Walk the beach and most kayak symposiums, and you'll work your way through a maze of brightly colored sails.

But don't turn completely around. Instead, stabilize your course until you're sailing at about 45 degrees into the wind, but now with the wind on your other side. You might not be able to sail directly into the wind, but you can zigzag your way upwind like this, and on average you'll be heading right upwind. You're covering more water, but you're working those switchbacks toward your destination.

Going downwind is almost intuitive. Turn your bow downwind. Let out your sheet until the sail is at right angles to the wind. You're on your way. In most cases you can lift both leeboards out of the water to reduce drag. With the wind behind you, you won't slip sideways.

A few warnings about downwind sailing: One, you're going to have a hard time estimating the force of the wind. It won't feel as powerful, because your speed will somewhat disguise the wind velocity. Two, the size of the waves is directly affected by the distance the wind blows over the water. The farther you sail downwind, the larger the waves will become. Third, it's a lot easier to be blown downwind

than it will be to battle your way back upwind. Fourth, if you absentmindedly turn a little off course, the wind can reach behind the edge of your sail and slam the boom to the other side with great force.

You decided to use your paddle to give a little extra power as you tacked into the wind, and you discovered one of the challenges of kayak-sailing with outriggers: The amas and the akas get in the way of a good paddle stroke. The leeboards are in the wrong spot, and even the mast is in the way! Stow your long paddle. Use a short canoe paddle instead. Short, because you are sitting low in your boat rather than kneeling, and you don't need a long shaft to reach the water. Some kayak sailors like to use a conventional canoe paddle, while others like a bent-shaft paddle. The bent-shaft allows you a longer effective power stroke, and probably takes some of the strain off your wrists throughout the paddle stroke. Most of us won't spend the time or have the need to learn bent-shaft paddling techniques. If you have wrist problems, it's something to consider.

CHAPTER 27

Why Go Kayaking?

Why go kayak cruising? We've shared a lot of tips on the *how* of kayaking.

But what about the *why* of this activity?

I'm not wise enough to link the symbolism of the salinity of the sea to the salinity of your blood, nor the pulse of the tide to the beat of your heart. Nor to reflect on the coincidence that your body and the surface of the Earth have about the same percentage of liquids.

I know we live in a stress-filled world, with constant demands eroding our own time and space. And I know that living on beach time with muscles tired from paddling rather than from being tense all day gives me a more positive outlook.

I've seen that folks who paddle along the shoreline under their own power seem not to trash the sea and befoul the shore. Perhaps while making their very good time, they have the breadth of vision to see the folly of not caring wholeheartedly for the land. I can't point with praise at an unblemished personal environmental record. My boats are plastic and 'glass. I wear synthetic clothing. I do the best I can, but I'm not about to crank the clock back to another time. I like the era in which we live, and technology used wisely is such an awesomely great benefit.

But the *why* of this activity?

All my life I've been in small boats on the water. A life without the language of water is a foreign tongue, and while I may attempt to translate it, I do not understand the nuances of it. Why go kayaking? How can you *not* go?

How can you not drift along on a sleek gray tide waiting for the sun to come climbing up in an explosion of reds and golds, changing the black sky to blue? How can you not watch rain throw itself into the sea? Or laugh at the quizzical expression on an otter's face moments before it leaps from its rock over your bow?

How can you not find that the speed of a cruising kayak matches your own curiosity, and that the ability to explore the byways immeasurably expands your horizons?

How can you not pass on to your children the understanding that the kayaker is responsible for himself or herself—that the freedom to paddle is based forever on the responsibility of paddling?

I launch from my dock and glide over deep purple sand dollars canted up on edge as they feed. How can you not delight in them and work to preserve them?

I met a Native American from the upper Midwest, a birch-bark canoe maker by trade and a person who understood that there are meanings underlying our actions.

"You," he said, "are responsible for the next seven generations." He didn't mean some vague, impersonal "you" floating over the population. He meant the person he was talking to, and he would mean the same thing speaking to each of you. Speaking to each of you in the singular . . . speaking to each of you one at a time.

If a cruising kayak can help any of us to see the magnitude of our task and the pleasures we find in meeting it, how can we not help but paddle?

Wind is the primary force in your paddling environment, not only pushing you and your kayak about but more important, creating most of the waves over which you bob. To make sense of this you have to place yourself at the center of the universe. From there you'll see the wind in its relationship to you. If a wind passes over you and on to another object, perhaps a shore or even a kayak, that object is to leeward of you. What does that tell you? That shore to leeward of you, the lee shore, is exposed to waves pushed along by the wind. The surf will be higher and more aggressive, there may be logs washed up on the beach, and the wind will push you that way. That direction is called "downwind," and it is kind of like coasting downhill. Think of the red kayak in the drawing at the right, with the wind shown as the blue arrow. If the wind passed over an object, such as an island, before reaching you, it is to windward from you. The island is upwind from the green kayak. Sometimes it is called "to weather" because the weather comes from that direction as it is blown along by the wind. It is also called "upwind" because paddling upwind is sort of like trudging up a hill. The greater the wind, the steeper the hill. On the plus side, as you paddle closer to that windward shore the waves will be smaller and usually less aggressive. As you approach the windward shore you are reducing the "fetch" or distance over the water the wind blows and thus the size of waves the wind can generate. It is not all peaches and cream, though. The wind close to that shore has to swirl and eddy to come around the land and becomes less predictable. Remember that leeward and windward are not fixed points or directions, but are always in relationship to you in your kayak at that specific moment.

The Beaufort Scale

In 1806 Sir Francis Beaufort devised a scale of wind speeds, vital to a navy that used wind as its fuel source. By using a set of accepted standards, sailors the world over could consistently describe and compare wind speeds.

Wind is the primary cause of waves in the cruising kayak environment. Wave height varies with the length of time the wind has blown, and the area of open water over which it has blown (the *fetch*). The heights given in this chart (see next page) are based on a twenty-four-hour wind and a fetch of no more than 10 miles—for the coastal paddler.

Be aware that today's meteorologists have expanded the traditional with five additional classes of hurricanes, peaking out with wind speeds of 118 knots.

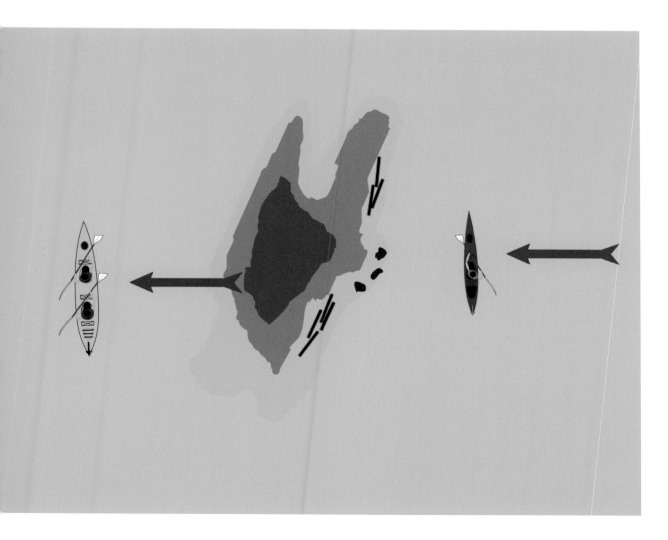

Beaufort No.	General Description	Sea Criterion	Landlubber's Criterion	Wind in Knots
0	Calm	Sea like a mirror.	Calm; smoke rises vertically.	Less than 1
1	Light airs	Ripples with the appearance of scales are formed, but without foam crests.	Direction of wind shown by smoke drift but not by wind vanes.	1 to 3
2	Light breeze	Small wavelets, still short but more pronounced. Crests have a glassy appearance and do not break.	Wind felt on face; leaves rustle; weather vane moved by wind.	4 to 6
3	Gentle breeze	Large wavelets. Crests begin to break. Foam of glassy appearance. Perhaps scattered white horses.	Leaves and small twigs in constant motion. Wind extends light flags.	7 to 10
4	Moderate breeze	Small waves becoming longer; fairly frequent white horses.	Raises dust and loose paper; small branches are moved.	11 to 16
5	Fresh breeze	Moderate waves, taking more pronounced long form; many white horses are formed. Chance of some spray.	Small trees in leaf begin to sway. Crested wavelets form on inland waters.	17 to 21
6	Strong breeze	Large waves begin to form; white foam crests are more extensive everywhere. Probably some spray.	Large branches in motion; whistling heard in telegraph wires, umbrellas used with difficulty.	22 to 27
7	Near Gale	Sea heaps up and white foam from breaking waves begins to be blown in streaks.	Whole trees on motion; inconvenience felt when walking against wind.	28 to 33
8	Gale	Moderately high waves of greater length; edges of crests begin to break into spindrift. The foam is blown in streaks.	Breaks twigs off trees; generally impedes progress.	34 to 40
9	Severe gale	High waves. Dense streaks of foam. Crests of waves begin to topple, tumble and roll over. Spray may affect visibility.	Slight structural damage occurs, such as slates removed.	41 to 47
10	Storm	Very high waves with long overhanging crests. Resulting foam is blown in dense white streaks. The surface takes on a white appearance. Visibility affected.	Seldom experienced inland; trees uprooted; considerable structural damage occurs.	48 to 55
11	Violent storm	Exceptionally high waves. The sea is completely covered with long white patches of foam. Everywhere the edges of wave crests are blown into froth. Visibility affected.	Very rarely experienced on land; horrific winds usually accompanied by widespread damage.	56 to 63
12	Hurricane	Air filled with foam and spray. Sea completely white with driving spray. Visibility very severely affected.		Over 63

Glossary

Abeam: On the side of the kayak, amidships, or at right angles to the keel line. "On the weather beam" means at a right angle to the keel in the windward direction, while "lee beam" means at a right angle to the keel in a leeward direction.

Aft: Toward the stern.

Amidships: In the center of the kayak.

Anchor: A weight that, when dropped to the bottom of a body of water and attached to a kayak by a rope, or line, holds the kayak in one place.

Astern: In the direction of the kayak's stern.

Asymmetrical: Pertaining to a hull shape in which the kayak's widest point, or beam, is either aft or forward of amidships.

Bail: To empty water from a kayak.

Bang plate: A reinforcing plate or "shoe" made of abrasion-resistant material that protects the stems of a kayak from scrapes and impact damage during beaching or launching.

Beacon: A post or buoy placed over a shoal or bank to warn vessels of danger.

Beam: The width of a kayak at the widest point.

Bearing: The direction to an object in relation to the person looking at it.

Bight: A rope bent back upon itself so that it is doubled. Also, a bend in the shore that creates a bay.

Bilge: Area where a kayak hull's bottom turns up into its sides.

Binnacle: The receptacle for a compass.

Bitter end: The end of an anchor line that is attached to a boat at a bitt.

Blade: The wide, flat area of a paddle.

Bow: The front of a kayak.

Brace: Paddling technique used to stabilize a kayak. The "low" brace and "high" brace are two common techniques.

Breaker: Waves broken by shoals or ledges.

Broach: A potentially dangerous situation that occurs when a kayak becomes caught in currents of different speeds. An example is when a kayak accelerates down the face of one wave and collides with a slower-moving wave in front, causing it to veer or yaw abruptly sideways.

Bulkhead: Transverse wall that creates a sealed compartment fore or aft in a kayak. Primarily used for flotation, but also used as a storage area with access via deck hatches.

Buoy: A floating mark that identifies a location or channel.

Can buoy: A buoy shaped like a cylinder. Most can buoys are black.

Canoe: An open craft with pointed ends that is propelled with one or more single-bladed paddles.

Chine: The intersection between the bottom and the sides of a vee- or flat-bottomed kayak.

Cleat: A device to which ropes or lines may be attached.

Compass: An instrument that points toward magnetic north.

Course: Planned route over which a kayak travels.

Cross bearings: Two or more bearings used to determine the position of a kayak.

Current: Water moving horizontally.

Current rips: Small waves formed on the surface by the meeting of opposing currents.

D-ring: A metal D-shaped ring for fastening ropes and straps.

Daymark: A structure used as an aid to navigation during daylight.

Dead ahead: Directly ahead.

Dead astern: Directly behind.

Dead reckoning: Calculation of distance from time on the water and estimated paddling speed. Derived from the word *deduced*.

Deck: Surface that covers the bow and stern of a kayak.

Depth: Vertical measurement from a hull's lowest to highest point, usually from the top of the gunwale amidships to the floor of the kayak.

Directional stability: Tendency of a boat to hold its course under way.

Displacement: The weight of the water displaced by a kayak.

Draft: The depth of water needed to float a craft.

Draw stroke: A stroke that is used to move a kayak sideways. The paddler places the blade in the water parallel to the kayak at arm's reach, then pulls the kayak over to it.

Dry bag: Waterproof storage bag.

Dry suit: Fully enclosed, waterproof garment with latex gaskets at the neck and wrists. Worn by whitewater and sea kayakers for protection from cold water.

Ebb: A receding or falling tide.

Eddy: Area of swirling water down-current of an obstruction.

Eddy line: Transitional area between main current and eddy current.

Eskimo roll: A self-rescue technique used to right an overturned kayak or canoe without exiting the boat.

Fathom: Measurement equivalent to 6 feet.

Feathered: Pertaining to a blade that is canted to present the narrow edge rather than the surface to the wind, thereby minimizing wind resistance. A feathered blade on a kayak paddle is offset at an angle from its opposite blade.

Ferry: To cross a current with little or no downstream travel, using the current's force to move the boat laterally.

Fiberglass: Glass-fiber cloth impregnated with resin that can be easily formed into hull shapes.

Flare: A hull cross section that grows increasingly wider as it rises from the waterline toward the gunwales. Also, a pyrotechnic device used to get the attention of someone beyond shouting distance.

Flat water: Lake or ocean water or slow-moving river current.

Flood: A rising tide.

Flotation: Buoyancy elements built into a craft to ensure that it does not sink when swamped.

Fore: The part of a kayak forward of the cockpit.

Freeboard: The portion of a kayak above the waterline.

Grab loop: Short rope or grab-handle threaded through bow or stern stem of a kayak or canoe. Most often used as carrying handle, but also useful as a handhold for swimmers.

Grip: The part of a kayak paddle held in the hand.

Gunwale: The line where hull and deck intersect.

Hatch: Access opening on front or rear deck.

Hull: The underbody of a kayak, which comes in contact with the water.

Hull configuration: Shape of a hull.

Inflatable kayak: An inflatable, open-top craft designed for one or two paddlers.

Initial stability: A boat's resistance to leaning; tippiness.

K1: One-person kayak.

Kayak: A watercraft that a sitting paddler propels with a double-bladed paddle.

Keel: A strip or extrusion along the bottom of a kayak to prevent slipping sideways under the pressure of wind.

Keel line: The shape of a kayak's bottom from a sideways perspective.

Kevlar: A DuPont aramid fiber used in kayak construction.

Knot: Rate of speed based on the time it takes to cover 1 nautical mile (6,076 feet).

Layup: Manner in which layers of fabric such as fiberglass or Kevlar are placed to form a kayak hull.

Lee: The downwind side. "Under the lee" of an object means having it between you and the wind.

Leeboard: A board fixed to the lee side of a kayak under sail to prevent the kayak from being blown sideways.

Lee shore: The shore upon which the wind is blowing.

Leeward: To the lee side.

Leeway: The distance a kayak drifts to leeward, or downwind.

Life jacket: Personal buoyancy device required by law for every person aboard a vessel of any size. Often called PFD, or personal flotation device.

Nautical mile: 6,076 feet.

Navigation: Determining and following one's route.

Neap tide: The period in the moon's first or third quarter when the low and high tides have the least amount of change.

Nun buoy: A buoy with a conical top. Most nun buoys are red.

Offing: Distance from shore.

Overfalls: Short, usually breaking waves that occur when a current passes over a shoal (or other underwater obstruction) or meets a contrary current.

Paddle: Primary tool for propelling kayaks.

Painter: A rope attached to bow or stern for tying a kayak to shore.

Peel-out: The act of leaving an eddy and entering the main current.

PFD: Personal flotation device.

Piloting: Navigation using geographical points.

Polyethylene: Thermoplastic material used in construction of kayaks.

Port: The left side of a kayak from the perspective of the paddler. Also, an opening or hatch.

Pump: A device for removing water from inside a kayak. Also called "bilge pump."

Put-in: The starting place of a paddling trip, where you put your boat in the water.

Ribs: Pieces of wood spaced along the inside of a hull to form its frame.

Rocker: Upward curvature of the keel line from the center toward the ends of a canoe or kayak. A great amount of rocker enables quick, easy turns.

Rudder: A foot-controlled steering device on touring or sea kayaks.

Sea: Waves caused by wind blowing at the time and place of observation, as opposed to "swell," waves caused by a distant wind.

Secondary stability: A hull's tendency to stabilize as it leans to one side.

Shaft: The rod or tube holding the blades, which the paddler holds.

Skeg: Rudder that is fixed laterally but may be raised or lowered and that improves a kayak's ability to move in a straight line.

Sound: To measure the depth of the water.

Spring tide: Tides that occur near the times of full or new moons when the range tends to be greater.

Starboard: The right side of a kayak from the perspective of the paddler.

Stem: The end piece of a hull at bow or stern.

Stern: The rear part of a kayak.

Surf: Large breaking waves along a coastline or tidal area. Also, to ride large waves on a river or the ocean in a kayak or canoe.

Surf ski: A long, narrow kayak used for cruising and racing across open water. The paddler sits in divots on the hardshell deck, not in an enclosed cockpit.

Sweep stroke: Stroke used to turn a kayak toward the off-side (non-paddle side) by reaching out and ahead, then "sweeping" the blade in a wide arc fore to aft.

Swell: Waves caused by far-off winds.

Symmetrical: Pertaining to a hull shape in which the kayak's widest point, or beam, is directly amidships.

Take-out: The end point of a paddling trip.

Tandem: Two-person kayak.

Tide: The vertical movement of water caused by the gravitational force of the moon and sun.

Tie-downs: Ropes or lines used to secure a kayak to the top of a car.

Tracking: The ability of a boat to hold a straight course due to its hull design.

Trim: Balanced and level both side to side and end to end. A trim boat is achieved by shifting the load or the position of the paddlers.

Tumblehome: A hull cross section that curves inward from the waterline toward the gunwales.

Vee: A hull shape.

Volume: Overall capacity of a given hull.

Wake: The path or track of a kayak in the water.

Waterline: The line that is formed at the edge of the water along the hull of a kayak. The shape of the waterline and the handling characteristics of the boat change as the load changes.

Wave: An undulation on the surface of the water, usually caused by wind. The water does not move, while the wave does.

Weather: In the direction from which the wind is blowing. If you are facing into the wind, you are facing into the weather.

Wetsuit: Gear worn by kayakers for cold-water protection. Typically made of neoprene, which creates a thermal shield.

Windward: The direction from which the wind is blowing; opposite of leeward.

Index

float coats, 47
floats for outriggers, 248, 252
flood tides, 161
flotation, 71
flotation bags, 37–38, 72
fog, 154–55
food
    allergic reactions and medical attention, 185
    children's menus and meal preparation, 182
    cooking and preparation of, 221, 226–28
    fuel *vs.* social event perceptions, 226
    packing and storage, 229–30
    resource planning, 169, 170
foot pegs and footrests, 35, 124
footwear, 178, 192–94
fore-and-aft sails, 247, 249
frame-and-fabric kayaks, 14–15, 21–22
fuel for stoves, 227

G

gel coats, 24
Giardia lamblia, 186
gloves, 184, 192
GPS devices, 144–45, 156–59
grab loops, 34, 50, 61, 208
Greenland bows, 8
gunkholing, 16
gybing, 250

H

hand signals, 207
hardshell kayaks, 13
hatches, 36–37, 71
hats, 177, 191–92
headaches, 185, 192
headwalls, 238
health, 184–85. *See also* safety
heaving, 215
heeling, 248
height, and kayak fitting, 123
high braces, 107–10
hip flicks, 104–5, 128–29
hip pads, 126
history of kayaking, 4–5, 19
hulls, 9
Hypalon coatings, 28

I

infants, 175–76
inflatables, 15–16, 27–28
iodine, 186–87

J

jackets, 178, 196
jibing, 250

K

kayak accessories
    anchors, sea, 41
    bilge pumps, 42, 135, 203
    bow lines, 40
    bulkheads, 35–37, 71
    carrying toggles, 39–40
    cockpits, 31–33
    compasses, 41–42, 137, 143–45
    flotation bags, 37–38
    foot pegs, 35, 124
    hatches, 36–37, 71
    paddle floats, 40–41, 43
    paddle parks, 41
    paddles, 39, 51–57
    personal flotation devices, 44–50, 62,
        176–77, 203
    rudders, 38–39, 95, 117–21, 122
    safety equipment, 42–43, 203
    seats, 30–31
    skegs, 38, 39
    spray decks, 33–35
    stern lines, 40
kayaking, overview
    history of, 4–5, 19
    learning, 1–4
    purpose of, 253–54
    sports categories of, 58
kayaking skills
    boarding, 62–64
    bracing, 102–11
    capsizing recovery, 71
    center of buoyancy assessments, 58–59
    Eskimo rolls, 127–29
    exiting, 64
    landing, 214–19, 242
    launching, 65–67, 203–4, 236–37

About the Author

Dennis Stuhaug lives much of the year on a drying bay in Washington State, dividing his time between writing, paddling, and researching his next trip in the wake of early European explorers along North America's northwest coast. "It's a twenty-minute paddle to the village, a two-hour bicycle ride to the city, and a month and a half's paddle to Alaska." Deer and otter are on the beaches; seals, sea lions, and a variety of whales patrol the deeper waters, but surface to watch a passing kayak. He's working on another book, and working with state and national agencies on a variety of boating and water safety issues.

Your next adventure begins here.

falcon.com